THE POLITICS OF
SCHOOL/COMMUNITY
RELATIONS

THE POLITICS OF SCHOOL/COMMUNITY RELATIONS

Frank W. Lutz
and
Carol Merz

Foreword by Laurence Iannaccone

Teachers College, Columbia University
New York and London

The information for the Scottsdale, AZ case is from Weninger, T., & Stout, R., Dissatisfaction theory: Policy change as a function of school board member–superintendent turnover. *Educational Administration Quarterly*, 25(2), 162–180, copyright © 1989 by Sage Publications. Used by permission of Sage Publications, Inc.

Published by Teachers College Press, 1234 Amsterdam Avenue New York, New York

Library of Congress Cataloging-in-Publication Data

Lutz, Frank W.
    The politics of school/community relations / Frank W. Lutz and Carol Merz.
        p.   cm.
    Includes bibliographical references (p.) and index.
        ISBN 0-8077-3162-5 (alk. paper). — ISBN 0-8077-3161-7 (pbk. : alk. paper)
        1. Community and school — United States.   2. Politics and education — United States.   I. Merz, Carol.   II. Title.
    LC221.C667   1989
    370.19'31'0973 — dc20   91-46303

ISBN 0-8077-3162-5
ISBN 0-8077-3161-7 (pbk.)

Printed on acid-free paper

Manufactured in the United States of America

99 98 97 96   8 7 6 5 4 3

To our students,
from whom we have learned
at least as much
as we have taught—
and without whom this book
would not have been possible.

Contents

Foreword

Any nation's system of education, especially its compulsory public education system, is an element and often a potent part of that nation's system of
governance. Schools play a central role in the political socialization of
society's youth, both through the educational system's implicit invisible
curriculum and through its explicit planned citizenship instruction. In
addition, education is usually the largest single fiscal item of state budgets
in the United States. The employees of the system, from classroom to
national civil servants — the entire public educational bureaucracy — comprise an enormous labor force whose salaries and perquisites are determined by governmental bodies and offices. Neither the processes by which
such employment decisions are made, nor the lobbying activities influencing these decisions, can be considered nonpolitical. Above all else, it is
inconceivable that the values taught by a society's educational system, both
through its planned instructional processes and its implicit operations,
could be divorced from the society's political future or living past.

Yet for much of this century the political myth of the separation of
education from politics held sway in the minds of most Americans, including public school employees. The belief that politics and education were
separable, and healthier separated, rests upon maintaining a narrow and
negatively weighed definition of politics. Nevertheless, it may have functioned usefully for educational administrators and others in the political
struggles of the first half of this century, as they sought to break the political patronage system of that day and to implement the tenets of municipal
reform. The separation of education from politics was a useful ideological
position, occupied in the struggle to protect the schools from political
corruption, especially that of urban political machines. However useful
that view may have been, it never described the reality. The statement that

public education and politics are separate or even separable simply does not reflect the facts, nor does it reflect the research of the last thirty years.

The ideological position expressed by the slogan of "keeping politics out of education" is itself a social weapon in the politics of education. It is in short a political myth, and political myths die slowly, if at all. As Nicholas Masters wrote in 1970, "There has been a temptation throughout the American educational experience to deny that anything labeled 'politics' is involved in educational decision-making" (Iannaccone and Lutz, 1970, p. v).

The almost universal belief in that separation, as the most desirable condition for American public education, was vehemently upheld by educators and their supporters. Whether beneficial or baneful, sincere or cynical, a view that is fiercely held with emotional commitment about any aspect of government is obviously a political ideology. The tendency to deny the manifold connections between politics and schools—woven into the very warp and woof of public education as an American institution—was a political strategy for some, an unfortunate matter of confusion for many.

Masters optimistically noted that attitudes on this topic were changing. He pointed out that by 1970 enough research had been done to disabuse people of the old myth that education and politics were separate or that they could be separated and therefore should be. The political power of the old myth has diminished since 1970, but much more slowly than might have been expected. Political myths live because they serve the interests of some and convert many other interested citizens into passive supporters. Slowly or not, the myth has given way on many fronts to a broader understanding of the relationship between politics and education, especially education policy.

One front on which the myth has not died is that of the public relations of local school districts. Superintendents and central office personnel all too often continue to act as if public relations can be handled with the mind set and orientation of American businesses—and the businesses of a previous generation at that. School officials who demonstrate a good grasp of educational politics in other areas often seem to set that understanding aside in their public relations programs. Little of the last thirty years of research into the politics of education has penetrated the public school's planned programs of public relations. The business ideology of a generation ago still dominates local school district thought and practice.

As Lutz and Merz indicate, this old-fashioned business ideology has a long historic record in American public education, ranging much farther than the public relations area. Their examination of the historical foundations of the American public schools, using political theories that have

guided recent decades of research in the politics of education, provides a
brief historical perspective on the study of school/community relations.
The *Gemeinschaft unt Gesellschaft* frame of reference from Tonnies via
Becker's sacred and secular communities functions as a framework for
locating communities for the rest of this work; more directly it suggests
appropriate variations in public relations for different communities with
their different policy assumptions and political processes. This approach
provides a useful recognition of the wide range of the secular to sacred
continuum, as an alternative to the more common single-right-way approach of so many other books written for school people.

Similarly, the authors' work on superintendent and school board relations uses concepts of school board culture from political anthropology. At
the same time they warn readers of the limitations of the view they use,
rather than falling into the more common reification of organizational
culture as the thing itself. The wide range of school board types and the
different sorts of representation of board members they present are like the
range of communities they report.

Lutz and Merz have undertaken a difficult task. While this is not a
technical how-to book, it is directed to the thoughtful practitioner rather
than to the research specialist. The authors keep readers aware of the need
for some situational analysis of particular school districts and communities, in order to decide which public relations approach is likely to be most
fruitful. They have presented readers with a range of cases involving different communities and school districts to help readers with such analyses.

These begin with a reexamination of the familiar Robertsdale case,
with additional data on the election of a challenger in a triggering election
at the beginning of a critical election era in a local district. The case is
examined using voter dissatisfaction theory, with an emphasis on some of
the practical tools—indicators of dissatisfaction—that indicate the ascen-
sion of discontent.

This is followed by a series of different school/community types.
Thompsonville, a community undergoing social composition change with
attendant value shifts, is an instance of superintendent turnover that precedes incumbent defeat, instead of the more frequent pattern in which
incumbent defeat precedes the involuntary turnover of the superintendent.

Scottsdale presents readers with an extreme case of repeated incumbent defeats, chief executive turnovers, and most significantly policy
changes reflecting the will of the voters. The point is made and made well
that this case—which comes closer than any other to representing the
dream of continuous competition theorists in democratic political theory—
is a case of continuous overturn in board incumbency and superintendent

tenure accompanied by real changes in policy outcomes. This is clearly a case of policy changes reflecting the choices of voters in a rapidly changing and politically active community.

Two other cases, Hamilton and Riverton, also display the familiar motor of critical election eras: community growth with its changes in social composition. The addition of changes in the racial and ethnic composition of these districts adds another significant dimension, increasing the complexity of social changes and conflicting social values, and fueling the dissatisfied voter pool in these school districts.

Lutz and Merz also use the voter dissatisfaction frame of reference to address some of the issues of the recent thrust toward site management. In doing so they take a revisionist position, reexamining the positive aspects of the old American political machine, that demonic target of turn-of-the-century municipal reform politics. Most readers are not likely to be prepared to accept the virtues of the old political machine as an argument in favor of the new reforms. The new attendance area linkages to the school that site management reforms create are presented as partially offsetting the effects of the centralization of municipal reform. Whether you agree with them or violently disagree, their arguments provide an unusual window on some aspects of the recent site management reforms.

The last chapters concentrate on the importance of paying systematic attention to the social composition of communities. The provision of specific indicators from recent research make it feasible for local policymakers to track changing value positions of district citizens. Equally useful is the closing chapter on public relations. Its emphasis on avoiding efforts to manipulate the public, instead combining honest information with two-way communication, so as to stay in tune with the community, is consistent with the political theory of voter dissent that runs through the entire book. It takes into account the wide diversity of communities presented in the earlier chapters.

In sum, Lutz and Merz have undertaken a difficult task. They have spanned the distance between the sociological and political theories used by researchers in the politics of education and the educational administrators' community relations work. Their approach uses a consistent frame of reference resting at bottom on voter dissatisfaction theory with enough flexibility to suit a variety of communities. They provide practitioners with useful tools without talking down to them, and without losing the strength of recent scholarship in the politics of education. "It is the purpose of this book to explain the 'grass roots' of politics in the local school districts and the local schools of America" (p. xi). They have carried off their chosen task well.

Laurence Iannaccone

Preface

Some books get written in the darnedest ways. This one began thirty years ago when one author was not yet out of high school, and the other was embroiled in school politics as the president of the school board in a school district known here as Robertsdale. Both, however, were involved in school politics for, knowingly or not, all citizens in the United States are involved in the politics of education to some degree.

Over the past years both of the authors became increasingly unhappy with the available texts in school/community relations. Those texts emphasize public relations methods, statistics about school boards, and public opinion polls about public schools. They say little about the political process that is the reality of school/community relations.

On the other hand, politics of education texts are adequate in the area of selected political theory with some application to the federal, state, and local processes that operate in American public education. They have little to say, however, about the actual application of those concepts to education practice where it counts, in the administration of local schools. Although some are adequate on local politics, all are largely lacking in the discussion of site politics — where public education actually meets the community. It is at the school level where school/community relations is practiced on a day-to-day basis. This is where the politics of dissatisfaction, or of failing to be dissatisfied enough to take action, usually takes place. This is where enthusiastic support for district policy and administration is developed, a factor little explored to date in the Dissatisfaction Theory of Democracy, which is at the heart of this book.

It is the purpose of this book to explain the "grassroots" of politics in the local school districts and the local schools of America. There the people can see and practice American democracy more successfully than they can in any other area or at any other level. There in public school politics, the

American people govern themselves, when they choose, as they choose, and about issues of concern to every American — issues concerning the education of their children. This is the heart of school/community relations.

F. W. L. and C. M.
1992

Conflict and Change in Modern School Governance

The politics of school/community relations is not often addressed, although it rests at the point where many fields of study intersect and is an implicit part of each of those fields. The relationship of the schools to their community is a political relationship, but preparation of administrators is often based on the myth that schools have been (or should be) removed from the political arena. Most people recognize that, in fact, schooling is very political and there has been a good deal of academic work in politics of education. That work has not become readily available to those who lead our local schools. Community relations courses have generally ignored political theory, choosing instead to study techniques of public relations programs designed for business. The authors of this book see community relations and politics of education as inseparable; we see any study of community relations that does not include political theory to be woefully lacking, if not irresponsible. Throughout the country, communities are demanding a greater voice in school governance. If we do not prepare school leaders for this reality, we will be preparing leaders who will be unable to cope with their world of professional practice. The purpose of this book is to lead school administrators to a clearer, more complete understanding of the relationship of schools and communities in order to create schools that are more responsive to their communities. We believe this understanding must include some study of political theory, sociology of community, and history of schooling in America.

Cuban (1986) writes that the superintendent serves in three roles: manager, politician, and teacher. Some administration programs do well in preparing administrators to be managers. Our constant adoration of business management and mindless acceptance of business techniques for school management has led us to pattern most school administration programs on programs designed for business administration. In no area is this

more true than in the area of community relations, where we have pat-
terned both instruction and practice after public relations programs of
business, forgetting that the public becomes both consumer and stockholder in its relationship to the schools. The dominant career path provides
school administrators who are relatively well prepared as teachers. If their
background fails to assure skills in this area, the recent reform movement,
emphasizing the role of administrators as instructional leaders, demands
that these skills be developed and maintained. Little is done, however, to
prepare administrators to lead the schools as political organizations. We
think there is no more appropriate place to address the topic of politics
than in the area of community relations.

School/community relations as a field of study has typically been limited to ways the schools can get their message to the community, based on
public relations techniques rather than on political theory. This is evident
in the fact that the terms *public relations* and *community relations* are
often used interchangeably in education. Some writers (Saxe, 1975) are
more careful to limit the term public relations to mean specific efforts on
the part of the schools to create a more positive public opinion of the
schools, and recognize that these efforts are but one part of community
relations, meaning all the communication that takes place between the
community and the schools. We believe that school/community relations
involve more than communication. They include assumptions and values
that are invisible a good share of the time. They include processes that have
many layers of meanings, meanings that vary and are imbedded in different segments of the community. In order to develop a conceptual understanding of the purposes and realities of school/community relations practice, we propose to address the nature of the schools, the nature of the
community, and finally the political processes of the relationship between
these two social structures. We will look specifically at some of the actual
cases that have led to the development of theory that underlies the relationship.

The relationship of schools to their community is nominally established by processes of government. In most places in the United States the
community elects a representative board that will in turn establish school
policy and hire administrators to carry out that policy in the day-to-day
operation of the schools. Educators are ultimately responsible to their
communities, a fact they often forget. The purpose of studying school/
community relations is to help educators establish a system that, first,
allows the schools to understand community values, preferences, and demands and, second, allows the community to understand the educational
programs and procedures carried out by the schools. This is, above all, a

communications system, which enables the process of democratic governance of education.

The common schools in the United States were established by communities to serve their needs as locally perceived. Schools were formed in order to teach the language and computational skills necessary to participate in the community and to transmit the culture and values of the community. As the country became more complex, schools became not only the vehicle for educating the children of the community to the standards of their elders, but also the vehicle for assimilation of immigrants. Through the schools members of immigrant communities could assure that their children would become part of the dominant community and thus be afforded the opportunity for full participation in American life. Gradually the immigrant communities began to assume a role of greater participation and they began to demand a voice in governance. The question of whose values the schools would impart and whose children would receive services became political questions. The relationship of the school to the community, which was once so clear, became complicated as the community became a mix of various groups with unequal political power.

While school people have often disregarded the political relationship of the schools to the community, we have long given lip service to democratic school governance. We have taught that school policy is established by representatives elected by the community and thus represents the values held by the majority in the community. Practicing administrators and other interested observers quickly saw that this was not always true. They saw the need to develop a more powerful theory to explain the relationship. If we are to understand the politics of school governance, we must address the question of whether schools represent the values of the community; more broadly stated, is school governance democratic?

POLITICAL THEORY AND SCHOOL GOVERNANCE

Over the past few decades political theory as a whole has moved from a linear model to a model that affords less prediction. Closely paralleling work in the physical sciences, political theorists, notably Easton, began in the 1960s to apply systems theory and to treat political systems as orderly, predictable entities. According to Easton (1965), demands from the public caused responses from the political system that became manifest in policy. Discontinuity between what members of the public wanted and resultant policy was attributed to a multiplicity of mechanisms working simultaneously, or the inherent nature of some systems making them more predisposed to certain types of demands. Later, other work, especially by Wirt and Kirst (1982), indicated that the connections were not as predictable as earlier thought. To reconcile these discrepancies, theorists considered the possibility that participation in the system was variable or that the working of the system was variable, the linkages not being as tight as previously thought (March & Olsen, 1979; Weick, 1983). This line of analysis again found parallels in the physical sciences. Studies of the ambiguous nature of organizations, like studies of chaos in the natural world (Gleick, 1987), have caused us to reconsider our understanding of political processes (Cronbach, 1988).

One must look only briefly at the process of school governance to see examples of discontinuity between community values and schools and the lack of political activity. To account for this we must consider the possibilities that schools are (1) apolitical, (2) political but not democratic, or (3) variably democratic depending on the political ability and participation of various community groups. School governance underwent a number of changes in the past century designed to distance it from politics of the community, intentionally weakening the political linkages on which representation in systems theory would depend. The reform movement, described in detail in Chapter 3, has left most states with nonpartisan elections, independent of general elections, electing board members at-large, and resulting in low participation rates and general apathy about the contests. Various studies have shown that about half of the school board members in the United States are elected unchallenged and another sizable segment is appointed by fellow board members during nonelection times of the year. The reform movement did not succeed in making school governance nonpolitical. Segments of the community continued to be able to exert considerable power and control over education resources. It appears that the reform movement simply made political participation more difficult for some segments of the community. Hence it has occasionally been concluded that participation in governance is available only to people who have sophisticated knowledge of the political process and that schools are therefore political but not democratic and represent a powerful community elite.

Many political theorists reached the conclusion, based on this general lack of participation, that school governance in America is a nondemocratic process. One of the most important studies to conclude that schools were governed through a nondemocratic process was done by Zeigler and Jennings (1974). Noting that participation is low, competition is infrequent, and incumbents are rarely defeated, they concluded that school boards are elected by a special class of citizens who participate in the elections. While not necessarily a social elite, this class is selected through their choice of affiliations and activities; thus the boards represent the civic leadership segment of community who elect them rather than the broader community.

Students of school board elections do indeed seem overwhelmed by the lack of political activity. Long periods in which nothing seems to change can persuade students that the electorate does not make its demands known during school board elections. But occasionally a great deal of activity occurs, even in the most placid communities, and incumbent board members are challenged and even defeated. Occasionally total board recalls occur and superintendents who have been hired by the leadership of a community and seem secure in their roles are fired. The capacity of a somnolent community to spring into political activity has interested students of school governance. Wirt and Kirst (1982) compare school board elections to the arroyos of the Southwest, which are usually dry but in times of flash flood can suddenly become the course of a rushing torrent of water destroying anything in its way. In their analogy to arroyos, Wirt and Kirst call school board elections channels of the political system that are seldom used (p. 99). Based on the political theory of Easton, Wirt and Kirst analyzed school governance from a systems perspective. They suggest that the community makes demands on the schools, these demands are designated "inputs"; the board as educational policymaker "converts" the inputs, combining, reducing, or sometimes absorbing them without reaction, and makes policy decisions called "outputs." The demands are often caused by stress in another system (a community group or special-interest group). Wirt and Kirst are struck by the dimension of political turbulence relating to resource allocation, curriculum, and other school decisions, but are equally impressed by the lack of participation in school board elections.

DISSATISFACTION THEORY OF DEMOCRACY

The Dissatisfaction Theory of Democracy proposes a model in which a stable community elects a representative board whose values are congruent with those of the community. This board then selects a superintendent, with similarly congruent values, who will administer an educational program that reflects these values and is appropriate for the community. According to the theory, when a community changes, a gap begins to develop between the values of the community and the values of the board, and the community no longer sees the schools as meeting their needs. When the gap becomes intolerably great, the community resorts to political action, removing board members through the electoral process until the values of the board and the values of the community are again aligned. In order to establish these new values in the school system, the superintendent must be replaced with one whose values are similar to those of the new board and the new community. This new administration enacts new policies and programs, reestablishing school/community stability. This theory is represented graphically in Figure 1.1. Where the three major strands representing community values, board membership, and policy (usually synonymous with the superintendent) are parallel, the system is stable; but when community values begin to diverge, a gap develops and tension results. Political activity, represented by incumbent defeat (ID), realigns the board to the new community and creates another gap between the board and the superintendent. This gap is closed by the event euphemistically called "involuntary superintendent turnover" (ISTO), which realigns policy with board values. This model is helpful in understanding why political activity is sporadic and dramatic. It also suggests interesting aspects of the relationship of the board and superintendent to the communi-

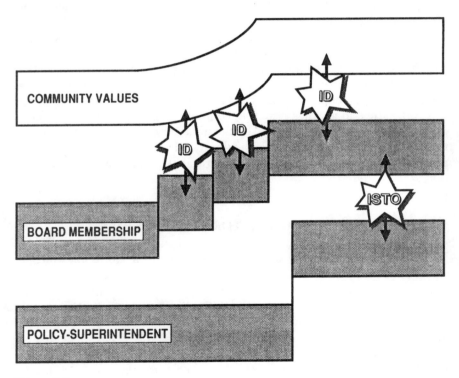

Figure 1.1
Dissatisfaction Theory of Democracy

ty. As communities change, the board and the superintendent are usually unaware of the change or refuse to take it seriously. In the words of Iannaccone and Lutz, the handwriting is on the wall but the board and superintendent do not understand or respond (1970, p. 176).

Varying Patterns of Community Change

A number of case studies have been done since the Robertsdale case, which is presented here in Chapter 5. These later cases advance and refine the theory. The Dissatisfaction Theory has always been considered contradictory to the work done by Zeigler and Jennings (1974), who find the school governance process notably undemocratic because of the low participation in elections and the lack of discernible differences between candidates. The Zeigler and Jennings work describes quite well the periods of quiescence that occur between conflict episodes described by Lutz and Iannaccone (1978), but fails to account for the occasional periods of intense political activity. In one study that examined the Iannaccone and Lutz theory, Danis (1984) describes a community that had only one conflict episode in fifty years. In communities in which conflict is so rare, longitudinal studies of great length are necessary to find conflict and it would be quite possible to assume that there was no conflict if one looked at a shorter period of time. It could be assumed that the two discrepant theories are cases of the blind men describing the elephant, each touching and describing a different part. In fact, much of the early research that has developed the Dissatisfaction Theory consists of case studies selected because the researcher knew that a conflict episode existed or longitudinal studies conducted in a selected group of districts with many variables in common. These selected populations may have presented only a partial picture of the political activity in school governance.

The clear implication of the Robertsdale case is that political turbulence is due to community change and incumbent defeat is one step in the establishment of a new value system and a new political equilibrium. The causal chain of events in the Dissatisfaction Theory has sometimes been considered an unvarying pattern: Changes in community values lead to dissatisfaction with school governance, which leads to increased political activity, which leads to incumbent defeat, which leads finally to superintendent turnover and outside succession. Attempts at predicting incumbent defeat and superintendent turnover have all been based on this pattern and have been, for the most part, unsuccessful. While this model is accurate in the original case, it is too narrow and does not adequately explain variations on the patterns of events seen in a wider variety of cases. Cases in which superintendents are fired before incumbents are defeated or without incumbent defeat and cases in which incumbents are defeated without superintendent turnover will be presented later. These cases are important to understand a more generalized theory of representational school governance. It is possible that political conflict is occurring, or perhaps always has occurred, in a variety of patterns. The possibility of a less tightly linked series of events must be considered. It would be more fruitful to consider schools as ambiguous organizations, with unclear goals, participation, and processes as defined by March and Olsen (1979). It would not be surprising to find varying, less predictable patterns of events that nevertheless show theoretical consistency but in a less linear model, still encompassing the original variables but in a variety of patterns.

ARE COMMUNITY VALUES REPRESENTED IN SCHOOL POLICY?

In ambiguous organizations, the link between community values and board values may not be clear. The very lack of participation characterized by Zeigler and Jennings's (1974) description of school governance may allow board members to be elected, or superintendents to be hired, whose values are very different, simply because the attention of the community is elsewhere. The election of board members by the community may be a case of especially uncertain outcome. Participation in school elections is notoriously low and campaign issues are rarely discussed; thus voters allow board members to achieve their position with little knowledge of what values they hold. The attention of the electorate is usually not on school board elections. During these times communities may select board members, and boards may select superintendents, whose values are inconsistent with their own. Competing value systems are not apparent because attention is elsewhere and values are treated as assumptions by different and competing groups. Several cases of this type will be presented in Chapter 6, explaining a more generalized theory of governance in which electoral conflict becomes an indication of ongoing alignment between board and community values, not only a manifestation of community change.

The question of whether the values of the community are represented in school policy must ultimately be answered yes, in the long run. There will be periods of nonalignment of values in the short run when communities change or representatives and policymakers are chosen without full understanding of the values they hold. When the discrepancy becomes intolerably great, however, the community, through the electoral process, will realign school policy with their values. Boyd (1976) describes a "zone of tolerance," which limits how far from mainstream community values school policymakers may deviate before encountering conflict. It is interesting to note that Thomas Jefferson, in a letter to James Madison in 1787, discussed this process in which citizens keep their government from overstepping the bounds of public norms, saying "a little rebellion, now and then, is a good thing, and as necessary in the political world as storms in the physical" (Koch & Peden, 1944, p. 413).

Choices in ambiguous organizations are opportunities to discover, define, or create values, according to March and Olsen (1979). Participants vary, and the roles they play vary, with the context of each choice. Often the process of making the choice can be prolonged as relationships and goals are defined or discovered. Surprisingly, the final decision is relatively unimportant compared with the process by which it was reached and it can even fail to be implemented. School policy decisions can be considered "choices" in March and Olsen's terms. Of all the choices a school board makes, the most important is the selection of a superintendent, because that decision can bring the operation of the schools into line with community values. Participation in the selection of a superintendent, as with any choice, is relatively fluid; the process is nominally established by the school board when it makes an initial set of decisions, such as how widely to advertise the job and how much to involve community members. From then on the process is unpredictable. Board members choose to participate to varying degrees; community members participate to varying degrees; the role of the press varies widely. In their analysis of the selection of a university dean, March and Olsen describe how the process changes several times; decisions are made and then changed and participation of many individuals changes over the course of the decision process before a final decision is made. In like fashion the choice of a superintendent can be an analogously tortuous situation; in other cases the selection can be made quickly with little participation beyond the board.

An organization does not treat all decisions as such choice opportunities. The vast majority of decisions are simply made on a routine basis and represent no particular value choice. These decisions resolve no organizational conflict and if there are no underlying conflicting values, the decision is implemented smoothly. However, if there are fundamental differences that need to be aired in a decision process that allows various participants to establish or reestablish community norms, a routine decision-making process will leave a residual conflict that will surface again. This seems to have happened in the Thompsonville case, which is examined in Chapter 6. In Thompsonville there were new elements in the community, but the school board and community leadership who selected the superintendent carried out their process as they had done for years. This routine decisionmaking precluded community participation and the opportunity to explain or define their values, leaving a residual conflict to be resolved later. It appears that a major conflict was lying dormant in the community; participants were only vaguely aware of differences that had developed and the selection of a new superintendent was the catalyst for a surprisingly strong reaction.

DIVERSE COMMUNITIES

The Dissatisfaction Theory of Democracy is based on the assumption that a community can establish some dominant set of representative values held by a plurality of its citizens. This assumption is usually true in rural and suburban communities. However, what happens when a community is so diverse, as urban communities often are, that no consistent set of values can be found or no school system can be established that is satisfying enough to the community and citizens are not motivated to take political action? Are these communities doomed to constant political turmoil? This question is beginning to appear in discussions of schooling today. School consolidation over this century has increasingly placed policy-making powers in the hands of individuals representing more and more people. In 1932 there was one school board member for every 46 pupils; by mid-twentieth century this ratio had become one to 300. Fully four-fifths of the school boards in existence in 1932 had disappeared by 1966 (*School Boards*, 1966). Spring (1988) suggests that political abuses by special-interest groups, especially business, have become so great that education policy needs to be established in an independent branch of the government similar to the Supreme Court.

Do communities deserve schools that represent their values? Yes — our system demands that we seek ways to provide such schools. Large urban districts have attempted to deal with their increasingly diverse communities by decentralizing school governance, turning more and more administrative decisions over to the individual school site. While this has not been a total success, the model of site-based management has become popular throughout the nation. In Chapter 7 we will examine site politics and consider some of the implications of school-site administrative responsibility replacing district-level administrative responsibility. Site-based school management is one way of making schools responsible to smaller and usually more homogeneous communities. While every site has diverse populations, these may be few enough to be managed. A principal and site council can know their community well, hear their demands, and be responsive to them in ways that a superintendent and school board often cannot. We will suggest that school-site councils, led by principals, function in school governance as ward-based boards did earlier in our history. In building a relationship to the community, the school site may be the most effective avenue to hear and respond to community demands.

Finally, we will turn to methods of establishing a community relations program that enables the communication necessary for aligned values of school and community. Chapters 8 and 9 will examine ways the schools can develop more effective relationships with their communities. Programs will be examined that can enable open communication, allowing the schools to respond to community demands and allowing the community to understand and participate in their schools.

2

The Foundation of American Public Schools

Knowledge of both schools and communities is a prerequisite for understanding school/community relations. What are these two social entities, the school and the community, between which we hope to establish a good relationship? Furthermore, why should we care about such a relationship? The answers are found in the historical roots of the American school *and* community.

Most of those studying or practicing school/community relations and the politics of education have a rather substantial personal experience within the public schools. What else is necessary? Broad as it may be, one's idiosyncratic experience is, in the last analysis, unique and limited, even though it may extend over decades and have occurred in various geographic locations. A more comprehensive view of America's public schools is still necessary for a reasonable examination of the school/community relationship.

With considerable agreement, education students report that the worst, least useful, and most unappreciated course in their undergraduate education program was the course in history of education. Unfortunately, those who teach school/community relationships may not possess sufficient knowledge of the important historical foundation on which that course should be built, namely the history of American schools and communities.

Educational professionals with two or three decades of experience in public education are sometimes amused and often frustrated to see the periodic reoccurrence of familiar problems, as well as suggested solutions, without recognizing previous success or failure by others. For example, asked to review the literature about "site management," a student recently reported on an article published in the mid-1950s and concluded, "If this research had been implemented we would have avoided many of the problems we face today." Like the proverbial tiger, we fall into the same trap again and again because we have short memories. History does repeat itself, perhaps because people were not taught history or, if they were, failed to learn their lessons. Educators are certainly not immune.

Cuban (1990) noted the phenomenon in education of "reforming again, again, and again." Reforming education is usually a matter of, like the tiger, getting out repeatedly from the same trap. The education reforms noted by Cuban were also often disguised in a slightly different fashion, with slightly changed labels (for very similar behaviors) and under slightly different conditions. He suggests that by studying the history of education's attempts to solve its problems one could define preexisting patterns and avoid old mistakes and the repetition of the same attempted reforms. Callahan says that "education is always influenced by the time and place in which it occurs. Education never exists in a vacuum or in the abstract; it always goes on in a particular society at a particular time" (1960, p. 107). Those sentences, which introduce a chapter titled "History of American Education," could not be better stated; they serve as an appropriate introduction to understanding school/community relations.

THE ENGLISH COLONIAL ORIGINS OF AMERICAN SCHOOLING

Not every citizen of the United States had ancestors who came over on the Mayflower or fought in the American Revolution. Not every Caucasian-American had ancestors who owned slaves. Not every African-American had ancestors who were slaves. Not every citizen is a Christian, nor is every citizen an entrepreneur running a business for profit. Yet the events suggested in the above ancestral scenarios profoundly influenced the configuration of today's public schools in the United States.

Many cultures and historic events shaped the history of the United States, enriched its culture, and influenced today's schools. We are unique in the wide range of native cultures, including Native Americans, Aleuts, Eskimos, and Hawaiians, that augment the immigrant cultures. The Spanish were in the Southwest before the English were at Plymouth, Russians settled Alaska before anyone else, and the French populated the Mississippi Valley from St. Paul to New Orleans. To this is added later immigrations of many peoples that newly comprise our "heritage" and influence our school curriculum.

Yet, when speaking of the nation and its public schools in particular, the old English tradition is entrenched. In the following chapter, there is considerable discussion of de Tocqueville's classic observations of American democracy (1945). This Frenchman notes again and again that it was the English traditions, the English language, the English colonists and their religions that dominated the building of the American democracy. When describing the democracy he observed in the early 1800s, he particularly noted the important role of the public schools. Historian after historian of American education also makes that point. The views of these notable scholars are accepted on merit and meaning for fair comparison with today's public schools.

COLONIAL EDUCATION

In what remains a classic work after thirty years, Callahan (1960) indicates the important role of the schools in the English colonies, as well as their continuing influence on today's schooling. He says, "Similarities are apparent in a comparison of education in colonial and modern America, . . . especially if one looks beneath the surface, for both were in the stream of Western civilization" (p. 107). Additionally, he states, in concert with others, that always in colonial days the notion of schooling was tied closely to the pursuit of religion and piety.

While the early establishment of public education in the development of American democracy was important, education was not the primary concern among colonists. Thus, Callahan notes, "It is not surprising . . . that schools and the means of [supporting] education were neglected" (p. 121). A logical conclusion is that, except during occasional periods in our history, excellence in public education and the "means" to provide it were and still are often neglected.

Cremin, in his monumental *American Education: The Colonial Experience* (1970), establishes the fact that the majority of colonies made provision for the schooling of their young during the last half of the seventeenth century and that religion and Bible reading were always of major importance, if not prime motivators of the colonists' interest in schooling. Furthermore, closely related to the considerable importance to the present structure of the curriculum and organization of the public school in the United States, the home was *always* a central element in schooling (pp. 127–131). Nash, in his *History and Education* (1970), sees religion as central in the establishment of schooling in colonial America. In this edited collection of the works of ten others, three chapters are devoted solely to the role of religion in education, and many other chapters mention religion in some way. Cremin (1970) titled the first chapter of his work "The Practice of Piety" and the second "The Nature of Civility" before launching into "The Advancement of Learning" as a background for understanding American education. He has a chapter on the church before presenting his chapter on the school. While noting the pluralist nature of America even in colonial days, Cremin calls attention to the central influence of the English tradition.

> Seventeenth-century American was as much a label of religion as it was of social class and ethnicity: in addition to English . . . there were French and Spanish Catholics, Swedish Lutherans, Dutch Calvinists, French Huguenots, and Spanish Jews, to say nothing of Indian and African. . . . Yet, in this realm as in others, English forms and customs came to predominate, providing the context within which other traditions developed, waned, or changed. (p. 148)

Both Cremin (1970) and Callahan (1960) point to Massachusetts as the keystone of American public education. Callahan emphasizes a quote from the 1642 Massachusetts law establishing public schooling, expressing the primary educational concern of the colonist as "especially of their ability to read and understand the principles of religion and the capital laws of this country." He continues by quoting the "Old Deluder Satan Act" of 1647: "It being one chiefe project of the old deluder, Satan, to keep men from the knowledge of the Scriptures. . . . It is therefore ordered that every township . . . should then forthwith appoint one within their towne to teach all such children. . . . " Cremin concludes that "the schools were established and supported by public taxation for the welfare of the community . . . [and that] set a precedent" for what was to follow (pp. 114–115).

Like others, Spring (1986) begins his discussion in *The American School* with the chapter "Religion and Authority in Colonial Education." Here again are the two themes in public education in the United States: (1) its English colonial origins and (2) its religious connections. Another theme suggested in Spring's work is the close tie of public education in America to a third influence, the family and parental control. Spring acknowledges this consistent tie between family and public schooling in colonial America but makes an important point:

> What distinguishes education in pre-Revolutionary and post-Revolutionary America is the concept of service to the broader needs of government and society. After the Revolution, many Americans begin to believe that a public system of education was needed to build nationalism. (p. 28)

The individual and the family began to become submerged within the larger society and, as we shall see, a national destiny. This constitutes a shift in emphasis but not a break with the family as an influence in public education in the United States.

In his more politically oriented work, Spring (1989) returns again to the theme of religion in American education and the right of the family to make decisions regarding the education of its children. Two important points emerged, each shaping and reordering important threads in American education. Both emanate from constitutional amendments. It is pertinent, however, that for all the discussion of the rights of citizens in the preamble to the Constitution of the United States, the Constitution itself guarantees almost no rights for citizens. Attention and concern for citizens' rights came with the first ten amendments and have played major roles in shaping today's public schools. The First Amendment directs that "Congress shall make no law respecting the establishment of religion."

This last concept was later interpreted to mean that there is a "wall of separation" between all levels of government in the United States and any church or religion. To a large extent this doctrine was ignored in public schools for almost a century after the fourteenth amendment was enacted; it is still ignored in some ways in some areas of the country. Regardless of operational neglect, the issue, for the present at least, was settled by the *Engel v. Vitale* (1962) U.S. Supreme Court ruling that prayers may not be offered in public schools, to include illegality of even a required period of silent individual prayer. Furthermore, an invocation before a Future Farmers of America banquet, or a prayer before a football game sponsored by the school and held on school property, is also illegal. Despite the ruling, many knowledgeable school people will recognize frequent, and some would claim flagrant, violations of this ruling in many geographic areas of the nation today. However, if based on tenets of colonial education, it would appear that such religious activities in publicly supported schools are not a traditional *violation* of American schooling but rather a continuation of *traditional values*.

Those who fear federal legislative and administrative interference in public education, please take note: It is clearly unconstitutional for the federal government to *establish* a single public education system for the nation — that is left to the mores and traditions of the American people and the legislatures of their states. However, the federal judicial branch can and has reestablished and restructured public education with rulings based on the first and fourteenth amendments. Perhaps the two major shifts in American public education from colonial days to the present are (1) the separation of public education from religion, based on the fourteenth amendment and affirmed in the "wall of separation" decision in *Illinois ex. re. McCollum v. Board of Education* (1948), and (2) the establishment of the principle that separate but equal schools are neither equal nor constitutional under the first amendment as affirmed one hundred years later in the decision *Brown v. Board of Education in Topeka* (1954). We strongly agree with both of those rulings, but it must be noted that both rulings broke with long-established traditions in American education and *restructured* the public schools of America *without providing a single penny* to accomplish those purposes. The costs of compliance was left to "the states and their people." Also note that it took a century after those rights were established by constitutional amendment for those same rights to be affirmed and operationalized for all citizens. Perhaps of greater import, it appears that more than thirty years after the just-noted court decisions, some schools still choose to ignore or evade those rulings in one way or another. Traditional and cultural change, right or wrong, legal or illegal, occurs slowly and with considerable pain in any society and in its schools.

In spite of such changes, the U.S. Supreme Court has, with some consistency, upheld the tradition in American public education that parents have the fundamental right to decide how their children will be educated. Spring (1989) cites numerous cases, the vast majority of which must be interpreted to mean that parents have the right to be prime deciders about what and how their children learn. They may also establish their own "private" schools to provide education. This upholds the colonial tradition that the school shall supplement the education given by the parents at home. The outstanding exception to this parental right to decide appears to be a parent's right to decide whether his or her child may be "beaten" in public schools (Spring, 1989). Perhaps this outmoded "tradition" will soon lose favor with the courts. If a wall of separation has been established between the school and religion, there is no such wall between the school and the home.

There is also the matter of the predominate upper-class influence in public schools, also having its roots in colonial America. Many have noted the predominately white, male, upper- and middle-class, Anglo-Saxon composition of local and state school boards (Spring, 1989) — and, for that matter, of school administration. Fortunately this condition is changing. In addition, a related, and perhaps more insidious, influence has been noted by some — the inordinate influence of American business in public education. Spring (1986) calls attention to the influence of American business and capitalism in determining the nature and curriculum of American public schools. He points to the hornbook and McGuffey readers, and refers to the scholarly controversy regarding whether public education most serves public need or corporate greed. Perhaps it is Callahan (1960) who best posits that question in his statement about the influence of business in American education:

> What was unexpected [at the outset of research] was the extent, not only of the power of the business — industrial groups, but the strength of

the business ideology in the American culture on the one hand and the extreme weakness and vulnerability of schoolmen, especially school administrators, on the other. (pp. ii–iii)

Summary of the Colonial Period. Public schooling in the United States has its roots in the English colonial period. It establishes education as a prerequisite for Bible reading and proper participation in religion. Schools were originally structured to supplement education by the family, not to replace it in any fashion. Additionally, the control of public schools was then, as it continues to be, largely in the hands of the upper and middle classes and heavily influenced by American business.

GAINING STABILITY AND BECOMING A NATION, 1800–1865

Cremin (1988) and Callahan (1960) suggest that the period between 1800 and the Civil War was concerned with establishing some measure of stability for both the nation and its system of public schools. It was also a period of growth and change for both. Immigrants from every European country were flooding the nation, mostly the urban areas, and to quote Callahan, "the barons of industry were beginning to make themselves felt" (p. 125).

In 1839, John L. O'Sullivan wrote "The Great Nation of Futurity," in which he developed the idea of "Manifest Destiny," which would propel the engine of national expansion for 150 years. O'Sullivan was, like many of his contemporary citizens, greatly nationalistic. He was a "true believer," and as such he not only espoused American values but actually believed in them. O'Sullivan was undaunted by the existence of slavery in the United States, and the fact that several southern states actually had laws *prohibiting* the education of slaves. He also failed to notice, or chose to ignore, the fact that the women could not vote and that, while freedom is infinitely better than slavery, the living conditions of many workers in the North were no better than the living conditions of most slaves in the South. However, he correctly recognized that the American nation was founded on *principles* of equality and freedom. He declared that in such a manner "our nation is destined to be the great nation of futurity" and that "the gates of hell" could not prevent the United States from accomplishing that God-given mission (O'Sullivan, 1839). Butts says, "We were 'on our way' and set out to win a continent by treaty, purchase, and war with Mexico and with the various Indian tribes. . . . The continent had to be won and . . . new markets were necessary . . . the road to imperialism was paved with high-sounding intentions" (1955, p. 433). By the mid-1800s another well-intentioned movement had put into place an organizational structure that 150 years later would seem like a new kind of imperialism (Lutz, Lutz, & Tweeddale, in press). Without doubt the move toward the state school superintendency and state control was intended to assist in the development of quality education and, in fact, it certainly has done so in many ways. On the other hand it has also tended to take the schools away from the people who send their children there to be educated.

Recognizing that "we should honor our colonial forefathers for their efforts to provide schools," Good (1960, p. 421) suggests that the colonists did not even envision the ladder that American public schools were to become. Noting that growth in the number of chief state school officers (superintendents) from the 1830s until 1861, when "of 36 states and organized territories . . . 30 had provided state school officers," he concludes that "the development of the state school office may be regarded as an index to the growing will of the American people to develop public education" (p. 421). The establishment and growth of the state superintendency does measure an intent and a determination to see to it that the nation would provide free public education for its youth.

During the period between 1800 and 1860, not only did the state superintendency grow so that every state in the union had a chief school officer by 1861, but the number of schools and the curriculum also grew. By 1860, the basis for a public school system extending from kindergarten through twelfth grade had been laid, although it had not been completely realized. This was to be supplemented by virtually free state-supported higher education in many states during the 1930s and 1940s, and aided by the federally legislated education benefits in the G.I. Bill of Rights following World War II.

Two other problems surfaced and were virtually solved during this period. The first was the question of whether some citizens should be taxed for the education of the children of others. The second was the question of whether the public schools should be nonsectarian, teaching values but leaving religion completely to the church. Both issues were reaffirmed under the leadership of Horace Mann, the premier state school superintendent in the history of public education. He led the fight for universal taxation for nonsectarianism schools. The years between 1860 and 1865 were truly a test of whether the nation would last. "Equality," "opportunity," "freedom," "destiny" — those were the things the nation was founded on and *floundering* toward in 1860. However, the reality for many during this period was disenfranchisement, poverty, lack of educational opportunity, actual prohibition from being educated, and even slavery. Surviving the Civil War, our nation moved during the next 130 years, often haltingly and slowly, toward those high goals, with the public schools always in the midst, if not on the front lines, of the battle.

Summary of Gaining Stability. While some measure of stability was established and the national purpose was affirmed, the major effect of this period was the recognition of its great failure to achieve its ideals for many of its citizens. While the Civil War did not eliminate the inequities that existed, it surely brought them into bold relief and turned the nation in the direction of solving them. It also began a trend in which corporate giants were placed near the top, if not in control, of government policy, including public education. All of these trends were to be continued during the next historical period and are recognizable in today's United States and its public schools.

WESTWARD EXPANSION AND THE INDUSTRIAL PERIOD, 1865–1900

With the Civil War over, but its value conflicts not resolved, the nation turned its full attention to accomplishing what it saw as its Manifest Destiny. Good (1960) suggests,

> The political evils of the congressional plan of reconstruction increased the sectional hatred aroused by war and the fear of Negro control, the burning issue of mixed schools, the outright opposition to Negro education even in separate schools tended to paralyze the agencies which might have developed public education. (p. 435)

In similar fashion, Butts and Cremin (1953, p. 293) note that "the years between 1865 and 1918 mark the transition from the old to a modern America." They see the Civil War as essentially "a struggle between two alternative ways of life — the decentralized agricultural way of the South and the centralized industrial way of the North." The victory, they say, was "a triumph of individual capitalism" (pp. 299–300). The "mopping-up" operation from that victory is still being felt by rural America, reflected in the education reforms of the 1980s and 1990s.

The period between 1880 and 1910 saw corporate America become a dominate force with a series of corporate mergers and the growth of industry, unparalleled since until the time of the Reagan administration nearly a century later. As industry grew, so did the urban areas and the urban schools. This was fueled by immigrants swarming to America to fill jobs largely unwanted by citizens who were the product of earlier immigrations. Consequently the nature of the population changed as well. Not unlike today, large groups of newcomers with different faces, languages, and religions created fear and suspicion among long-settled citizens. By the end of World War I, immigration to the United States would virtually dry to a trickle for half a century (Butts & Cremin, 1953).

The period between 1880 and 1910 was a period of national growth and expansion for industry; the corporate captains were in control and were aided by a government that believed that the "business of the United States is business." This fact was not lost on public education. Spring (1986) notes that while some historians, such as Cremin, label all

> educational changes of the late nineteenth and the twentieth cen-
> turies . . . progressive, . . . many scholars have opposed [that] . . .
> view [and argue] . . . that the political and administrative structure of
> education changed to assure elite and corporate control of the education-
> al system and to produce cooperative and docile workers. (pp. 152–153)

Both of these positions, as Spring suggests, are probably overdrawn. Certainly everything done by corporate America is not altruistic. Neither does big business care to control, or try to control, everything in government and surely not everything in public education. As Dahl (1961) so clearly points out, power in the United States is unequally distributed. That is, the United States is not ruled by any single oligarchy of corporations. Issues at all levels of government are decided by shifting polyarchies of power, coalescing because of shared interest in some particular issue.

Industrial corporations in the United States are interested in having a pool of capable workers who can be motivated by "reasonable" wages and who will produce a "reasonable" profit. They are also interested in seeing to it that the public schools, whose job it is to provide that pool, do not become so expensive, and taxes so high, that the profit margin is not reasonable or that the market price is driven too high. To this end private business and corporate America have always exercised a considerable influence in our public schools. Although perhaps not a Machiavellian plot to produce docile workers, corporate influence may not always have been seen as in the "best interest" of public education. Iannaccone (1990), reviewing Callahan's work, sees the decade of 1890–1900 as a "turning point" in American education politics. Agreeing with Burnham (1970) and Schattschneider (1960), Iannaccone sees this period as establishing the basis for three decades of conservative policy in education. This political watershed was created partly by a conservative fear of the massive immigrations of the late 1800s and the fear, particularly in the South, of the African-American population, recently freed and struggling for equality.

While agreeing that American business is influential in public education, as it is in all American politics, Iannaccone (1990) thinks that "ideo-logically the two systems are profoundly different." The one, business, is operationally exclusive and secret, concentrates power and fosters inequal-ity; the other, American democracy, is broadly egalitarian and public, and rests in "disbursed inequalities. . . . Thus the business system with its values and the governmental system with its dissimilar ones are the Gemini twins of American society and its governance as a whole" (pp. 162–163).

Summary of Expansion and Industrialization. This period overlaps more with the next period than do other periods selected for description and analysis in this work. The westward expansion continued into the next period until the last of the western territories became part of the continen-tal United States during the early 1900s. The influence of business contin-ued at least through the administrations of Harding, Coolidge, and Hoover in the 1920s and early 1930s. The growth of the immigrant population continued until World War I. These major influences — (1) westward ex-pansion and Manifest Destiny, (2) the heavy influence of business in gov-ernment and public education, and (3) the growth and change of the population of the United States centering largely in the cities — were all established by 1890 but continued well into the first third of the twentieth century and were marked by conservative ideas and the growth of urban schools.

NATIONAL CONSERVATISM AND GROWTH IN URBAN SCHOOLS, 1900–1950

The United States was an emerging world power during the early 1900s. Its industrial wealth and world influence were growing. Butts and Cremin (1953) make this clear: "The years before 1918 also witnessed growing American influence in the political and economic life of Europe and Asia, a fact which was ultimately destined to change the power structure of the world" (p. 309). Unlike Europe, the United States emerged from World War I stronger than it went in. While Europe was economically and social-ly decimated, the United States, having fought a "war to end all wars," drew back and became more conservative. Its urban schools grew and thrived, although in many places African-Americans were still segregated and under-educated. They and other groups were not encouraged to enter the professions or even to stay in school beyond attaining the minimal skills in reading, writing, and figuring needed to produce in the marketplace. Nonetheless even individuals with few skills could find employment during the first half of the twentieth century, when much work required a strong back rather than a strong mind.

It was during this period that Frederick Taylor laid out his principles of "scientific management," addressed management groups, and published his "theory" throughout the world. The efficiency movement swept public education, its administration, organizations, and the newly developing university programs in education administration (see Kimbrough & Nunnery, 1988). Cubberly's (1920) embrace of the concept was to have lasting effects throughout the twentieth century. There were three major influences during this period: (1) the work of Counts and Dewey, (2) the adoption of scientific management as a model for education, and (3) a great world depression straddled by two major world wars. The first, not so overt or immediately felt, resulted from the ideas of two educators: John Dewey and George Counts.

Two Great Education Thinkers

"Dewey's philosophy of education took the form of a restatement of the aims of education in the light of the rapid changes that had taken place in American society in the nineteenth century," according to Butts and Cremin (1953, p. 480). Dewey, in his "progressive school" at the University of Chicago, stressed both the social and psychological aspects of the "whole" child, always emphasizing "experimentation" and "experience" as essential elements of the learning process. In such a manner Dewey broke with the usual separation espoused in traditional education, that of mind and body and of the rote learning style and punishment. In many ways Dewey's ideas ran counter to the conservative nature of American politics and business during the first half of the twentieth century. Dewey's commitment to experience as an important aspect of education fitted nicely with the business need and demand for vocational education, and those programs developed during this period. For Dewey, however, experience meant more than learning a trade, and education meant more than being minimally prepared to enter the workplace.

As this present work deals with the politics of school and community, it is fitting to note that Wirth (1966) concurs with C. Wright Mills's criticism of Dewey based on the nature of politics and modern bureaucracy. Mills (1964) argues that Dewey's ideas "proved to have inadequacies when applied to the social process within bureaucracies" (p. 294) — schools are surely bureaucracies — and that "Dewey's concepts of reflective behavior did not involve an adequate accounting of the functioning of power in a society of contending interest groups" (p. 295) — the United States is surely a society of contending interest groups. Wirth concludes that while Dewey might have accepted these criticisms, he would never have accepted nor been defeated by "nay-sayers who have concluded that man's fate is sealed" (p. 295).

George Counts proclaimed public education as the means of social reform, a means out of poverty and ignorance for the sweltering masses in the American urban slums and into a magnificent world society of free people. For him this was the great possibility of public education in the United States.

Counts conceived of an education system that would move the American nation out of the past and into the future. He suggested that "the present age calls for a great education, for an education liberally and nobly conceived . . . for an education that expresses boldly and imaginatively the full promise . . . and strength of America" (1952, p. 21). In words clearly suggestive of the preamble to the first National Defense Education Act, Counts stated, "If the democracies are to triumph in this *struggle for the minds and hearts of men*, they will be compelled to derive from their civilizations conceptions of equal power" (p. 37, emphasis added). Therefore, he says,

> the time has arrived to relate our thought about education to the whole sweep and substance of our American civilization — its history, its finest traditions, its present condition, and its promise. . . . We must fashion a conception of civilization that will respect the rights of all nations and champion the cause of liberty at home and before the world. . . . Such an education . . . [would prepare the American people] to discharge with honor and strength the heavy responsibilities which history has placed on their shoulders. (pp. 37–40)

In other words, Counts saw public education in the United States as the center of a changed society and that changed world as the purpose of public education.

The ideas of these two giants in American educational thought remain unrealized but still visible in educational thought today. Probably, with the possible exception of Thomas Jefferson, no two Americans contributed more to the conception of what public education in the United States should be.

Dewey and Counts were extremely controversial. The conservatism of the 1950s, epitomized by the McCarthy era, fell heavily on the ideas of these two brilliant thinkers. As both had rejected the domination of people for the purpose of profit and particularly rejected American business as the controller of public education, those who embraced the threat of communism as an opportunity to advance their careers made Dewey and Counts favorite targets for "McCarthyism."

Scientific Management

The second major influence in public education during this period was the finalization of a movement that started in the last period, noted above. In 1887, Wilson (1941), while a professor at Princeton, had begun to press for the dichotomization of public politics and public administration as a methods of reforming the corrupt politics of the machine in large American cities. About this same time, Taylor (1947) had developed his method of scientific management and it was becoming widely accepted as a method of management in the private business sector. Callahan (1962) documented scientific management's movement into public education administration and noted its use as the basic framework in newly emerging university programs to train educational administrators. In such a manner, educational administrators became "school executives rather than scholars of education who make administrative decisions." Callahan believed this was an American tragedy. Whether one agrees or not, it is the period between 1900 and 1950 that clearly established the management orientation in educational administration that continues to dominate the field into the 1990s. This is, therefore, one of the significant events of this period.

The Great Depression

We speak today of recession and unemployment in terms of single-digit numbers. In 1930, 30 percent or more of the workforce was unemployed and that workforce consisted mostly of persons from single-wage families. A depression of that magnitude could not help but affect the public schools. There was simply no money for anything. Even the noblest of school boards had to cut teacher salaries, and some were required to issue "script" instead of paychecks. To their credit, many urban boards did not make major cuts in curriculum, although the cost-accounting procedures discussed in Callahan's "Cult of Efficiency" (1962) were pursued. Such education "management" was prevalent and often a matter of necessity during this period.

Actually this period and the years following it, climaxing in the 1940s and 1950s, could be referred to as the "Golden Years" for urban public schools in America. Still, many citizens were left out. Dropping out of school after grade six or eight was an accepted practice for male children of poor families in the 1930s. Even a very small wage, if it could be earned, was needed. Females were not encouraged to go beyond high school, or if so only to normal schools or teacher colleges. Entrance into engineering, law, medicine, or politics was nearly unheard of for women. African-Americans largely attended segregated schools, which were clearly below the standard of white schools. Even in nonsegregated schools, African-Americans were usually not encouraged to aspire to high achievement, such as going to college or entering the professions. In fact, they were often deliberately *discouraged* from doing so — accomplishing such goals, when they did, largely because of support from parents and family or some close friend.

The economy and the conservative nature of waging a war in the 1940s, followed by enjoying the benefits of victory in the 1950s, left the schools larger but little changed.

Vocational Education, High School, and Higher Education

Two additional influences of importance emerged during this half century. One was the vast expansion of the numbers of students continuing on to high school, particularly after 1935, and the inclusion of greatly expanded vocational education programs in those high schools (Butts and Cremin, 1953; Callahan, 1962; Good, 1960).

These factors affected higher education. Following the end of World War II and the enactment of the G.I. Bill of Rights, tens of thousands of veterans entered college with the education benefits provided for them in that bill. The result was threefold: (1) colleges and universities grew extensively and their curricula became more practical and more student-oriented, and faculties grew proportionately between 1950 and 1965; (2) the university was democratized — never again would it be seen as a place for only the wealthy; and (3) high schools were forced to be concerned about the possibility that any and all students, regardless of wealth, race, or sex, might be applying to colleges and universities and thus could not be ignored by college preparatory programs.

Summary of Conservatism and Growth. To some extent this period could be seen as an extension of work begun in the previous half century. The nation fulfilled its Manifest Destiny uniting a country comprised of forty-eight states and three major territories. The industrial revolution was completed; business was firmly established as the "business of the United States," and our nation grew to become one of the "superpowers" — if not *the* superpower — of the world.

Additionally, Harry Truman's Marshall Plan established the framework for political and economic freedom for Western Europe and could be seen as the "bulldozer" that eventually destroyed the Berlin Wall. Under his leadership, a major civil rights bill was passed that was to plant the seeds for the civil rights movement of the 1960s.

Major influences on public education included: (1) the work of Dewey and Counts, which changed the philosophy of schooling; (2) a major increase in industrial capitalism's influence in government; (3) a worldwide depression that fed the conservative political outlook and bounded by two major world wars, each of which, in different fashion, affected world government, economics, and politics, including those of the United States and its public education system.

A HALF CENTURY OF EDUCATIONAL REFORM, 1950–1990

At the beginning of this chapter we introduced Cuban's (1990) notion of "reforming again, again, and again." What we have written so far about the history of education tends to look like a steady stream of progress toward better, more expensive, more comprehensive and inclusive public education (Peterson, 1985). Many of these advances, shifts, and alterations in public education prior to 1950 were labeled "school reform." Certainly the press to make schools "efficient" through scientific management from 1900 to 1930, reviewed by Callahan (1962), was labeled "reform." Between 1950 and 1990, however, there have been three major attempts to reform education. Taking the 1983 *A Nation at Risk* as the initiating agent of the most recent reform effort, we are nearly ready for the next, provided current trends continue.

Plank (1986) has argued that education reform is often more rhetoric than reality. That is, reform seems to push public education farther and deeper in the direction it has been going. So it may be. Yet those historic events labeled "reform" are major benchmarks of "recharging" and "revitalizing" public education. There were also events during the latter half of the twentieth century that, though not called reform, had a major influence on public education and could be thought of as reform.

Brown v. Topeka School Board

We have already labeled this Supreme Court decision as one of the two *major* restructurings in the history of American education. Some might declare that the decision is only rhetoric, for many public schools, particularly those northern and urban, are more segregated today than at the time of the decision. Yet it seems clear that *Brown v. Topeka School Board* reformed public education and provided a major impetus toward the fulfillment of the promises of freedom and equality for all Americans.

The National Defense Education Act

Enacted by the single Republican president between the Hoover and Nixon administrations, this reform had its "conservative" elements. For one thing the act was couched, both in its title and its preamble, in defense-military terms and values. It was hardly a broad education support bill, aiming only to increase education for the college-bound in math, science, and foreign languages. However, it did infuse large amounts of money into public education in an effort to specifically increase student achievement in these areas.

The Great Society

Lyndon Johnson, like Franklin Roosevelt, had a distrust of professional educators. Johnson's Great Society, like Roosevelt's New Deal, was not centered in the philosophy of George Counts. Johnson placed his bets in areas of the private and public sector largely outside organized public education. Although we had the first Elementary and Secondary Education Act, supplying federal money for the first time to public schools across the board, most of the effort and money of the Great Society to help the condition of the poor went to other agencies, often for literacy education and job training outside of the public education bureaucracy.

The Great Society was a continuation and extension of the New Deal of Franklin Roosevelt and the Fair Deal of Harry Truman. The period from the mid-1960s to the mid-1970s was one of turmoil. There was unrest and rioting in the cities. There was a major civil rights revolution. There was a war in Vietnam — the only war the United States ever lost. Whether because the war absorbed too much money, or because it was ill conceived, or perhaps both, the Great Society reform, largely not a public education reform, failed.

The Vietnam War stimulated vigorous protests on college campuses. Having been taught by public schools to think for themselves, students thought for themselves. When the "old men" in government said "Go fight and die in this war," young men and women on college campuses said "Hell no — we won't go!" The issue came to a head in 1974 at Kent State University when several students were shot to death by government forces. These campus incidents helped influence public opinion and undoubtedly helped bring the war to an end. Conservative politicians have never forgiven schools or universities. Schools had taught young people to think for themselves, and government could not control that thinking process. Independent thinking, while a laudable goal in American democracy, can be an embarrassment to entrenched politicians.

The loss of the war, the resignation of Richard Nixon as president, and the hostage situation of the Carter administration left the American public decimated psychologically. There was probably no period during which national pride was lower. Now enters on the scene Ronald Reagan, "The

Great Communicator," and another realignment election, changing the nature of national politics, including education politics. There was a return to the conservative politics of a not-so-silent majority, and to a Coolidge ideology in government. This resulted in at least twelve years of conservatism in American politics. Corporate America was again King.

The *Nation at Risk* Reforms

Part of President Reagan's "new federalism" was an attack on public education, on the premise that schools were not doing their job. The report of Reagan's education commission labeled *A Nation at Risk* specified that the federal government's responsibility was to point out the failure of public education and then let states and local government pay the cost of correcting it. Thus the education reforms of the 1980s were launched. All were to be *state* reforms. Nearly all centralized power in state education agencies, all required new tax money at state and local levels, all were oriented toward producing a pool of workers so corporate America could compete in world markets. The reforms of the 1980s increased standardization of curriculum, centralization of state authority, and a drive for accountability similar to the "cult of efficiency." The reforms struggled between a quest of meritocracy (raising achievement standards) and egalitarianism (a concern for reducing dropouts). Conservatism in the schools called for constitutional amendments to permit school prayer, for vouchers for private schools, for a better pool of workers for business, and for English as the official language.

This was a period of enormous accumulation of wealth for some, but dire poverty for others. The gap between rich and poor became greater, a larger proportion of the population lived at or below the poverty level, drug use became almost a national pastime, crime increased in urban areas to a point where many viewed the cities as "unsafe," and the number of homeless people became a national disgrace.

These events of the 1980s had a tremendous impact on our large urban centers. Their infrastructure had been neglected for several decades and was crumbling. Roads, sewage, water, transportation, bridges — all the things people had become accustomed to in large urban centers — could no longer be taken for granted. As poverty, homelessness, drugs, and crime increased in the urban centers, more money was needed and given to combat crime. As the cost of crime-fighting accelerated, crime accelerated and politicians pontificated.

Additionally, legal immigration to the United States increased during the 1970s and skyrocketed in the 1980s. Unlike previous waves of immigration, most of the new immigrants were from Asia or from Central and

South America. "In 1988 alone, the U.S. admitted 643,025 immigrants, a 52 year high. Two hundred thousand people — or more — also entered illegally that year, pushing the total close to the record highs set during the so-called Great Wave of immigration" (Harrington-Lueker, 1990, p. 19). What all of this suggests is that American schooling, particularly urban education, will change again, whether by plan or fiat. What it will become we cannot yet see — yet we have had periods in the past when poverty and pockets of newly arrived immigrants populated our great cities. There are differences — but surely we could learn something from history, if only we would.

At this point there is much debate but little evidence that the *Nation at Risk* reforms are succeeding. There is much discourse about "restructuring" schools, but the reforms seem to reemphasize rather than restructure. Assessing the impact of the reforms of the 1980s, Nowakowski and First (1989) raise a serious question about why local school boards were so neglected as an aspect of implementing the reforms. This answer is obvious — the reforms were intended to increase the power of state agencies and decrease the power of local boards. Yet we write now about events and opinions — not history. The events of the 1980s and 1990s are too close, the feelings too personal. With the passage of time, other authors will write the subsequent pages of this history. It is likely that the *politics* of school/community relations will play some role in that process. Counts reminds us that "since education must always be one of the major concerns of any advanced culture, it should be recognized as one of the *central* problems of politics" (1930, pp. 181–182; emphasis added).

Summary of Half Century of Reforms. The major threads of American society, community, and politics are all observable in this half century, including:

1. religion and family influence in schools
2. Anglo-Saxon dominance of schools (although perhaps diminishing)
3. influence of business
4. efforts to reform again, again, and again
5. an effort to push civil rights forward and the back-and-forth struggle between the "haves" and the "have-nots"
6. a continuation of centralization of authority in state education agencies

All of these things and their origins can be seen in the history of American education. One can also see revisions of the ideas each time they resurface. Perhaps that is what we call progress and perhaps that is the best that we, with our frailties, can accomplish.

CONCLUSION

The presentation in this chapter is not a substitute for the study of history of education, nor for reading any of the many fine works written by scholars of the history of education. Rather, this chapter is intended to provide a brief overview of the history of American education as a basis for the study of the politics of school/community relations. Those who study and practice school/community relations should understand the foundations of both the American school and the American community.

Some scholars claim that the influence of American business in public education has been in its own self-interest and pervasive, even to the detriment of the people. The question is raised whether that influence has served the public need or private greed. Others suggest that while the influence of business in public education has been pervasive it has benefited education and the changes resulting from business influence have been progressive. A middle ground suggests that American capitalism is good for the country but that the wholesale adoption of scientific management techniques in the organization and administration of public education in the United States to provide excellence in public education reflects an opportunity lost and therefore was a terrible mistake.

None, however, argue that American business does not influence American politics and that as public education is a political matter, it influences public education. No one or no group is likely to spend time, energy, and money influencing politics against their own interest. We have noted that the United States is not ruled by an oligarchy but by different polyarchies (depending on the issue) of "dispersed inequalities." The American political system is a system of inequalities, but in that system of inequalities some are *more* unequal than others. Corporate America is clearly *not* among the least equal, and this inequality is often to their advantage.

Business and politics have different systems of valuing and operating. Corporate America concentrates power and decisionmaking among a few and uses secrecy as a means of deciding. On the other hand, American politics is generally egalitarian and public, and requires support in one form or another, usually votes. Thus, we have a system of "dispersed inequalities." Corporate America has considerable power and money; those working for a salary or those unemployed have little money individually, but they represent a very large number of votes. Still the resources of corporate America can be, and have been, used to influence the votes of middle-class and poor America, and with the media technology available today this is considerable power indeed.

Regardless of the political power of any one group, it does not always choose to exercise that power, for the exercise of political power has not only big payoffs but, also, big costs. Hunter (1959) studied the U.S. Congress and found that the single most influential power elite was the American Medical Association (AMA). How does one explain that finding? Was Hunter simply wrong? Or does the AMA influence decisions about war and peace, defense spending, spending for social programs, or whether the Corps of Engineers builds dams or bridges? Of course the AMA does not care to nor does it actually influence the entire range of congressional legislation, but during the year that Hunter studied the Congress the AMA used its considerable power to defeat the first potential national medical insurance program, the forerunner of Medicare. They cared to use their influence; they had power; they used it; and they won. That does not mean the AMA controls Congress. In similar fashion, corporate America does not control Congress, nor all public education policy at the federal, state, or local level. Its lobbyists have been extremely effective in influencing public education in the interests of business when they have chosen to do so.

Generalizations about any group do not fit every group member or every situation. Many American businesspeople have altruistically served American education, whether on local boards or through supporting higher taxation in order to improve education, as occurred in Detroit during the 1930s. Business supported Tom Dewey, but Harry Truman won. Harry Truman was the product of a corrupt political machine, and he never repudiated those "friends." History notes, however, that Harry Truman never took or gave a bribe. Generalizations need not hold true in every case in order to be useful. Corporate America has consistently influenced public education in ways of interest to corporate America. It is not a Machiavellian plot to subvert and subject workers; it is American politics. In American democracy—particularly in public education, so long as it remains governed largely by locally elected school boards—the American people can get about what they want by going to the polls and voting. Therefore, it can be contended that in the United States, insofar as public education is concerned, *the people get more or less what they deserve*. A good school/community relations program is the process of helping the public decide what it is getting from the public schools, and what it would like to receive.

As we have seen, the public school system in the United States is unique. In all likelihood, the two-party system in its role in political realignment, along with the local school board, represents structures particular to American politics. The *local* governance of public education has its roots in the basic idea of American democracy and, although not universal among the fifty states (Hawaii has no local districts), it is uniquely American. The local governance of American public education is as much a product of our history as is the freedom to participate or not to participate in the governance process. Both are essential to liberty.

Dissatisfaction and protest were the seeds of our American nation, and the right to express these sentiments was among the concerns of the newly formed national Congress as it enacted the Bill of Rights. No less than these issues must be the concern of those who conduct school/community relation programs, and it is the duty of those who participate in the politics of local school governance to model the tenets of American democracy.

3

The Foundation of the American Community

When people speak of community, whether a particular community or their own community, they often have only a vague notion of what it means. Do all Americans have the same thing in mind when they discuss community? Is a community a geographic place? Must it have political boundaries? When speaking of "the community" do you mean the place where you live, your entire city or town, or only your neighborhood? Are you a member of more than one community (e.g., a church community, a civic community, a professional community, a world community), and which of these is your reference point when you speak of community? Might each of the above be a part of or different from the community of which you are speaking?

In writing about community power, Cunningham (1964) stresses the confusion about the concept or term *community* for both scholars and laypersons.

> I am overwhelmed by the ambiguity surrounding the term "community." It means all things to all people. . . . What is community—really? Is it an epitome of the world as some would argue? . . . Is it a kind of collectivity that possesses *some* sort of central nervous system which responds to stimuli? . . . does it have an intellect which permits it to act on itself . . . or fail to act upon itself—[and therefore] to rot, decay and wither away? (pp. 29–30)

Most people never bother to think about questions such as these, much less spend time wrestling with their answers. Yet the answers to these questions are prerequisite to the study and understanding of school/community relations.

People want community, want a sense of belonging. They want something to believe in and to be a part of. In the last analysis they want a community of which they are a part. Understanding those basic principles should make building a strong school/community relations program as easy as selling snow cones in midsummer at the Little League ballpark.

THE HISTORY OF AMERICAN COMMUNITY

Perhaps the most universally quoted and historically relevant source regarding early American community and government is de Tocqueville's work *Democracy in America*, first published in 1834. The translation used here was published by Knopf in 1945, and in introducing that edition Harold Laski says:

> The *Democracy* presented the whole panorama of politics, observed in detail in one country. The first part treated specific aspects of government and politics in America, even more specifically local government (where de Tocqueville found the taproot of democracy in self-government). (p. xviii)

De Tocqueville seems an appropriate place to begin when trying to understand the relationship of the Dissatisfaction Theory of Democracy to school/community relations. The Dissatisfaction Theory identifies local school boards as "the grassroots of American democracy" (Lutz & Iannaccone, 1978, p. 132). De Tocqueville's views of America's early local government as the "taproot of democracy" is suggestive of a parallel to Dissatisfaction Theory's notion of local school boards as the "grassroots of American democracy."

De Tocqueville emphasized that all nations "bear some marks of their origin" (p. 26). The original elements that precipitated the beginning of this nation can be seen in the present and will contribute to future development. It is in those elements that one can find an explanation of events and behaviors that otherwise seem inexplicable.

The fact that the United States began as a group of Anglo-American settlements, devoutly religious communities or colonies, was extremely important in de Tocqueville's view (p. 28). He noted that both the French and Spanish had established a foothold in the New World. He also predicted that the continued colonization and expansion of the population from the Anglo-American colonies, when it finally came in contact with the French and Spanish, would result in the absorption of those other cultures into a single Anglo-American nation. Although he did not make a specific prediction regarding the Russian settlements (now Alaska), he certainly hit dead center regarding the Spanish and the French.

Furthermore, he was particularly prophetic in his prediction of events that would occur in Texas within the following half-century.

> I have already alluded to what is taking place in the province of Texas. The inhabitants of the United States are perpetually migrating to Texas, where they purchase land [actually many were *given* Spanish land-grants]; and, although they conform to the laws of the country, they are gradually founding the empire of their own language and their own manners. The province of Texas is still part of Mexican domains, but it will soon contain no Mexicans; the same thing has occurred wherever the Anglo-Americans have come in contact with a people of a different origin. (p. 431)

The plight of the Native Americans and African Americans was also noted by de Tocqueville. His comment regarding Native Americans is instructive, coming from a man who greatly admired American democracy. "The Spanish were unable to exterminate the Indian race . . . , nor did they succeed even in wholly depriving it of its rights . . . but Americans have accomplished this two-fold purpose. . . . It is impossible to destroy men with more respect for the laws of humanity" (p. 355). Regarding African Americans he states:

> Oppression has, at one stroke, deprived the descendants of the Africans of almost all the privileges of humanity. The Negro of the United States has lost even the remembrance of his country; the language which his forefathers spoke is never heard around him; he abjured their religion and forgot their customs. (p. 332)

With these words we can reflect on the persistent problems and opportunities in our present schools and communities, as seeds sown in our distant past. To understand today's American community it is prudent to know America's past.

EARLY NEW ENGLAND TOWNSHIPS AND SCHOOLS

If our present community is the result of its history, as de Tocqueville (1945) suggests (and de Tocqueville was the classic observer of past American democracy), what does he have to say about early American communities and schools? Again, de Tocqueville focuses on New England townships. While there was colonization in America by other nations, some even prior to the Mayflower's arrival, de Tocqueville believed that it was the English colonies that set the tone for what was to become the national culture of the United States. Other nations had colonized, and there are ethnic groups whose presence in our nation is due to later immigrations, but English remains the pervasive language and our *common* customs and politics tend to be more influenced by Anglo traditions than by others. In fact, "the tie of language" was an important element, according to de Tocqueville, in shaping American democracy (p. 28).

From the beginning, while recognizing the governance of the British Empire, the English colonies still saw the "independence of the township." Here was the center and heart of "interests, passions, rights and duties" of the people (p. 40). Here people lived together, worked together, organized for protection, aided one another, worshiped together, and lived so as to "satisfy a crowd of social wants" (p. 41). It was the township that was the heart of American democracy. "But it is by the mandates relating to public education that the original character of American civilization is at once placed in its clearest light" (p. 41). Thus, de Tocqueville welds the concepts of community and school into a cornerstone of the American democracy.

Basic to this foundation of American democracy (the township and public schools) is the idea of the sovereignty of the people. "In America the principal of the sovereignty of the people is neither barren nor concealed . . . , it is recognized by the customs and proclaimed by its laws, it spreads freely, and arrives without impediment at its most remote consequences" (p. 55). It is clear that de Tocqueville saw community in the township and the township principle as essential to American democracy. "The village or township is the only association which is so perfectly natural that, wherever a number of men are collected, it seems to constitute itself" (p. 60). Further, he notes that centralized and autocratic governments cannot "tolerate local independence," and that "municipal institutions constitute the strength of free nations . . . [bringing liberty] within the people's reach, they teach men how to use and how to enjoy it" (pp. 60–61). De Tocqueville goes on to describe how the township in America, which at that time averaged somewhat fewer than 2,000 people per community, brought legislative and administrative action close to the people. He enumerates the duties of township officials, often putting public schools first among those duties (p. 63), concluding that "not a man can be found that would acknowledge that the state has any right to interfere in their town affairs" (p. 65), and that "without power and independence a town may contain good subjects, but it can have no active citizens" (p. 67).

It was clear to de Tocqueville that the election of the legislative body by "the people *directly* and for a *very brief term*" (his emphasis) provided access of the will of the people to modify their government. His emphasis on a "very brief term" is particularly noteworthy in light of today's criticism of members of Congress regarding their propensity to perpetuate their tenure and privileges. De Tocqueville went so far as to assert that it was necessary that elected officials be subject "not only to the general convictions [of the people], but even the daily passions of their constituents" (p. 254). Although totally supportive of the "will of the majority," de Tocqueville saw a danger in it, for when "the power of opinion . . . [might operate] so that no obstacles exist which can impede or even retard its progress, so as to make it heed the complaints of those whom it crushes upon its path, this state of things is harmful in itself and dangerous for the future" (p. 256). Such a condition may presently occur when public opinion is easily influenced by mass media at the disposal of rich and powerful oligarchies and centralized seats of government at both the state and federal level. In support of this thesis de Tocqueville states, "If ever the free institutions of America are destroyed, that event may be attributed to the omnipotence of the majority, which may at some future time urge the minorities to desperation" (p. 269). Could it be that the continual movement over the past 150 years, from local community governance of public education toward strong state education agencies and centralized state control, is part of just such a move?

De Tocqueville places public education at the heart of democracy. He declares, "It cannot be doubted that in the United States the instruction of the people powerfully contributes to the support of the democratic republic; and such must always be the case" (p. 317). But education alone is insufficient to maintain the democracy, he declares. Hands-on experience with democracy is essential and, without recognizing it, de Tocqueville states the essential tenent of the Dissatisfaction Theory of Democracy — that, as one of the last remaining local-public governance structures, *locally* elected school boards are essential to American democracy in the complex political world of American democracy today. De Tocqueville adds, "The American learns to know the laws by participating in the act of legislation; he takes a lesson in the forms of government by governing. The great work of society [the process of democratic government] is ever going on before his eyes and, as it were, under his hands" (p. 318).

In America today there is some sense of "loss of community." This is undoubtedly due to the large and complex nature of today's society as opposed to the one de Tocqueville saw. Today there are few individuals living in incorporated towns with populations of fewer than 2,000, where de Tocqueville saw the "taproot" of American democracy in operation. It may be that local school districts are the last, or at least the best, place in the United States where that hands-on participation in government is still possible for all of the people. Even in cities as large as New York and Chicago, meaningful efforts at decentralizing and democratizing school governance have taken place in the form of school/community control boards. Perhaps the local governance of schools is the place where citizens can find a sense of community today.

The notion of direct hands-on participation in governance is important not only for school/community relations but, perhaps, even for American democracy itself. Those who advocate massive consolidation of local school districts into supercentralized complex organizations of 100,000 or more pupils might consider the consequences of the loss of that sense of community which accompanies and is inherent in the concept of *"my school district."* The loss of the opportunity to see the operation of the will of the people in a local governance system where your neighbor is actually your representative and where your vote makes a difference in so important an issue as the education of your own children is much to be lamented and is usually opposed by those whose political power is thus diminished.

The views of de Tocqueville and the application of those views to school/community relations are important for several reasons. Many historians and sociologists regard de Tocqueville's observations of American democracy as classic, describing the foundation on which our nation was built. The original source is somewhat extensively quoted here because educational administration often gets too far from the primary source on which its precepts are built. Occasionally generalization is piled on generalization until one no longer recognizes the original idea. The concept of American democracy and that of community are so essential to the practice of school/community relations that risking distortion by the use of only secondary sources is not justified. Without a clear vision of the roots and wellsprings of American democracy, public schools risk losing both of those precious institutions simply for the sake of efficiency.

CHANGES SINCE DE TOCQUEVILLE

Almost at the same moment de Tocqueville was writing, changes were taking place both in the United States and in the world that would modify some of what he had observed. As indicated in Chapter 2, the notion of Manifest Destiny was beginning to be played out in the history of the United States. Actually, de Tocqueville's (1945) observations were amazing, accurate, and foresighted. He saw that the events already taking place would eventually shape a nation, not only from coast to coast but to the mid-Pacific and into the Arctic circle as well. He clearly saw the evolution of events in California, Texas, and even the Missouri and Mississippi valleys, where the Anglo culture would dominate the Spanish, Mexican, and French cultures and languages. He saw the subjugation of the Native Americans and the impossible condition of slavery.

He generally failed, however, to foresee the impact of the immigrations of people from other nations, which would reshape the nation. He gave no hint of the massive influence of Asian culture or of the immigrations from Mexico and Central and South America that today play such a major role in reshaping American culture. He totally failed to envision the separation of church and state in the schools, or the bilingual programs in today's schools; in fact, he asserted that it was "the tie of a common language" (p. 28) and the strong influence of religion "as the safeguard of morality" (p. 44) that made democracy in America unique. If de Tocqueville was correct in those assertions, and if they are true today, our government and its courts must rethink some decisions.

De Tocqueville could not have foreseen the advances in communication that make instant audiovisual world communication a matter of fact in every living room; the transportation and agro-business technology that permits, if not mandates, the continued demise of the small isolated community and the family farm. He could not have envisioned the population expansion that fuels large and geographically extensive metro-corridors encompassing millions of people. These changes contribute to a sense of loss of the community observed by de Tocqueville. Still, it was the Anglo-American township/community with its political/historical/cultural traditions that began and still serves as the taproot of American democracy and culture.

Cubberly pointed out that an important factor in the growth of the American public school was "the rise of cities and manufacturing" (1920, p. 667). This of course also effected changes in the nature of community. He noted that until 1820, about the time of de Tocqueville's visit, there were only thirteen cities with populations above 8,000, and that the entire population housed in cities comprised less than 5 percent of the nation's population.

Between 1620 and 1820 towns grew not so much in size as in number. Transportation and the agrarian nature of work required small population centers. When towns grew too large, people moved on, setting up new communities, usually mirroring the community its inhabitants had left, both in style and culture. A significant part of the transplanted culture was always religion and education. As Good (1960) points out, in colonial America, education, religion, and community often went hand in hand (pp. 376–386). Thus, American public education and American democracy are, from their beginnings, inseparable.

While education varied from community to community and from region to region, there was concern in all the colonies that education be part of the community and a recognition that it was a necessity for citizen participation in government and religious worship (Cremin, 1970). According to Cremin, "Within such a community, household, church, school, and college both supported and reinforced the informal nature of daily life. With such a community too, responsibilities moved easily from one institution to another" (p. 237).

CONCEPTS FOR UNDERSTANDING COMMUNITY

As previously indicated, community means many things to many people. More difficult still, for the purpose of mutual understanding and analysis, it can mean many different things to the same person so that meaning may fluctuate as discussion proceeds. The work of Tonnies, first published in 1887 under the title *Gemeinschaft unt Gesellschaft* and translated by Loomis (1957) as *Community and Society*, is helpful in solving this problem. That work provides a basic and essential insight for the discussion of today's community.

Writing just before the turn of the nineteenth century, when Western Europe and the United States were deeply immersed in the industrial revolution, Tonnies was concerned about the relentless movement from an agrarian society to an industrial society. This trend involved people leaving their small communities and their extended families and moving to large cities where they had no traditional support systems. More explicitly, Tonnies was concerned with the changes this movement signaled for social interaction and the human conditions accompanying such changes.

Although Tonnies (1957) translates *gemeinschaft* and *gesellschaft* as "community" and "society," those German words are not directly or literally translatable. As the concepts are used to define and describe community and society, another meaning may be suggested, a meaning more useful to us in understanding the community or the society. We suggest "folklike" for the concept gemeinschaft-like, and "urbanlike" for gesellschaft-like. The concepts gemeinschaft and gesellschaft are not a dichotomy, that is, exclusively this or that. They define an ideal-typical, conceptual continuum, as explained by Bender (1978). Thus, a community or society, or a subunit of that community or society, can be more gemeinschaft-like (folklike), or gesellschaft-like (urbanlike). As these terms are cumbersome, we will simply refer to gemeinschaft or gesellschaft and rely on the reader to remember that these concepts are not dichotomous and separate but rather represent an ideal-typical continuum.

Using this continuum, as illustrated in Figure 3.1, person A might describe the city in which he or she lives as (1) extremely gesellschaft; the neighborhood as (2) somewhat gesellschaft; the workplace as (3) rather gesellschaft; church as (4) rather gemeinschaft; and family (5) as very

Figure 3.1
Persons A and B along a gemeinschaft/gesellschaft continuum

Person A	(5)		(4)	(2)		(3)	(1)
Person B IV		I	II	V		III	

Gemeinschaft   Gesellschaft

gemeinschaft. Each of these places of social interaction can be positioned separately along the ideal-typical continuum.

Person B works for the same organization (III) but lives in a small commuter town (I), has little neighborhood contact (II) due to a commuter style of living, has no family (V) within 500 miles, but attends a small and very close-knit church (IV) in a neighboring town. This person's social interaction settings are represented in Figure 3.1 by roman numerals. It is obvious that these two people A and B will have a different personal sense of community. Each may think about some different social entity when thinking of "my community."

Tonnies's Ideal-Typical Continuum

A sense of community suggests and is parallel to a *personal* sense of social relationships. Discussing this, Tonnies says, "Social relationship or bond implies interdependence, and it means that the will of one person influences that of another, either furthering or impeding, or both" (1887/ 1957, p. 242). Tonnies was referring to the fact that different individuals in the same geographic place may have different views of or sense of community. This is similar to the phenomenon illustrated in Figure 3.1. Tonnies explicitly defined Gemeinschaft and Gesellschaft.

> In contrast to Gemeinschaft, Gesellschaft is transitory and superficial. Accordingly Gemeinschaft should be understood as a living organism, Gesellschaft as a mechanical aggregate and artifact. (p. 35)

And again,

> Gesellschaft . . . is to be understood as a multitude of natural and artificial individuals, the wills, and spheres of whom are in many relations with and to one another, and remain never-the-less independent of one another and devoid of mutual familiar relationships. (p. 76)

Although some contend that Tonnies preferred gemeinschaft over gesellschaft and lamented its loss, that argument is of no real importance
here. The point is simply that there exist, theoretically and empirically,
two generalized types of social relationships. One is a bonding together of
people with other people, roles with other roles, and lives with other lives.
In the gemeinschaft community things are not separated. You are not a
good councilperson and a poor worker. You are not a poor mother and a
good church member. There is a tradition, and that tradition, as Tevia
informs us in *Fiddler on the Roof*, tells everyone who they are, what they
are to do, "and what God expects of them. Without tradition life would
be—as shaky as a fiddler on the roof!" Anatevka is a prototypic Gemeinschaft community.

As Tonnies says, "in the Gemeinschaft they [the people] remain essentially united in spite of all separating factors" (p. 65). Continuing in the
same sentence, Tonnies identifies the essential element in the gesellschaft
community: "they [the people] are essentially separated in spite of all uniting factors" (p. 65).

In the gesellschaft community, not only are people separated from
other people, but any one role a single individual may play is separate from
other roles played by the same person. One group is independent of the
other group, and values held by one group are often different from, and
even in conflict with, values held by the other group.

Tonnies may be interpreted as saying that there was an evolution
throughout the last century, driven by industrialization and technology,
moving society from gemeinschaft to gesellschaft, which in turn destroyed
community (gemeinschaft). While it is true that Tonnies can be read that
way, Bender (1978) sees it differently.

> Simply placing Tonnies and his development of the Gemeinschaft–Ge-
> sellschaft typology into proper historical context begins to reveal the real
> meaning of his concept and its usefulness for the study of community.
> Gemeinschaft and Gesellschaft were not places; they were forms of hu-
> man interaction. Whereas he [Tonnies] indicated that Gesellschaft was
> gaining significance in peoples' lives, he did not say that *all* relationships
> were or would become what he called Gesellschaft. "The force of Ge-
> meinschaft persists," he wrote, "even within the period of Gesellschaft."
> (p. 33)

Other Sociological Concepts

One can recognize some similarity between Tonnies's concept of gesellschaft and Weber's concept of bureaucracy (1964). Both have been
commonly misunderstood and misapplied. Both concepts were invented by

German sociologists in an effort to explain and understand the historical-social movements embracing Western Europe, particularly Germany, in the latter part of the nineteenth century. Like Tonnies, who clearly did not look forward to a totally gesellschaft society, Weber did not relish a society reduced to the perfect bureaucracy. At one time he warned that such an organization would be an "iron cage" for humanity (see Mitzman, 1970, for a discussion of the Iron Cage and Weber's relationship to the work of Tonnies). Can you imagine the "perfect" bureaucracy without the problem of human emotions, without anger, jealousy, revenge, or greed, but also without friendship, kindness, charity, or compassion? Extended to the total society, that notion becomes even more deadly. Thus it is easy to understand not only Tonnies's lack of enthusiasm for the gesellschaft society but our own dislike of the rapid trend toward gesellschaft and our use (or misuse) of the word *bureaucrat*.

Another German sociologist living in the late 1880s and early 1900s comes to mind who also thought that the trend toward industrialization was driving humankind to despair. He thought that because of this trend toward industrialization individuals were losing their dignity. Robert Michels (1966) suggested in 1911 that there was a tendency toward an "iron law of oligarchy" within which a very few individuals inevitably dominated and ruled the many. Given the conditions of a gesellschaft society, regardless of how egalitarian or democratic a society or organization was when it began, he believed that it would eventually evolve into one where an oligarchy would make the decisions for and rule the masses, in the interests of the oligarchy.

In similar and more revolutionary fashion, another German sociologist of this period, Karl Marx, saw a clash of the class structure driven by these same forces, resulting in violent revolution and, finally, the fall of that iron oligarchy — the bureaucracy — resulting in the dictatorship of the people (for a general discussion see Magill, 1981). Marx's predictions clearly were off track. Perhaps that was because there is an iron law of oligarchy, and it dominated the USSR, particularly under Stalin. The most prominent German sociological/philosophical movement of the late 1800s and early 1900s was "Critical Theory." This movement rejected Soviet communism under Lenin and Stalin as more insidious than capitalism because of the domination of the Russian people by an intolerable and totalitarian bureaucracy ruled by one man. While some intellectuals have attempted to explain away this bureaucratic totalitarianism, it has refused to go away. It has been wonderful to witness the Berlin Wall and other symbols of iron cages coming down in Eastern Europe. Even the USSR experienced an upheaval and democratization unimaginable under the Soviet bureaucracy. These events are proof that within any people there exists the seeds of a gemeinschaft society and of democracy of the American kind, no matter how gesellschaft, bureaucratic, and totalitarian a society becomes. Always for these people "freedom" meant and means *American* democracy, a community in which people express and experience democracy in a hands-on fashion.

A MODERN PERSPECTIVE ON COMMUNITY

The literature on the politics and sociology of community is enormous and impossible to cite in its entirety, much less review here. The option taken is to present a brief, succinct, classic, and historical review of the sociology of community. Bender (1978) developed such a historical perspective of community by examining the concepts of Tonnies in parallel with more recent works of Cooley (1909), Durkheim (1933), Lewis (1951), Parsons, Bales, and Shils (1953), Redfield (1941), and Wirth (1938), to mention but a few.

As explained above, Bender does not see gemeinschaft–gesellschaft as dichotomous and descriptive of one place as opposed to another. He notes, "Gemeinschaft and Gesellschaft describe . . . two patterns of social relationships that *coexisted* [emphasis added] in everyone's social experience. [They] . . . were not place; they were forms of human interaction" (p. 33). He points out that community must be studied within the larger context of a complex society in which there are "multiple loyalties" — some belonging to communities and others to roles an individual plays, such as "professional, cooperate employee, homeowner, citizen" (p. 59).

Bender insists that "the study of community must focus on tension and interaction [between gemeinschaft and gesellschaft]. . . . Although the equilibrium between community and society shifted [since the early 1800s] community never disappeared. It was, however, transformed" (p. 119). This transformation has, apparently, left some students of community confused and myopic when attempting to deal with the concept of community in today's modern complex society. People live in two social contexts, which constantly compete for time and other resources in a society that has "involved men and women simultaneously in gemeinschaft and gesellschaft" (p. 136). This greatly complicates their world and the attempts of social scientists and school politicians to explain and understand it.

Bender points out that the relationships between school, family, and other social institutions used to be fluid across institutional boundaries. Since the industrial revolution, the boundaries have become more clearly defined. These more rigid boundaries tend to establish more exclusive roles and to make the job of school/community relationships more complicated and difficult. Bender seems to suggest the school as a bridge between the family, or the gemeinschaft society, and the larger, impersonal, competitive, economic-political gesellschaft society in which children and adults must exist.

The American democracy observed by de Tocqueville has changed but not disappeared. It is there we find the taproots of social experience that allow it to grow, blossom, and bear fruit. All was not wonderful in the gemeinschaft society of the *Scarlet Letter*, however; just ask Hester Prynne about Salem. Bender notes:

> [the] societal development [the movement toward gesellschaft] has profoundly complicated our lives, but it has also made it richer. The experience of living in two social and psychological worlds, gemeinschaft and gesellschaft, may produce tensions, but it also offers the prospect of a creative disorderliness in the interstices of these imperfectly integrated social forms. (1978, p. 146)

What better description of *chaos* (Gleick, 1987) in the social sciences could be offered? The search for community fails because people "have misunderstood the changing character of community. By looking for the experience of community in areas that had become public, they found themselves bereft of community and ignorant of public culture" (Bender, 1978, p. 150).

Sacred Versus Secular Communities

Another concept useful for understanding community is Howard Becker's (1968) continuum of community valuing, sacred versus secular. Like gemeinschaft–gesellschaft, the sacred-secular concepts of Becker do not represent dichotomous and mutually exclusive concepts but ideal-typical concepts at the extremes of a single continuum of human group behavior. Sacred, like gemeinschaft, was clearly part of the origin of the American democracy described by de Tocqueville. To quote Becker, "It may well be possible that democracy, as a kind of secular society in moving equilibrium, may sometime reach a point where the sacred elements which *called it into being* and which still sustain it will be left behind—but that point has not yet been reached" (1968, p. 74; emphasis added).

It is unlikely that such a complete shift toward the secular end of the continuum will ever take place, yet the largely sacred community of the *Scarlet Letter* was surely not the essence of what we cherish today as American democracy. The social mobility afforded through secular elements of society is extremely important to citizens, surely just as important as the sacred elements found in their families and associations.

It is clear that a strong parallel exists between the gemeinschaft — gesellschaft and sacred–secular continua. Again, it is well to seek a way in which each tool for assessing community can prove useful without being completely overlapping. We suggest using gemeinschaft-gesellschaft to describe the structural elements of the community and, following Iannaccone and Lutz (1970, pp. 29-51), using sacred–secular to understand the valuing process of that community. Even within a single school board some members may hold sacred values while others hold secular values. This range of values among board members may represent a range of values in the community. As Merton points out, "People may work at cross-purposes precisely because they are living up to the norms of their respective positions in society" (1968, p. 68). This not only accounts for the behavior of some special-interest groups in school district politics, but also occasional sharp differences of opinion and caustic public exchanges between school board members. Unfortunately, neither school board/superintendent literature nor professional programs prepare board members or superintendents to reasonably manage political conflict. The norm and expectation is for unanimity and consensus. Thus, the occurrence of political conflict is often a matter of considerable consternation and difficulty in school/community relations. Actually, conflict is more natural and usual in secular valuing and gesellschaft organizations than is unanimity and consensus. As any single community can exhibit both sacred *and* secular values, as well as both gemeinschaft and gesellschaft structure elements, it is predictable that conflict about public education will sometimes arise within school boards.

Vidich and Bensman (1968, pp. 174-202) present an excellent case of a small, generally sacred valuing and gemeinschaft town, in which school politics during the fifteen-year study was couched in high conflict and managed by the board through "stonewalling" tactics. Although they report that "despite these crises, the decisions of the board stand and the social composition of the board remains the same" (p. 178), it is our belief and experience that such a condition was soon to change.

Becker, who arguably best understands the concepts sacred–secular, declares that "societies which impress upon their members modes of conduct making for a high degree of resistance to change are for us sacred societies" (1968, p. 44). Explaining this definition, he continues, "The means by which these ends [preventing social change] are sought are chiefly of traditionally nonrational and sanctioned rational types" (p. 45). Thus, Becker emphasizes that sacred societies are very likely to become "isolated" (p. 47).

On the other hand, a secular society is not likely to become isolated because "a secular society is one in which resistance to change is at a

minimum . . . where change in many aspects of life is usually quite welcome. . . . Secular is the photographic negative of sacred" (p. 67). Therefore, "secular societies are ordinarily accessible — the antithesis of isolated"
(p. 68).

Emphasizing that problems also exist in open, secular societies, as well
as in closed, sacred societies, Becker states: "Because of its 'social accessibil-
ity,' the secular society tends to be open, without rigid barriers where
. . . gangsters and socialites mingle in the tolerant haven of the Stork
Club, Number 21, or other modish hangouts." Such a mingling of values
and flaunting of virtue would never be openly tolerated in a sacred society.
As Becker points out, this apparent normlessness may result in "easy disre-
gard of matters once held as sacred, also in their ostentatious flaunting" (p.
69).

Within a given community one finds some groups that value tradition
and the way things are, or more accurately perhaps, the way they *were*.
Such individuals "know" because they have been there. "It" has been tried.
One does not "fix what isn't broke." Little trust is put in research as a tool
of decisionmaking. Everything from medical decisions to what is wrong
with the car to how to educate the children is decided within the "good old
boy network." A great deal of what is known among such individuals is
based on oral tradition. The local newspaper verifies that tradition; it
seldom, if ever, challenges it. As these values are exhibited by the majority
of the citizens, and particularly the powerful, the community can be described as a sacred valuing community. Sacred valuing communities resist
change and value tradition, utilizing "controlled" rumor and gossip as a
means of communicating and knowing. It is obvious that in today's world
of the six o'clock network news and of computer-transmitted newspapers,
no community can be totally divorced from all views and opinions that
challenge their own. In such a world, no person and surely no community
can be totally cut off from the secular world. Some communities, particularly religious ones such as the Amish, go to elaborate means in order to
isolate themselves from the secular world. Still, they fail to totally isolate
their own sense of community and values from change.

In any community one will find individuals and groups with secular
values that challenge the traditional sacred values. The traditional country
doctor is confronted with medical research printed in *Woman's Day* or
broadcast on the evening news. The doctor is challenged by some patients
armed with this information, and the old community hospital is struggling
to survive, or failing to survive, as patients reject the sacred values, abandon "Old Doc" and *his* hospital — accepting a young, newly trained, fe-
male physician who is on the staff at the large, well equipped hospital in
an urban center a mere seventy miles away.

Likewise, the mechanic, down at the old gas station, is having a difficult time dealing with new cars that require computerized diagnosis and the replacement of modular components in order to make them run correctly. Parents both work, but they read Gallup's poll about education, see on the evening news a special report about teen pregnancy and drug abuse in the schools, and learn that public schools are failing. Too tired to attend the open house at the school, they have not met their children's teachers or principal since they enrolled them six years ago. As such individuals increasingly become the majority of the residents of any community, the sacred traditions and values are challenged and often abandoned as secular values are adopted and finally prized. Thus, school/community relations become more complex.

Often individuals holding secular values do not trust those holding sacred values, nor do those holding sacred values trust those with secular values. They do not trust one another because they do not trust the other value system. As one group vies for the power held by the other, distrust becomes the norm and conflict management and negotiation become increasingly difficult.

Ideal-Typical Continua

In the foregoing we have been careful not to present sacred and secular as dichotomous concepts. Dichotomies are useful, but often artificial, constructs. As we say tall or short, bad or good, sweet or sour, we communicate useful information to others, but each of these "artificial" dichotomies assumes a specific though arbitrary reference point. The fact is that most of the reference standards we use as dichotomous are not true dichotomies. Rather, they represent continua on which individual cases will fall more toward one "ideal" construct or the other. Most dichotomies are false — becoming dichotomies only because it is convenient to create them.

This is exactly the case with the constructs gemeinschaft–gesellschaft and sacred–secular, which are provided here for understanding community. Communities are not *either* gemeinschaft or gesellschaft. They are not *either* sacred- or secular-valuing. Rather, they are more one or the other, and very likely any single community will exhibit some elements tending toward both ends of the continuum.

How Can a Single Community Be Both?

Imagine a large urban community of 500,000 or more. Many individuals commute daily to jobs they may not like in the city and return in the evening to homes and families they hardly see. They know only a few of their fellow workers and those they do know do not know their spouses or children. These people do not know the parents of their children's friends. They may go to church once in a while but have no time to linger after the service or to attend church groups.

In that same city are neighborhoods, often ethnic neighborhoods of Italians, Irish, Germans, Hispanics, Greeks, African Americans, and so forth. Often these neighborhoods have colloquial names (e.g., The Hill, The Patch, The South Side, Germantown, etc.) that typify their norms, values, traditions, and ethnicity. Sometimes "others" are not totally welcome in these gemeinschaft, sacred-valuing communities — not even as visitors or "passers-through." The occasional outsider who does live in the Italian neighborhood is known simply as "The Dutchman." He does not need a name. Everyone knows who he is because there is but one "Dutchman," who goes to a different church and speaks with a different accent. Such an Italian neighborhood is surely an example of gemeinschaft.

The point is that even within the most gesellschaft, secular-valuing cities, there exist gemeinschaft *communities* that carefully guard their sacred values. Although hardly to be prized, the violent teenage gangs that terrorize many urban areas are, in fact, examples of gemeinschaft and sacred-valuing community for their members — gemeinschaft and sacred are not always good or moral.

Tonnies (1887/1957) himself pointed out that gemeinschaft exists with gesellschaft communities. Violent gangs demonstrate how difficult it is to change the gemeinschaft when we wish. With the exception of such antisocial behavior, we would not want to change it if we could. Although sometimes hidden by the complexities of the modern society, community is not gone in the United States. Human nature seeks community, and by seeking it will find it in spite of us, if not because of us.

Remaining Rural America

In society's rush toward gesellschaft, as lamented by Tonnies (1887/1957), it is easy to believe that rural America will soon pass into oblivion, if it has not already done so. Nothing could be further from the truth. There remain more rural school districts in the nation than there are urban school districts. Often suburban communities, with their green lawns and gardens, local churches, and community centers, have at least as many gemeinschaft and sacred-valuing characteristics as gesellschaft and secular-valuing characteristics.

Of some philosophic, if not practical–political, concern is the question of how to deal with the remaining rural schools. Tonnies (1887/1957) was correct. There has been, and continues increasingly to be, a movement

from gemeinschaft toward gesellschaft in the larger society. The entire
"reform" of the 1980s has surely not changed this trend. It has not altered
the bureaucratization and centralization of the public schools, but rather
reinforced them. We are too often driven by fear and greed to compete in
an expanding industrial-gesellschaft world society. The public schools are
recognized as an important element in that process. Can the gemeinschaft
community exist in this gesellschaft world? If it cannot, where can human
beings find the sense of community they so desperately seek and seem to
require? Can we consolidate rural schools out of existence? And if we can,
do we want to? Without the rural schools can there be rural community?
Without rural communities as a model, can the gemeinschaft community
exist in this "iron cage" for humanity? Can we be inventive and compas-
sionate enough to encourage gemeinschaft experiences within a gesellschaft society? Must those with power crush those without it? If they do,
what is left for those who rule and for the rest who do not?

CONCLUSION

Perhaps the university community can serve as a useful example of differences and similarities within a political community. Alvin Gouldner (1957/
1958) suggested the concepts of local-cosmopolitan as useful for examining
that "community of scholars" comprising the university. In Gouldner's
terms, a professor who is a "local" cares most about the institution, serves
on local committees, adheres to institutional norms, and advances within
the organization usually by befriending powerful or influential locals. Locals exhibit sacred values and gemeinschaft behaviors. Conversely, the
professor who is a "cosmopolitan" cares most about the discipline, relates
to a national network, and works at producing research and publications
in journals referred by other cosmopolitans at distant institutions. A cosmopolitan usually advances in rank and salary and toward tenure because
other institutions bid for services, whether the cosmopolitan actually ac-
cepts another position or not. Such a professor exhibits secular values and
gesellschaft behaviors.

This dichotomous picture of the university is, however, oversimplified.
All locals know professors at other universities, who may also be locals.
Some professional organizations are structured as "watering holes" for locals. At meetings of such organizations, locals are joined by locals to discuss mutual concerns, exhibit gemeinschaft behaviors, and reinforce sacred values. Thus the locals look like cosmopolitans as they attend national
meetings and publish, though usually in nonreferred journals edited by
fellow locals.

On the other hand, every cosmopolitan seeks some campus colleague to befriend, generally abides by some of the local norms, occasionally plants a tree or bush, and, after leaving the institution, wonders if it has grown. Most professional organizations, even the most cosmopolitan ones, have norms that members are expected to follow, and gatekeepers who pass judgment before the association's professional honors are bestowed on a recipient. Even the most cosmopolitan will occasionally wonder, "If I say this or write that, will my colleagues think well of me?" and then modify what otherwise would have been written or said.

Community is not simply a place. It is not simply a set of norms or values, or a group of people, some with and others without informal power. It is all of these at different times and, sometimes, all of them at once. One can be a member of more than one community. Everyone seeks to be part of a community, yet also becomes uneasy when too many obligations are demanded by too dominating a community. At some point sacred and gemeinschaft become unbearable. The community seeks interaction with the school but will reject its domination. They demand gesellschaft opportunities, but seek gemeinschaft understanding and acceptance.

Bender (1978, pp. 136–137) suggests that today's "bifurcated society" requires people to operate simultaneously in both gemeinschaft and gesellschaft modes of behavior, producing psychological conflict. This requirement calls for a dual "psychological repertoire," and when a behavior from the inappropriate repertoire is selected in a given instance, unhappiness and frustration are certain to result.

Speaking specifically about schools, Bender contends that

> in colonial towns, the school as a setting for social interaction was not much different from the family or any other social institution. . . . By the mid-nineteenth century, when the quality of social relations in the middle-class family became distinct from that in other social institutions, a more complicated program of socialization was needed. (p. 138)

Because this sociological fact has generally been ignored for 150 years, it is quite past time to develop "a more complicated" school/community relations program based on well-established sociological concepts.

A final comment related to both research and practice in school/community relations must be made. Much of what has been said here suggests that community is at least as much in the "mind of the beholder" as it is a matter of observable, empirical, and measurable quantification. Community is a matter of personal social relationships and perception of those relationships. This suggests that the phenomenological perceptions may be as important as the empirical reality of whether opportunities to participate and shape decisions are provided for citizens. Do citizens "feel" involved and listened to, and are their demands responded to properly? If you want to know, ask the people what they *think*. It is not nearly so important (operationally at least — and perhaps even as an element of research) to know what the public relations director can show based on printed brochures, meetings conducted, and letters mailed — all of which, to be sure, can be counted.

There is a saying — "if you can't beat 'em, join 'em!" School people might take that saying to heart. If you want a strong school/community relations program, join the community. Recognize the diverse and pluralistic values, aspirations, and wants represented within the community. Understand that several people with the same interests become a special-interest group — not to be shunned and beaten down, but to be heard, understood, and helped. Banfield and Wilson (1963) in their book *City Politics* demonstrate that it was not the corruption of the political machine that kept it in office, but the *friendship* established between the machine and the voters. When a voter needed something (e.g., a job, a ticket fixed, a street light repaired), she or he went to the machine and got what was needed. When the machine wanted votes it went to its friends (i.e., the voters it had helped) and got votes. This may be the best way of operating a school/community relations program — not to beat them, but to join them.

4

Superintendent/School Board Relationships

Much has been written about the role and duties of the superintendent. A case has been made for the superintendent as philosopher (Callahan, 1962), as school executive (Downey, 1984), as community leader (Fields, 1988), as budget manager (Hartley, 1989), and as politician (Iannaccone & Lutz, 1970). Each of these images contains some truth and becomes a reality at some particular moment in the life of a superintendent.

The single most important job of any superintendent from a practical point of view, however, is getting along with the school board. One perspective suggests that the superintendent is in an extremely vulnerable position (Callahan, 1962) and does what must be done to keep the position, so as to do any good at all. Colloquially we say "One goes along to get along."

There are, of course, more specific recommendations to be made in an effort to establish a good superintendent/board relationship than simply to go along and get along. In fact, that notion itself will never work, not for very long at least. Not with any school board. Actually the "popular" literature and even some research literature has several alternative suggestions about how to maintain a good superintendent/board relationship.

One of the ideas often offered is for superintendents to always remember that they serve at the "pleasure of the board" and for a fixed period (Shannon, 1989). Such a suggestion carries the notion of vulnerability and getting along. That advice results from numerous studies suggesting a "shopping list" of areas that could generate conflict between the board, or board members, and the superintendent. Generally superintendents are admonished to *avoid* such conflicts rather than taught how to manage them (Blumberg, 1985; Krajewski, 1983; Trotter & Downey, 1989).

One particular area in board/superintendent conflict often chosen for special note is how to avoid getting involved in role conflict with the board by failing to recognize the "proper" roles played by boards and superintendents (Alvey & Underwood, 1985; Bisso, 1988; Hentges, 1986). In an effort to establish clear lines of role behavior and to avoid role conflict, superintendents are admonished to see to it that their boards receive proper training in the way a board member and the board as a whole should behave, that is, "rules and recipes" of board behavior (Plunker & Krueger, 1987; Trotter & Downey, 1989). Another method often suggested in order to avoid board/superintendent confrontation is to clearly establish regular and bureaucratic means of evaluating the superintendent (Braddom, 1986; Brown et al., 1985).

Some studies suggest that superintendents get into trouble by trying to dominate their boards (Awender, 1985) while others almost suggest that such domination is the expected mode and accepted by some school boards (Tallerico, 1989). A more reasonable approach, however, may be one in which boards and superintendents "learn" to work together in compatible styles (Katz, 1985). Thus, by using the board president as a buffer or sounding board for the entire school board/community, the superintendent can stand aloof from any conflict (Freund, 1988). These and other policies are often suggested to superintendents as sources of conflict management and methods of avoiding vulnerability.

Zeigler, Kehoe, and Reisman (1985) disagree about the vulnerability of the superintendent, at least as compared with other top organizational management positions — in particular that of city manager. After all life itself, and certainly management positions, is vulnerable and superintendents are paid pretty well for their job vulnerability. Superintendents may tend to avoid necessary risk taking and sometimes "use" the vulnerability thesis as an excuse for not taking those reasonable risks necessary in order to provide the *leadership* required for excellence in public education. Excellence requires leadership and excellence requires money. In order to get that money some risks must be taken.

Regardless of one's viewpoint, it remains true that if a superintendent wants to remain in the well-paid superintendency at "Paradise School District," that superintendent is well advised to maintain a good relationship with the "Paradise School Board." The first and most important job of a superintendent who wants to remain in any particular position is to create and maintain a good strong superintendent/school board relationship.

THE SCHOOL BOARD AS A CULTURAL SYSTEM

The concept of culture, like many others used in this book, is at once familiar to everyone and at the same time poorly defined by everyone. White states: "Virtually all cultural anthropologists take for granted, no doubt, that culture is the basic and central concept of their science. There is, however, a disturbing lack of agreement as to what they mean by culture" (1959, p. 97). When so important an anthropologist as White asserts that culture is not well defined within the discipline, is it any wonder that the educator attempting to understand school/community relations will be confused about the concept and wonder about its relevance to the subject at hand?

Bernard (1988) suggests that culture is not a variable but a concept to be defined. "Conceptual definitions," he says, "are at their most powerful when they are linked together to build theories that explain research results" (pp. 33–34). We would add that they are most powerful when they assist in understanding and, perhaps, explaining *real* social behavior. Culture is just such a concept. It unifies a wide set of human and group behaviors so as to make them more understandable. When applied to school board behavior, the concept of culture permits the participant or observer to understand and occasionally predict behaviors that are otherwise misunderstood or misinterpreted.

In their work *Anthropology as Cultural Critique*, Marcus and Fischer (1986) present an excellent view of the use of the culture concept as a means of understanding the social processes in which people engage. In that work they suggest "interpretive anthropology" as the way to best understand those processes, by eliciting the "native point of view" (p. 25). That is, if you want to know how local school boards govern and how they relate to superintendents and community, you watch and listen to school boards in the process of doing just that and you ask them what they are doing and why. You let the "natives speak." When explaining the notion of interpretive anthropology, those authors cite Clifford Geertz as "the major spokesman . . . whose work has made it [interpretive anthropology] the most influential style of anthropology" (p. 16). It is to Geertz (1973) and his work *The Interpretation of Cultures* that we turn for the definition of culture to be used in this effort to understand the politics of school/community relations.

Geertz suggests that culture is "a set of control mechanisms" (1973, p. 44), the rules and recipes used to understand how a person must act under the range of possible conditions encountered in organization, tribe, community, or state. Culture shapes Mankind and Mankind shapes culture. Without Man, he says, there is no culture, but without culture there would not be Mankind — not as we understand it (p. 49). The same can be said for local school boards. Without a culture, local school boards would not be as we know them. They would be more unpredictable without their rules and recipes for behavior. Others have skillfully used the concept of culture to assist in the understanding of public schools, their administration, and their governance. Major among them are George and Louise Spindler (1987), Solon Kimball (1974), Harry Wolcott (1973), Francis Ianni (1967), and Flora Ida Ortiz (1982), to mention a few.

Local school boards can be said to operate in their own culture because they exist in a milieu of rules and recipes that tell them how to behave within a multitude of circumstances. They are provided a state code of laws and regulations. They have a local policy book covering every possible contingency. They belong to state and national associations that publish journals and conduct regular, systematic meetings and workshops to socialize and enculturate them into the "proper" way for individual members and boards, collectively, to behave. Clearly there is a dominant local school board culture.

Elite and Arena Boards

Borrowing another concept from anthropology, school boards can be classified as either "elite" or "arena" councils. These terms were first applied to general governing councils by Bailey (1969) and later expanded on by Richards and Kuper (1971). Lutz (1980) applied those concepts to local school boards. Following the anthropologists' use of the terms, elite school boards think of themselves as trustees for the people and separate from the people. They usually strive to reach consensus in private and informal ways, and enact that consensus, in the public meeting, by a unanimous vote. Arena school boards, on the other hand, think of themselves as "community in council." That is, they act to represent the variety of values and demands inherent in the community as they sit in "council." The relevance of that process, community in council, is obvious and significant in school/community relations. Further, arena boards think of themselves as representatives of the people, dedicated to enacting policy the people demand rather than policy the board, in its wisdom, believes best for the people. Because there is likely to be some variety of values and aspirations among the people represented by the arena school board, and some conflict about which are the "better" values, there is often open and public debate about issues. Disagreements about correct policy to be enacted are decided by debate and counter-debate and the board decides, usually by nonunanimous vote. Easton (1965) defines politics as the *authoritative* allocation of *values*. Whose values? Those of the people or those of an "elite oligarchy?" The answer is meaningful in terms of school/community relations.

It should not take those with any experience with local school boards long to recognize that the majority of local school boards tend to behave in a somewhat elite fashion. In fact, such behavior is commensurate with the rules and recipes for behavior prescribed for school boards that we call "the culture of local school boards." Superintendents expect and work for consensus on the board. Boards are, in their training programs, told how to "work together." Both boards and superintendents strive for consensus and harmony and feel "uncomfortable" when such is not the general condition.

There does, however, seem to be a tendency for more school boards to exhibit arena behavior. Often the "necessary and sufficient" condition for a shift toward arena behavior seems to be that the community grows more heterogeneous and diverse. This is often, but not always, due to an increased sense of power in the "minority" community, regardless of how one defines minority. The global definition of minority is whichever group — racial, economic, or other with common interest — had previously felt powerless and unrepresented. Dissatisfied with not being able to influence the school board to "authoritatively allocate their values," they muster enough votes and elect someone to represent their values on the school board. One such person is sufficient to turn an elite board into an arena board.

Homogeneous communities, with monopolistic power elites, without significant minorities, feel comfortable and satisfied with elite school board behavior. Diverse and heterogeneous communities feel alienated from elite boards. Seeking representation and an occasional "win," or at least vocal support on the board, minorities in the community prefer arena boards. If they cannot win, at least they can cheer their spokesperson. Superintendent training programs, including graduate programs in educational administration, have ill prepared superintendents to deal with arena school boards. Superintendent preparation programs and the majority of their experienced faculty have embraced the culture of elite school boards. In fact, they are an important part of that culture formulating and perpetrating the rules and recipes that comprise the elite culture.

What then of school boards that behave in arena fashion when the rules of the culture tell them to behave in elite fashion? They do what individuals do when they find themselves in a "normless" society. When the rules fail to help one understand how one should behave, or to explain the behavior of others, such individuals and societies become "anomic" or normless. According to Durkheim (1933), suicide increases in anomic societies.

Trained to believe that school boards ought to operate in harmonious and consensual ways, both board members and superintendents become anxious and occasionally angry when a board member or two begin to disagree with the board majority frequently and publicly. The culture of school boards requires that everyone should "reason together," seeking consensus in private. If total consensus in private becomes impossible, the minority should "retire" in favor of the majority in order to preserve a common and united front before the public for whom they are trustees. After all, the board is a group of trustees for the people and how can people trust a group of trustees who are unable to agree on what is best for them? As both the traditional superintendent and the board struggle in vain to bring the board into harmony, they become increasingly frustrated and angry. Their ability to work with the arena board members decreases. Out of frustration, other board members may begin to act in arena fashion themselves. Some of the public that supported the old elite board will begin to wonder about the board's ability to govern the schools. Soon the old board and the old superintendent are gone. They very likely have committed political suicide by failing to adapt to the changing politics and culture. Unable to operate any longer within the only norms they know, they find themselves "outside" their culture and normless—a perfect description of Durkheim's concept of anomie. They commit suicide.

In addition to the culture of school boards in which boards must exist and operate, they also live and operate in another culture, the same culture in which the community lives and operates. The vast majority of school board members have lived in a culture dominated by Anglo-Saxon, middle-aged men—the same one in which most superintendents have lived. That made things easier for all concerned—that is, easier for all except those segments of the community that did not share that culture and did not feel represented by individuals who espoused only the values of that culture.

Superintendent Vulnerability

Callahan's (1962) "vulnerability thesis" has previously been noted. In that work he not only makes the case for the superintendent as "educational philosopher" who deserves protection from political vulnerability but also builds a strong historical argument for the notion that American values and public education have been dominated by a business ideology. This, coupled with the extreme vulnerability of public school professionals, particularly superintendents, accounted for some serious failings in American public education. It has also been noted that some have disagreed with Callahan about this, both politically (Peterson, 1985) and in terms of pressure and conflict to be tolerated (Zeigler, Kehoe & Reisman, 1985). The vulnerability thesis is important enough and accounts for sufficient data, however, to require careful explanation and consideration when discussing the superintendent/school board relationship.

Callahan (1962) perceived a perhaps fatal flaw in the way public schools are governed. Local schools have been governed by elected boards heavily dominated by individuals with business orientations. In addition, particularly during the formative period in school administration and governance about which Callahan was writing, a business ideology dominated national values, from President Coolidge, to the Congress, to the "man in the street." Of major import, the notion of scientific management came into vogue during this period and was adopted wholesale, first by American business and then by the public schools. To make matters worse, it was during this period that graduate programs in educational administration were initiated, first at Teachers College, Columbia University. Later, at other universities with professors trained at Teachers College in the ideology and methods espoused by Teachers College, scientific management became the standard of professional training for superintendents. Thus, for sixty years school administrators have thought of themselves more as business executives than as educators. Further, this was not unlike what business-oriented school boards expected them to be. Given these expectations, coupled with the fact that the majority of the money necessary to operate public schools in most states must come from local school districts and be voted on by elected local school boards, the superintendent is in a vulnerable position. That is, if the superintendent fails to exercise great fiscal prudence and constraint, the board will find another who will. Callahan recommended a three-step remedy for this condition. First, programs in school administration should become more academic, teaching more history, philosophy, sociology, anthropology, and political science. Second, better-educated superintendents should be freed of the constant threat of dismissal by a lay board, untrained and therefore unqualified to make such decisions. Finally, Callahan thought that the inequities in public education as well as the vulnerability of superintendents could be alleviated if the burden of funding public schools were shifted from the local level to the state or (preferably) federal level. None of these things have happened.

What has happened, however, is that others have begun to question the correctness of the vulnerability thesis. We have previously noted that Zeigler, Kehoe, and Reisman (1985) find superintendents not particularly vulnerable, at least in comparison with city managers. Perhaps school superintendents have chosen to be superintendents knowing the risks and the rewards. Further, everyone risks losing when they take an unpopular stand and superintendents are compensated for the risks they take in comparison with the pay of other public education professionals. Thus, it might be contended that the vulnerability thesis too often becomes an excuse for superintendents not to take stands on important issues because they fear losing their jobs. Regardless of whether Zeigler, Kehoe, and Reisman are correct or whether Callahan's thesis remains valid, the facts are clear. Superintendents still work at the "pleasure of the board." Unless they maintain good relationships with the school board they will soon be looking for another board with which to build a relationship.

For these reasons, many superintendents operate in a fashion so as to assume that they are part of the school board culture. They align themselves with the current board, recommend policies they believe acceptable to that board, adopt the norms of that board, and often act politically to support that board and its incumbent members in their reelections. As long as a gemeinschaft society with sacred values supports elite board behavior, that strategy seems to work well. It has real dangers, however. If the community changes, precipitating incumbent defeat and a shift to arena board behavior, it is likely that the emerging power structure will also view the current superintendent as a part of the "old" power structure and the "old" board. In such a case the new power structure will probably perceive the current superintendent as their principal enemy.

There is another problem even more dangerous to the incumbent superintendent: because the superintendent is a member of the culture of the board, a power shift will surprise the superintendent as much as it will the old board members, who probably think they are still representing the "real" community as they have done for years. Both the board and the superintendent thus labor under the same delusion — that the community is unchanged, that the opposition is insincere in its beliefs and represents a small "special interest" that will soon disappear. They sincerely believe that the present board and superintendent will soon emerge as the true champions of the people. There is nothing hypocritical about these feelings. They are simply naive. More to the point, they are self-defeating for both board and superintendent and are the result of poor school/community relations.

Another, somewhat more practical kind of superintendent/board relationship is available to the superintendent. It fits a "school executive" model and the culture of school board expectations. It can be recommended over the "join the culture of the board" behavior just described. In such a role the superintendent is careful to assess the political factions of the community and the cliques operating on the board, particularly as they represent the community. When conflict arises due to value differences, the superintendent formulates several appropriate alternative recommendations and suggests probable effects. The superintendent then encourages open discussion of the alternatives. Without taking one side or the other, the superintendent works with the board discussing the best solution. When the issue is decided by the majority of the board, the superintendent administers that decision expertly, so that the maximum benefit accrues to the students. In such a manner the superintendent is the executive for the entire board and avoids the appearance of siding with one or another clique. This is not to suggest that the superintendent should never express an opinion or take a stand. Rather, it recommends that such positions not always favor a single set of values or side with a single community faction or board clique. A superintendent might also remember that not every issue requires the superintendent to take a position or to state the position as an ultimatum.

A caution should be noted here. The role of the professional expert sometimes degenerates to one that resembles the role of "philosopher king." There are some aspects of board culture that suggest that the board must rely solely on the information and recommendations of "their" superintendent. As that norm develops, the role of expert changes to become a behavior in which the superintendent appears to be the central decision maker. As noted, this can be a mistake.

Delegates, Representatives, and Politicians

Both school board members and superintendents can be described as exhibiting behaviors similar to those of the delegate, the trustee, or the "politico" (Mann, 1975). Many of the above descriptions of superintendent behavior could be placed in one or another of these three categories. Like many three-concept models in school administration, this may be a two-concept model with the third concept, "politico," describing a selective behavior, borrowing first from one and then from the other based on the person's understanding of the specific situation. As with other models, it is that "contingency" (Fiedler, 1967) class of behavior, based on the specific assessment of the situation, that can best be recommended.

Mann (1975), having introduced the concepts of delegate, trustee, and politico representation, discusses the use of such representation in the school/community public relations program. He suggests that the notion of "telling" and "selling" the public, seen as a single body with similar interests, is unwise and unproductive. He says that schools have not been good at handling citizen discontent and that real community involvement requires real sharing of control. Community involvement occurs, he says, when the community is given something *meaningful* to do. These ideas have obvious import for which role — trustee, delegate, or politico — a superintendent assumes.

Trustee-type superintendents will tend to operate within the culture of the board and according to the norms set by the training programs through which they are enculturated. Trustee superintendents operate as educational experts and executive managers. They often assume that they are the "official" education experts in their districts and, as such, behave as trustees not only for the people but also for the board. Such behavior is often consistent with an elite board and over the years an elite board may even come to expect such behavior.

We have already spoken about a superintendent who behaves as the "delegate" of the board. Such a superintendent makes recommendations to the board, often with the explicit comment, "Of course we will defer to the wishes of the board." Such behavior, which always defers to the wishes of the board, surrenders leadership to others and forces the board either to assume authority itself or to turn outside for new ideas. While such behavior prevents the superintendent from being seen as siding with one or another faction of the board or community, it also forces everyone to look elsewhere for educational leadership and, when they do, puts the superintendent in a difficult position.

As suggested, it is the politico role that is to be recommended. In such a position the superintendent assumes neither the trustee nor the delegate role as a single posture. Operating as a politico, the superintendent studies the coalitions and cliques on the board and possible changes in the school system. The knowledge about the changing coalitions, value differences, subcultures, and factions in the community is constantly assessed and addressed. As the occasion dictates, the superintendent acts as a delegate for the board or as the trustee of quality education. If such a posture seems too crassly political for the reader's taste, consider the alternative. The board represents the community, either well or poorly. The superintendent represents the educational organization of the community, either well or poorly. If we are correct that a good superintendent/board relationship is essential to a good school/community relationship, it becomes clear that both those relationships become the major task of the superintendent. We believe this is necessary for the good of the public schools — not to mention for the security of the superintendent's job.

The Meaning of Grassroots Democracy

Earlier we said that school boards are the "grassroots of American democracy." Just what is grassroots democracy? As noted previously, de Tocqueville described the "taproot" of American democracy as the community, where the people had hands-on experience in the political process and could satisfy a host of their wants. That is what grassroots democracy is about and why local school governance is democratic in the unique sense of American democracy. The people may not get involved and may not vote, but never forget that they can vote, and when they are dissatisfied enough they will vote. The democratic but disruptive process described in the Dissatisfaction Theory could be tempered if the superintendent were a better politico and could better represent the school system while helping the board to represent the community, or at least assessing how well they are representing it.

CONCLUSION

It is said that at Waterloo, after Napoleon had lost, the "Old Guard" was left to fight the rear-guard action as Napoleon retreated. Wellington's forces attempted to cut him off. The Old Guard, a brigade of a few hundred old men who had fought through the Napoleonic Wars, threw themselves against Wellington's center, thus preventing him from moving to cut off Napoleon's retreat. Again and again they charged. After three assaults Wellington's brigadier came out of the lines under a white flag. "Surrender," he said. "You have done all that is honorably expected in war." The Old Guard's response was, "The Old Guard dies — but *never* surrenders!" In their next assault, it is said, every remaining man in the Old Guard died.

Superintendents who never surrender will surely die! Not every battle is worth dying for. The superintendency is risky enough without vowing to fight to the death in every skirmish. No superintendent should lay his or her job on the line for every issue. That is neither wise, reasonable, nor correct. Yet there must be *something* worth the final charge, something for which one will take a stand. That is the essence of the superintendent/ board relationship.

5

Community Participation in School Governance

Are the values of a community represented in the decisions made by a school board? The public education system in America is built on the concept of community governance. Having looked historically at representational democracy in America and the notion of community, we are now ready to address the question of how the community makes its values manifest in its schools. In theory, the community elects representatives that share its values and will make policy decisions in the interests of their constituents. But the processes of representational democracy are not always obvious in school governance and the concept of community has become complicated. The purpose of this chapter is to examine the connections between community values and school board policy. To do so we will look at theoretical connections and a case that has become a classic example of community change.

As described in Chapter 1, over the past few decades political theory as a whole has moved from a linear model to a less predictable, more random model. Closely paralleling work in the physical sciences, political theory began in the 1960s to apply systems theory (Easton, 1965) and to treat political systems as orderly, predictable entities; demands from the public caused responses from the political system that became manifested in policy. Discontinuity between what members of the public wanted and resultant policy was attributed to a multiplicity of systems working simultaneously, or the inherent nature of some systems making them more predisposed to certain types of demands. On the heels of this work came a group of studies indicating that the connections were not as predictable as earlier thought. To reconcile these discrepancies, theorists considered the possibility that participation in the system was variable or that the working of the system was variable, the linkages not being as tight as previously thought. This line of analysis again found helpful, parallel work in the physical sciences; studies of the ambiguous nature of organizations and chaos in the natural world has contributed greatly to our current understanding of political processes.

ROBERTSDALE CASE

Although this case is nearly thirty years old, it is included here for two reasons. In its original form, it signaled the beginning of the Dissatisfaction Theory research. It is perhaps the single piece of dissatisfaction research that actually used the participant-observer ethnographic methodology and focused on the school board rather than the superintendency. As such, it is rich in school board politics.

The Robertsdale case (Iannaccone & Lutz, 1970) was first published as a three-year extension of the original one-year participant observer study (Lutz, 1962). The case presented here is a reduction of that original study and focuses on recruitment of Prentice as challenger to an entrenched, traditional school board; the campaign leading to Prentice's election; one year of board infighting, which led to two more incumbent turnovers; and the election of Prentice to the school board presidency. A brief postscript reminds the reader of the next two years of board politics leading to the forced retirement of the old superintendent (Iannaccone & Lutz, 1970).

Historical Perspectives

Robertsdale is a school district in the midwestern section of the United States. While Robertsdale was over 120 years old in 1960, this study is concerned with its history between 1938 and 1963. In 1938 Robertsdale faced a school crisis that ushered in a new superintendent, who was still serving in the district at the time of the study. The first record of this crisis is a special school board meeting called on April 2, 1936. This meeting considered the question of giving its superintendent a three-year contract. The matter was tabled and not brought up again until a special meeting on April 21, 1938.

That meeting shed some light on how the board of education was operating in 1938 and how many still operate. The fact that there were visitors at this meeting was unusual. The board had to move from their usual meeting room in order to accommodate the "delegation." The president opened the meeting by asking if the delegation wanted to speak. Their reply, "that a taxpayer could attend any meeting without special reason," caused the board to retire to the office for a conference.

After the executive session, the board returned to its regular open meeting. The purpose of this meeting was then made explicit. The board was to determine whether to "retain or reject" the present superintendent and principal. Again the delegation was given the opportunity to speak but remained silent. A vote of the board was taken, which was unanimously in favor of dismissing the superintendent. When the president directed that a vote be taken on the retention or dismissal of the principal, someone from the delegation rose to speak and was ruled out of order. The director of the Mid West Baptist Orphans' Home rose to ask that the delegation be allowed to speak. The president's ruling was sustained by the board and the principal was dismissed by unanimous vote.

The minutes of the next meeting demonstrate that there were some segments of the community supporting the principal but not the superintendent. Leaders of these segments can be identified in the minutes. One segment was the Baptist group in Robertsdale, the other was a section of the community represented by the Little family, who owned the community bank. Both were still active in Robertsdale more than twenty years later.

During the executive session, the board split 3–3 on whether to rehire Webster, the principal, demonstrating that those citizens who petitioned for Webster's rehiring had some board support. A compromise was reached allowing the new superintendent to make the decision about Webster. It is likely that those who had voted to rehire Webster expected this new superintendent to recommend rehiring Webster. The meeting closed with the appointment of F. W. Joyce as the new superintendent. He was still serving in that capacity in 1960, the time of this study.

On May 19, 1938, the board met and Joyce recommended a Mr. Chod for the principal's position instead of Webster. Chod was still principal of Robertsdale Elementary School at the time of this study. Joyce's recommendation was accepted by the board by a vote of four yes and two no.

Lakeside, the oldest part of the Robertsdale School District, had been established on February 23, 1943, by the merger of two towns laid out under an old Spanish land grant. That made Lakeside the oldest town in the Mid West County. While it was the oldest, it was also one of the farthest from the City of Mid West, and, therefore, late to start its urban growth. In 1953, a series of annexations began and Lakeside started to grow into a large municipality. In 1956, Lakeside became the largest city, area-wise, in Mid West County, encompassing eleven and one-half square miles. Later annexation brought this total to seventeen square miles. Yet in 1958, Lakeside still had only one person on its municipal payroll. About that time a shift began that established a new Lakeside. Extensive subdivision growth began in the areas of Bluffview, Elm Grove, and St. Joseph, which bordered Robertsdale. This growth had a significant effect on the

Robertsdale community. Between 1950 and 1960, Robertsdale School District grew in assessed valuation from $3.4 million to $44 million.

Background for the April 1960 School Board Election

F. N. Prentice moved to Bluffview, then a new subdivision in Lakeside, during the last of March 1959. He had formerly been a resident of another suburban community in the metropolitan district of Mid West.

In December 1959, a Bluffview resident and longtime resident of Lakeside approached Prentice about a meeting that was being held to discuss the public schools. It was obvious that there were many things with which some of the people were unhappy. Prentice said he would be happy to attend the meeting if the superintendent, Joyce, was also invited. Joyce declined the invitation to the meeting but willingly gave information that was requested.

As is the case on many school boards, once someone was elected to the board, that person often stayed until retirement. There were several things operating in the Robertsdale District that tended to support that pattern. Information about the schools was not easy to get. While anyone was "welcome" at board meetings, very few people came. The school board took no action to change this. During elections, incumbents almost always spoke at Parent-Teacher Association (PTA) meetings, but no one else running for office was permitted to speak. Incumbents' names appeared first on the ballot, with all other candidates following in alphabetical order. The lack of information limited the issues and the inability to campaign fostered small turnouts in elections.

In January 1959, Prentice filed as a candidate for election to the board of education of the Robertsdale School District. During February 1959, he attempted to obtain invitations to speak before all PTA groups in the district. His first reply from PTA leadership was that they could not allow a candidate to speak, because the PTA was nonpolitical. When Prentice pointed out that an incumbent was speaking, he was informed that the man was speaking as a school board member and not as a candidate for election. Prentice contacted Superintendent Joyce, who saw nothing wrong with that procedure.

What Prentice could not accomplish by frontal attack was in part accomplished indirectly. An active PTA member spoke with the president of the Robertsdale Elementary School PTA, who invited Prentice to speak. Due to conflicting dates, Prentice was unable to appear. The president, however, read a statement written by Prentice regarding his qualifications for election to the school board. Subsequently, the Elm Grove PTA invited all candidates to speak and the St. Joseph and Mt. Olive PTAs followed suit.

At the St. Joseph PTA, Prentice met Mr. Clubb, an incumbent member of the school board. Clubb was very friendly and during the conversation with Prentice, Clubb said, "I probably cast more 'no' votes than any other man on the Board." He went on to indicate that he did not care for Dyke, an incumbent who was running for election. Clubb said Dyke would tell people whatever they wanted to hear. Clubb also indicated he had little chance by himself of getting anything done, saying that once he had gotten through a motion refusing to renew Joyce's contract only because one member had been absent. At the next meeting the contract was extended for another three years.

Dyke spoke at the senior high school meeting but Prentice was not allowed to speak. After the senior high school meeting Prentice spoke to Tally, the senior high school PTA president. Tally was also on the Lakeside Town Council and was president of the Republican Club, an office formerly held by Dyke. Tally indicated he had no intention of allowing candidates other than incumbents to speak and that there was no point in discussing it.

The April 1960 Election

School board elections were held each year in Mid West. There were six members on a school board, each serving three-year terms. Each year two positions were open and were filled by the two candidates polling the largest number of votes in an at-large election — no plurality required.

The school election was held the day after the regular Lakeside City election. The city election had held a great deal of interest, and it was difficult to get out a large number of voters just the day after. Two men from the community spent the afternoon in a sound truck campaigning for Prentice.

The morning of the school board election, twenty-four names of Bluffview residents were removed from the election books because it was claimed that it was not clear whether they lived in the Robertsdale District or the adjoining district. (The line cut through Bluffview.) These residents had been allowed to vote in the general election the day before but were not permitted to vote in the Robertsdale School election, even though they produced tax receipts from the Robertsdale district. Neither were they permitted to vote in the adjoining district. There was also a transfer of names at the St. Joseph's polling place and some six to ten people failed to get to the correct poll in time to vote. All Bluffview residents concerned were reinstated as residents of the Robertsdale School District two weeks after the election.

Prentice polled the largest vote in the election and Dyke followed. These two men were, therefore, elected. Usher, another challenger, was only four votes behind Dyke. Usher, from the St. Joseph area, had run for the board before and would run again.

Selected Items from Prentice's Personal Diary, April 1960–April 1961

The reader should remember that usually 80 to 90 percent of the school board business caused no controversy and unanimity on such items was usual.

Special Board Meeting April 5, 1960: Prentice Joins the Board. At the special board meeting on election day, Prentice was welcomed by the defeated incumbent, Jones, and by Wilke, Clubb, and Mahan. Neither Dyke, Scott, nor Superintendent Joyce said a word to Prentice. The following Thursday was the regular meeting at which Prentice was to be installed.

The day before this regular meeting, on April 6, Prentice received a call from Clubb informing him that the annexation of Mid Meadows would be taken up at the meeting the next day. There were at this time no agendas sent to board members before the meetings. This allowed some members to appear completely "cold" as to what would be discussed in the meeting. At the time of the phone conversation, it was clear that Clubb favored annexation. Prentice was to discover that such individual phone calls were a major avenue of information and decisionmaking among board members.

Regular Meeting April 7, 1960: Joyce Attempts to Stop Annexation. This was the first school board meeting Prentice attended as a member. The Mid Meadows annexation was brought up and Superintendent Joyce handed out a set of figures given him by the Mid Meadows superintendent. Those figures indicated a projected one-year growth for Mid Meadows of approximately 67 percent over the present year and projected the same growth for the following three years.

Dyke make a motion that the Robertsdale board reject the annexation of Mid Meadows because the projection presented to the board indicated that this new community would overwhelm Robertsdale's seriously strained resources. Prentice said that he would vote against the motion because the board had already printed a notice in the local papers of a meeting to be held later that month at the high school to discuss the annexation; privately Prentice wondered about the accuracy of the figures. That meeting was to be held April 21. The board agreed with this and Dyke withdrew his motion. As the meeting adjourned, all members seemed to agree that the figures presented to the board could not be correct, but if they were correct, it would be impossible to annex Mid Meadows.

The following Saturday Prentice toured the Mid Meadows district with residents of Mid Meadows and spoke to builders at the subdivision sites. He obtained a count of what was built, what was under construction, and what would probably be constructed by September 1960. These figures showed the original set of figures to be 300 percent too high. Prentice called Joyce and gave him these figures and asked him to indicate on Thursday what these new figures would mean when considering annexation.

Special Meeting April 21, 1960: Prentice Learns Board Procedures. Immediately before the "problem" meeting that had been called to discuss annexation, the board met in executive session. Joyce had not revised his recommendation in view of the new figures. He recommended that the board reject the annexation. In spite of the fact that the entire board had agreed a week before that they would have annexed had not the projected enrollment been so high, Dyke, Mahan, and Scott still refused to annex. Dyke said that Joyce had recommended that the board fail to annex and that, if the board did not take his recommendation, he did not "see why we had him here." To this Clubb returned, "I don't see why we have him here either."

After much discussion and no agreement, Dyke accused Prentice of having some ulterior motive in obtaining the new figures on the Mid Meadows projected enrollment. Dyke then made a motion to reject the annexation and Scott seconded it. The roll call was Dyke, Scott, and Mahan in favor of rejecting annexation; Clubb, Wilke, and Prentice against rejecting annexation. Clubb suggested that Joyce could cast the deciding vote. Prentice objected that this was illegal. Joyce confirmed Prentice's objection. The board went before the public meeting split 3–3 and knowing that the county superintendent, who favored annexation, could legally be petitioned to decide the issue.

In the public meeting Clubb made some remarks about why he favored annexation. His words carried definite antagonism toward Dyke personally. Dyke returned in kind, opposing annexation. The 3–3 split was then announced and Clubb informed the public and the board, for the first time, that he would not sign the petition necessary to allow the county superintendent to cast the deciding ballot. This ended the issue for all practical purposes, as three signatures were necessary to petition.

Prentice initiated a discussion of the school mailing list and how information was provided to the public. He felt more could be done in this regard. At this time only parents of children in public school received information. During the ensuing discussion there seemed again to be a 3–3 division of opinion. Finally, it was decided to use the registered voter list plus whatever other lists were available to develop a mailing list. Dyke made such a motion and all six members voted to implement this decision.

The plans for the dedication of the junior high school under construction indicated further division on the board. There had evidently been a discussion sometime before the April 1960 meeting about dedicating the building and placing a plaque to Superintendent Joyce and his wife in the building, to be named "Joyce Junior High School." Clubb and Wilke insisted that no such discussion or agreement had taken place. After some discussion, the entire board agreed that nothing could be done at this point as the name was already on the building.

Chris was introduced as the new administrative assistant for business and finance. The minutes were then read and Joyce presented a proposed school calendar. Prentice questioned whether the proper number of teaching days had been included. Dyke took exception, saying that the board should not dispute the superintendent's word. Prentice suggested that even the superintendent could make a mistake and asked that the calendar be verified. Some discussion ensued and the calender issue was dropped. Prentice thought that it would be on the agenda for the next month, but he did not have to wait that long.

After the disposal of several items on the agenda, Dyke, without comment, made a motion to accept the calendar as the superintendent had recommended. Scott seconded the motion. The calendar was passed at this time with five votes in favor and Prentice voting no. Actually neither Clubb nor Wilke voted, but according to law they were recorded with the majority.

As the meeting adjourned, Wilke and Prentice walked out of the board room and turned toward the main exit of the high school Clubb had left the meeting early. Dyke stopped momentarily as Joyce, Mahan, and Scott entered the principal's office. Mahan returned to the corridor, looked at Dyke, and said "Good-night" to Wilke and Prentice. Dyke entered the office saying "Good-night" and leaving Wilke and Prentice alone in the hall.

As they left the building, Wilke commented to Prentice, "I guess you see they're having an after the board meeting to decide what to do. That's probably where they decided to name the junior high." Wilke went on to say that he would not go along again favoring extending the superintendent's contract. He said he was "fed up," and "If you and I pull together we can change that in the next election."

Special Meeting June 22, 1960: School Tax Issues. The meeting was called because a reassessment of the district made it necessary, by law, to reduce the school tax levy to bring in the same revenue as the old levy at the old assessment. During the discussion, Prentice was surprised to hear Dyke say he would like to hold back on the reduction because the district was in need of money. Scott, however, was in favor of reducing it as much as possible. Prentice urged that a great deal of publicity be given to the fact that the Robertsdale district had one of the lowest per-pupil expenditures in the county and, while the reduction would help taxpayers that year, the board would probably have to seek a higher levy for 1960–1961. In spite of Prentice's urging, little was done except to take credit for a reduction.

As the final item on the agenda, they approved salary raises for non-teaching personnel. Prentice asked if maintenance personnel and mechanics were on a salary schedule or if each negotiated independently. On finding that there was no schedule, Prentice suggested that one be developed. During the discussion Scott said that several bus drivers had come to see him personally about some wages they felt were owed them that they had been unable to collect. Joyce said simply, "We paid all the men for all the driving they did!" That ended the discussion.

Mid West County Joint School Boards Meeting June 26, 1960: Prentice and Joyce. Prentice and Joyce were the only ones from the Robertsdale district attending this meeting. At the meeting Joyce told Prentice he thought it was very difficult to convince older residents that more money needed to be spent on education, but that the people moving into the new communities believed in education and were willing to spend money to get it. Indicating recognition of the situation, he stated there was a new type of person in the community. Joyce clearly saw the situation at hand but was so closely linked to the older residents that he could not change.

On June 29 Prentice called Wilke and asked if he remembered the board acting on the employment of the new administrative assistant, Chris. Wilke said he had no recollection of any action and suggested that the two get together to do something about this situation.

On July 8, 1960, Prentice and Clubb spoke on the telephone. Clubb said that he had heard nothing about hiring Chris and added that, although the board received only the name of the teacher recommended, he thought that the top personnel should have interviews with the board before hiring. Prentice reminded him that the board was supposed to get a paragraph on each teacher to be hired from now on. Clubb said, "I'll make you a little bet. I'll bet Joyce does it for a while and then drops it. That's what he always does with anything the board passes he doesn't like or want."

Prentice asked about the problem of legal advice the board was or was not getting. "That's a Republican deal, too," he said and went on to tie the thing up with the fact that Dyke and Little had been presidents of the Republican Club and that the board attorney had held high offices in the Republican organization.

Special Meeting July 14, 1960: Prentice Questions Board Procedures. A letter was read regarding the formation of an organization of citizens interested in the public schools. The majority of these people came from the Elm Grove area. The letter assured the board that the group was anxious to help.

After several routine items were taken care of, the dedication of the new junior high school was discussed. Joyce left the room and Edmonds, administrative assistant in charge of curriculum, took over. Edmonds presented the proposed program, which included Baptist ministers from both churches Joyce had attended, one opening the program, the other closing it. Edmonds went on to say that there would be a section reserved for special guests of honor, people Joyce had known for a long time, and that Joyce wanted Dyke to make the address. Dyke agreed and Joyce returned to the meeting.

As agreed, Clubb brought up Chris's employment. Joyce claimed that not only had the board voted to hire Chris, but had reviewed his credentials. Prentice broke in, "I didn't see any credentials or vote to employ anybody. I think Mr. Chris is a good man and we should take the correct formal action." Immediately Dyke, Mahan, and Scott agreed with Joyce. They remembered the entire proceeding, while Clubb, Wilke, and Prentice claimed they had heard nothing before Chris was presented as employed. Prentice said to Dyke, "If we acted on his employment find it in the minutes, I can't." Dyke started to look. Joyce told him not to look but just to make another motion, but Dyke insisted that he could find it. Finally he admitted, "I can't find it but I know it's there!" Clubb replied, "Why isn't it in the minutes then?" With no further comment Scott moved the board hire Chris, and Clubb seconded the motion. The motion passed unanimously. Prentice suspected the discussion to hire Chris had taken place in a private conversation among Joyce, Dyke, Mahan, and Scott.

The district depository was then discussed and a great deal of interaction occurred. Joyce said that he thought it was good public relations to continue to use the Community Bank for all funds except the activity fund. He went on to relate how well the Littles had always supported the district and the favors they had done the district. Clubb finally said, "This business of good public relations amounts to this. These people are friends to yourself and the other people here."

In the middle of the discussion Scott moved that the meeting be adjourned and Dyke seconded it. The motion passed with Clubb and Prentice voting no. Clubb got very angry and had sharp words with Mahan. Mahan said nothing could be voted on unless it was on the agenda. Mahan said he would reopen the meeting, however, and did so. Prentice asked how board members could know what was to be voted on under this "new agenda policy," as they never saw an agenda until the night of the meeting.

Clubb then made a motion that the board have regular monthly meetings during the summer months (in the past all summer meetings were "special meetings") and the motion failed, with only Clubb and Prentice voting yes. Prentice then made a motion that tentative agendas be sent to all board members the Monday before the board meeting. The motion passed with some facial expression indicating that Joyce was not too happy with the idea.

As was usual, the official minutes took little note of the confusion and disagreement about the adjournment and failed completely to mention the discussion in progress during the first adjournment. Dyke was board secretary and he wrote the official minutes.

The problem of the school calendar came up again when several of the residents of Bluffview said they were very unhappy about the calendar. They said they had been told, however, that it would be all right for their children to miss the first few days of school as school was starting so early. Prentice was very unhappy with this report after his stand on the calendar from the beginning. Also, the question was brought up of where in Bluffview the Robertsdale district boundary ran. Prentice assured these people that he would try to straighten out the situation. Prentice could no longer operate in a totally nonpartisan manner. He felt obligated to identify with the constituency that had elected him.

On July 29, 1960, Usher, a St. Joseph resident, called Prentice and asked to be placed on the committee to study the Mid Meadows annexation. Usher had been an unsuccessful candidate for the school board for several years and thought this appointment would help him. He also told Prentice that word had gotten to him that Dyke had told some residents of St. Joseph, who were unhappy with the calendar, that Prentice had been the person who insisted on the early starting date.

Chris and Prentice met on August 7, 1960. They had talked a week earlier and Chris told Prentice that he had been offered another job at a college, paying a considerably higher salary. Chris indicated that he had some difficulty in performing his job presently, particularly bill payment, due to conflict with Joyce's secretary. Chris told of misplaced checks and late mailing of checks signed and approved. He said that many of the professional staff were talking about the situation between Joyce and his secretary, and that the secretary "hovered over him" so the principals could no longer get to see him to get their jobs done. Prentice suggested the possibility of appointing Chris assistant superintendent with a bookkeeper so that Chris could perform his job better.

A telephone conversation on August 9, 1960, between Clubb and Prentice brought agreement between these two regarding the problem discussed by Chris two days before. Clubb volunteered the information that a friend had come to him unhappy with Prentice because he thought Prentice had insisted on the early starting date for the next school year. Clubb said he had assured his friend that this was far from the fact and that actually Prentice had strongly opposed the calendar as it was approved. During the conversation Clubb said his friend had told him that he had gotten his information "via Dyke." Clubb asked, "Do you think they're running scared, Prentice?"

Special Meeting August 11, 1960: Prentice Learns More About Finances. Regular business was conducted as usual. Scott was absent. When communication regarding the school calendar was in order, Prentice said he had heard that some residents thought that he was responsible for the calendar. He said he wanted no credit for the present school calendar and wondered how anyone could get that impression when he had so often opposed it. Dyke said, "I don't understand how anyone could have gotten that information from anyone on the board." Prentice did not press the matter.

There was considerable discussion on the motion to change the administrative assistant title to that of assistant superintendent. When the question was called, all were in favor. Prentice noticed, with some surprise, that during the discussion Joyce offered no particular opposition to changing the title of administrative assistant to assistant superintendent, questioning only whether setting up a separate office where all finances were to be handled was meant to by-pass his authority.

At Prentice's suggestion, $2,500 was appropriated for libraries, $1,000 of it for the junior high and $1,500 for the senior high. Account numbers were provided for the board when approving bills, in accordance with a previous motion. This was the first time the board had received such account numbers.

On August 22, 1960, Prentice found out that the high school principal, Brook, had not been notified that he was to expend $1,500 for improvement of library facilities. Neither had the junior high school principal been told that he was to spend $1,000. Nothing had been done to establish an independent office to handle the paying of bills.

During the discussion with Brook, Prentice suggested that the local teachers' association appoint a salary study committee. Brook asked, "Who would protect them?" Prentice asked the meaning of his question and Brook said that, up until now, anyone who initiated these steps would probably have lost his job.

Joyce informed the board that the bookkeeper had been employed and pointed out that his secretary had put in many extra hours doing that job as well as her own work over the past two years. The board agreed, on Joyce's recommendation, to pay her $1,000 for the extra hours. Clubb made it clear that he felt this was irregular and the practice of overtime should be discontinued.

Regular Meeting September 8, 1960: Prentice Confronts Dyke; PTA Becomes Interested. Mahan and Wilke were absent and Clubb presided. Prior to this meeting Prentice talked to Clubb about having the teachers' association form a salary and welfare committee, and about sending the board minutes to all principals to post in order to prevent delay in dissemination of board policy. Clubb thought these were good ideas, and now as presiding officer recognized Prentice to discuss these topics. Prentice made a motion about the matter.

There was considerable discussion without a second. Clubb finally asked if there was a second, and Dyke said he would not second it as he did not believe there was any necessity for a teachers' association salary study committee. He said that the teachers had approved the salary schedule when they signed their contracts in the spring and anyone who did not like the schedule could have gone somewhere else.

At this point Prentice angrily replied to Dyke, "You wouldn't have the nerve to stand before the teachers' association or the PTA and say what you just said, that if teachers didn't like our salary schedule they could get out!" Dyke replied, "I didn't say that and, if you say I did say it I'll sue you for libel." Prentice continued, "I know exactly what you said . . . and I'll repeat it any place I please. I'm not the one who's known for misquoting other members of this board."

This was the angriest exchange ever to take place between Dyke and Prentice. It also marks the high point of division on the board. The minutes made no mention of any controversy. They merely state that Prentice's motion lost for want of a second.

Clubb initiated a discussion about sending board minutes to each principal to be posted on bulletin boards in the various schools. Prentice made the motion and this also lost for want of a second. Dyke said, however, that he would check with the attorney to see if this would be legal and, if so, he would not oppose it. Prentice promised to continue to make these motions (those that had failed for want of a second) until they passed.

In the parking lot, Prentice spoke to Mr. Frank, the district's assistant superintendent for business and finance, who had replaced Chris. Frank said that some progress had been made in getting the bills handled in his office, but some operations were still being handled by Joyce's secretary in the superintendent's office.

Frank said that he had been introduced at the opening of school as the new assistant superintendent in the area of business and finance. Joyce then said that the title of Edmond, the director of curriculum, had been changed to that of assistant superintendent. Joyce laughed and went on, according to Frank, "I don't know why they're assistant superintendents but that's what we'll call them because one member of the board decided that's the way he wanted it." Frank said Joyce had then assured the staff that the jobs were just the same as they had always been, and there was no new responsibility or authority connected with the jobs.

On September 19, Prentice received a call from Lindzey, president of Elm Grove PTA. He had heard of the lack of backing for Prentice's motion regarding the education plan and the teachers' association salary committee. He asked what he could do to help. Prentice suggested attendance at board meetings. On October 5, Lindzey called again to say that he had sent a letter to other PTA presidents asking that each PTA be represented at board meetings and that PTAs take a more active interest in the district's affairs. The PTAs were to become a vehicle for political participation from the new areas, representing the parents who had high educational expectations for their community.

Regular Board Meeting October 13, 1960: Prentice Blind-sided on Teachers' Salaries but Gains Support of Association. All members were present and the meeting was held in the library due to the large number of visitors present. Just before adjournment two motions were presented by Prentice, and passed unanimously, one regarding the submission of an educational plan by the superintendent, the other regarding the distribution of a summary of board minutes to building principals. Both of these motions had been made at the September meeting and both failed for lack of a second. Prentice then started to make a motion regarding a teachers' salary schedule, but the chairman ruled that it should be discussed in the executive session to follow. The board appeared to be recognizing Prentice's new power but would not go so far as to risk salary discussion in public.

The board adjourned to executive session to discuss several problems concerning individuals. After these items, Joyce presented material regarding the salary schedule, which he had told Prentice he was preparing. However, instead of presenting salary information, he presented very vague plans regarding the amount of the upcoming tax levy. Joyce told the board this proposal had nothing to do with Prentice's proposal for a teachers' association salary study committee, but should the board approve one of these plans, or state an amount at which the levy might be fixed, there would be little use for a teachers' association committee.

Prentice felt he had been blind-sided again. He made a motion that the teachers' association be asked to form a salary study committee and report to the board at the December meeting. During the discussion it was apparent that Prentice had at least three votes for the motion. Dyke angrily said that he would vote for the motion regardless of what the teachers asked for. He added that he felt the teachers' request would be ridiculously high and require a tax levy higher than the district would support.

The motion carried with Prentice, Clubb, and Wilke voting for, Scott voting against, and Mahan, who said nothing was wrong with the motion as he saw it but nothing good either, abstaining. In spite of Dyke's proclamation that he would vote for it, he also chose to formally abstain.

On October 27, 1960, Prentice visited the high school and talked with Joyce and later with Brook and Frank over coffee. Before leaving, Prentice spoke to the teachers' association president, F. N. Hahn, and discovered that, just after her election as president, she had been warned that salaries were a board matter and the teachers' association was to keep hands off. No such comments had been made since the recent board motion to form a salary committee, according to Hahn, and she was receiving cooperation from Joyce. Prentice assured Hahn that he stood firmly behind the teachers' association in this matter and she could call on him at any time. The time arrived that same evening. Hahn called saying that Brook was concerned because Joyce had told him that "those on the salary committee had better be careful." Hahn went on to say, "You know our teachers' association has never had any strength, never had any recognition or rights. We feel this will be an opportunity to build this organization." Thus Prentice acquired another constituency, the teachers' association. Representing two groups, Mid-Meadows citizens and the teachers, Prentice was gaining political ground.

Regular Board Meeting November 10, 1960: Prentice Learns to Compromise. There was again a large number of visitors. After the October meeting it would be a very rare meeting that would not have visitors in attendance and meetings were routinely held in the library to accommodate them. No unusual interaction took place during the regular meeting. After the board adjourned into executive session, the following occurred. Again the official minutes make no mention of this action, behind closed doors.

Wilke "expressed his displeasure" because Frank's old bookkeeper had quit and, most particularly, that some new person had been hired at $50 per month more than Wilke's friend, the old bookkeeper, had been receiving. There was much discussion. Dyke said that the board had approved an increase in pay, if necessary, to hire a bookkeeper. Prentice agreed that he had some recollection of this and perhaps he was the one who made that statement. He said that misunderstandings would occur as long as the board failed to keep a more complete record of meetings. Wilke made a motion, and Clubb seconded it, that the new bookkeeper should receive no more per month than the former bookkeeper. The motion carried with Dyke voting against, and Mahan and Scott remaining silent. Prentice later mentioned to Clubb that he felt Dyke had been correct, but the only way to keep the coalition among Clubb, Wilke, and Prentice intact was to vote for the motion. Thus Prentice's role had changed his behavior: While early in his tenure he would have clearly voted his conscience, he now is willing to compromise in minor ways to support his allies. He had become able to shift his explanation to an organizational rationale, blaming the poor minutes.

On November 19, the White House Conference on Education was held in Mid West City. At this meeting Prentice was approached by Dyke, who, attempting to call Prentice on his previous behavior, said that something had to be done about the situation that had occurred over the hiring of the new bookkeeper. He said some people had "just lied" about what the board had agreed to previously. Prentice said that such misunderstandings were unfortunate and mentioned the naming of the junior high as an example of misunderstandings. He suggested that meetings should be tape recorded; this would eliminate such differences of opinion as to what had been said. Dyke immediately agreed. Prentice said that, if Dyke wished to present such a motion, he would support him.

During the first few days in December, Prentice received the teacher-proposed salary schedule and discussed it with Hahn, the association president; he also received a call from Clubb, who had been given a copy and wanted to talk to Prentice about it.

Regular Meeting December 8, 1960: Teachers' Salaries Again. Regular business was handled as usual. Prentice again asked about steps toward annexation of Mid Meadows. There was agreement among the board members on this issue. The salary schedule developed by the teachers' association was presented by the chairperson of that committee. A discussion ensued regarding the schedule, but no action was taken.

Clubb called Prentice on December 13 to discuss several problems. Teachers were questioning what the board thought about the salary schedule their committee had presented. He said the teachers had told him they hoped the board would not act "in the old pattern and throw it all out the window and expect us to be happy!"

Special Meeting December 15, 1960: Board Discovers That Joyce Has Married His Secretary. The elementary principals submitted a preliminary report of equipment needs for the coming year. Additionally, the board gave approval for the submission of an $850,000 bond issue.

Mahan called Prentice on December 22 to indicate that additional rooms would be needed at Elm Grove and the board should probably hold off on the addition to the high school. He said that the board had another problem. The superintendent's wife was still working as his secretary in violation of board policy. Prentice said that he did not know, except by way of a Christmas card, that they had been married.

Mahan replied, "They knew this was coming. It was nothing that happened all of a sudden. They know the policy. If he doesn't mention it, we'll have to at the next meeting. He just can't let it ride along without any idea of when it will end."

Prentice agreed, and then added that, due to the opposition last year, it might be better if the extension of the superintendent's contract were not brought up. Mahan said he was not sure how he would vote on a new contract. He agreed that not bringing the matter before the board was the best way to handle the situation. Mahan then told Prentice that he did not plan to run for reelection in April. He felt he had done his part and wished to retire for "personal reasons." Prentice expressed his regrets, but indicated he felt Mahan had certainly earned the right to retire from office.

On January 11, Clubb called Prentice to discuss some of the items on the agenda for the board meeting the following night. Employment of teachers, Joyce's secretary, and teachers' and principals' salary schedules were discussed.

Regular Meeting January 12, 1961: Joyce's Contract Comes Up; Prentice Assumes Leadership Role. Several items were discussed before Prentice asked about two items that were not on the agenda. These concerned a letter that was to have been sent to Mid Meadows and an insurance report the board had asked for. Joyce said that the letter had been sent to Mid Meadows, but no reply received as yet, and the insurance people had asked to have until the end of January to make their report. The items on the agenda concerning salary schedule, budget, and tax levy were postponed until a special meeting to be held on January 19.

At this point, Mahan asked if Joyce and both assistant superintendents would allow the board to meet without them for a few minutes. After they complied with the request, he brought up the situation regarding Joyce's wife, who still served as his secretary. The board agreed that they would be willing to pay in order to get someone quickly.

Mahan then brought up the superintendent's contract, contrary to what he had agreed. He said that it had been suggested that the board fail to take any action on the present contract, which still had two years to run. Dyke said there was no reason at this time to decide not to extend Joyce's contract. Scott, however, after hearing the discussion, agreed that perhaps it would be better not to take any action this year. The board, with the exception of Dyke, agreed that this was the best way to handle the situation. Showing a new pattern of affiliation, Scott said, "I'll go along with that. Just let it ride."

After the meeting adjourned, Prentice drove Wilke home. The two had a conversation regarding the board after the coming April election. Wilke said he thought Prentice should be president of the new board. Prentice suggested Clubb, but Wilke said he had already talked to Scott about Prentice for the job, and Scott had been willing to go along.

On January 15, Prentice, who was now very active in establishing board agendas, called Edmonds, Joyce's administrative assistant, and Clubb regarding the salary schedule. He also spoke to Hahn about the schedule and the proposed insurance program in which the teachers might participate. On the sixteenth, he went by Joyce's office and, unable to reach him, gave a salary schedule to Frank with the message to give it to Joyce and ask him to duplicate it for all board members. Frank said "I've heard a lot of good comments about letting the teachers participate in setting the salary schedule. A lot of bouquets have been passed." The teachers, he indicated, were pleased that they were to be permitted to be at the board meeting when the board acted on the schedule. He also said that the principals had been warned to be at the meeting on the nineteenth to protect their interests regarding salaries.

School Bond Election January 17, 1961: Shifting Political Power. The people of the Robertsdale district voted in favor of an $850,000 bond issue for new school buildings. The bond issue was to cause no increase in the tax levy due to the increased valuation in the district. The vote was 473 for, 164 against. The political clout of the formerly powerful areas paled in comparison with that of the newly developed areas.

Special Meetings January 19, 1961: Joyce Takes Credit for Teachers' Salaries; New Candidates for the Board. As the major reason for this meeting was discussion of the salary schedule, many teachers and principals attended. Joyce presented a salary schedule that he said he had been working on and thought was a good one. The schedule was exactly the schedule Prentice had prepared for the board just two days before, with the exception of the recommendation of administrators' salaries. On the pages containing the administrators' schedule, each principal and assistant superintendent had been listed and after each name were five columns of figures. The first four were headed: (1) present policy, (2) normal increase, (3) principals' recommendation, (4) requested schedule. The fifth contained the adjustment factors Prentice had suggested for use with the principals' salaries, only all adjustments were applied as though the principals had zero years experience. All had been placed at the beginning of the schedule. Prentice had not suggested this. A sixth column contained recommendations by the superintendent. The same adjustment factors were applied, but with the correct placement of administrators for experience. Joyce was recommending exactly what Prentice had suggested, but it did not appear so in the recommendation. Prentice questioned this, stating that the columns misrepresented his request. Joyce quietly admitted that this was true.

The recommendations for salary schedule made by the superintendent were approved. It encompassed practically all of the recommendations the teachers' association had made and was, with one exception, exactly in accordance with Prentice's proposed schedule. This may have been an attempt on the superintendent's part to take credit for a change he saw as inevitable and to discredit Prentice in the process. The exception is interesting. The teachers' association recommended that a certain number of college credits be required in order to advance on the schedule. Prentice had suggested that some activities other than college courses might occasionally be beneficial and asked that this requirement be one of "professional growth" rather than only college credits. Clubb had agreed to this in private conversation, but completely abandoned Prentice and the idea, and the motion lost for want of a second. More interesting is the fact that the minutes called Prentice's suggestions a motion for a probation period. The minutes state: "A motion was made by Mr. Prentice dealing with probation of teachers resulting in withholding their increment upon the recommendation of the principal. The motion failed to receive a second."

On January 28, Prentice had a talk with Troy, a community member from St. Joseph who said that he understood that someone was to file for the board from that area who would have the total support of the Democratic Club in the township. The reason for this action, Troy speculated, was to obtain political favoritism. He further said he did not like this policy and would not work for this person. Troy urged that a Bluffview candidate join with a candidate from another area in order to beat this Democratic-sponsored candidate.

On February 5, Prentice saw Troy at his gasoline station. Troy said he had asked Becker, from Bluffview, if he would run for school board in the coming election. Becker had said he would. Troy had nothing but praise for Becker. Troy went on to say that there were three men running from the St. Joseph area: Clubb, the incumbent; Usher, an unsuccessful candidate in three former attempts; and Farley, the person supported by the Democratic Club.

Prentice called Becker, who when questioned said that he had attended Casper University, that he would work hard to be elected, and his only interest in the election was improvement of the schools in the district. Prentice warned that only on this platform could a resident of Bluffview hope to win, and only on this platform would Prentice support anyone.

The following day Prentice called the president of the Bluffview Elementary PTA and told her of Becker's intention to run for the school board. She was not enthusiastic, inasmuch as Becker had not been active in the PTA, but agreed that possibly he was the best candidate under the circumstances.

Regular Board Meeting February 9, 1961: Search for Candidates Continues. As the first order of business, Prentice insisted that the item be corrected indicating that he had suggested that teachers be held without salary raise. With this corrected, the minutes were approved.

A letter from Mid Meadows was read inviting the Robertsdale board to meet with them February 20, 1961. The budget was then presented by Joyce for approval by the board. Frank, who had prepared the budget, assisted in the presentation. The board had not seen the budget before and Prentice suggested that they delay approval in order to give members time to study the proposal. Everyone agreed.

Final filing date for candidates in the April election was set as March 10, 1961, and it was agreed that the polling place for Bluffview residents would be in Bluffview. It had formally been in the Lakeside Elementary School but that poll was to be closed in the April 1961 election.

On February 17, Prentice stopped by to see Troy. Troy said that the person who was to file from the Republican Club had decided not to file and was to support Becker, the Bluffview candidate. There was also indication of support from a member of the Democratic Club who lived in the old Robertsdale area and from Tally, who was president of the Republican Club. Prentice said that he did not believe that Tally or the other Republican Club member would support anyone Dyke did not support, and that Dyke would not support anyone from Bluffview.

On February 21, in a telephone conversation, Clubb told Prentice he would like to back Becker in the coming election. Prentice said that he was doing what he could for Clubb and Becker and had heard that Troy was also. Clubb then told Prentice that Farley was running because Ms. Gram, wife of the Democratic committeeperson, was in the insurance business and, while she wrote some of the district's insurance, Gram wanted her to have more. This comment received validation just three months after Farley's election, as he requested placement on a board committee to study the district's insurance program. At the October and November meetings Farley made recommendations that, if accepted by the board, would have allowed Ms. Gram to write an additional $100,000 of insurance.

Joint Meeting Robertsdale and Mid Meadows Boards, Feb. 20, 1961: Candidates Fail to Recognize Important New Constituencies; Becker Loses Ground. This meeting showed general agreement about annexation. There was for the first time general agreement between the boards that annexation should occur. The president of Mid Meadows said: "In the length of time I've been associated with this community [obviously including both districts], the change which is indicated by this meeting is hard to believe."

On February 24 Clubb called to say that at the recent meeting of PTA presidents to form a PTA executive council, all candidates for the board had spoken with the exception of Becker. Clubb went on to say that Farley received rough treatment at the meeting and Clubb felt that Farley could count on no votes from that group.

The meeting was interesting for three reasons. First, Prentice had urged that such a group be formed. It was now being formed. Second, it began a pattern that was to cause Prentice's predictions of who would be elected to go completely afoul. Becker did not attend this meeting. He had told Prentice in their first conversation that he would attend all PTA meetings from that time on. However, he attended only one of the nine meetings. Third, Farley received no encouragement from these people and he would receive none, but he worked hard with those who nominated him in the first place and got their complete support.

On Sunday March 5, another development occurred that caused Prentice's initial prediction to go amiss. Originally Prentice believed that Clubb and a Bluffview resident could be elected. But Lindzey, president of the Elm Grove Elementary PTA, called Prentice to say that he had been asked to run for the school board. Lindzey questioned the approximate time it would take to perform the duties of a school board member. He also inquired as to Prentice's opinion of his chances to win. Prentice said he would have originally supported him but thought it was rather late to file, as four people had already filed and most of the people who were willing to work in school elections were already committed to others. Prentice urged Lindzey to wait until the following year, when he could receive more support. Lindzey said he would call Prentice again.

Lindzey was president of the Elm Grove PTA. He had supported Prentice. As Elm Grove and Bluffview were the higher-priced housing developments in Robertsdale (representing the higher socioeconomic class citizens), they were usually political allies in school matters. This made Lindzey's entrance into the race difficult for Prentice.

After talking to Lindzey, Prentice called Becker and asked him if he had been going to PTA meetings. Becker said he had not, but planned to during March. He also said he planned to talk before the Lakeside Businessperson's Association. This association represented the older elements of the community. It had occurred to Prentice at this time that Becker was asked to run not just by Troy, but by a faction concerned with politics in Lakeside. This faction was actually made up of both Democrats and Republicans, as Lakeside elections are nonpartisan. Prentice again emphasized the importance of PTA-meeting attendance and in getting some statement of what Becker believed about education before the voters in the district.

Later the same day, the editor of the Bluffview community paper called Prentice to ask who was running for the board. Becker had not even bothered to call her. Prentice gave her the information and the community paper carried the names of Becker, as a resident of Bluffview, and Clubb, as an incumbent. Prentice also called Troy and Wilke and suggested that perhaps it would be better for Becker to withdraw if he were not going to work.

Regular Board Meeting March 9, 1961: Lindzey Declares Candidacy. Nothing appeared on the agenda regarding the tax levy and Prentice asked if it was not necessary at this meeting to adopt a levy for presentation to the voters in the April 4 election. It appeared that the superintendent and most of the board felt this had been taken care of, but the minutes showed no record of such action. A levy of $3.52 was then unanimously adopted.

A list of names of candidates for the coming election was read by Dyke, and Lindzey's name appeared on the list. In the executive session, Scott moved that the board extend Joyce's contract. He said that inasmuch as the board was talking about annexing Mid Meadows and they had extended their superintendent's contract, Joyce's must be extended. Dyke seconded the motion, and Wilke, in a surprise move, immediately agreed that under the circumstances the board should extend Joyce's contract. Prentice had been blind-sided again. During the discussion Clubb and

Prentice both spoke against the motion. When the vote was taken, Prentice and Clubb voted against; Dyke then suggested that since Joyce's contract would be extended anyway, the board might want to make it unanimous. Prentice agreed but Clubb would not go along. When Joyce was asked to return to the room, he was told his contract had been extended. Clubb interjected that he had voted against the extension.

Becker called Prentice on March 11, and said he had talked to Wilke, who felt that Becker must do more if he were to be elected. On the following day Prentice received another call — this time from a new community person, Ms. Master. She and Prentice's wife had been sorority sisters in college and the Masters were friends of the Prentices. The Masters also lived in Bluffview and were active in many social clubs. Master said she wanted to do everything she could to help Lindzey get elected to the school board and asked advice. Prentice told her the situation and indicated that it was rather late to start but he would give her what help he could.

On the thirteenth Lindzey called Prentice and told him that he was going to run and asked for whatever help Prentice could give him. Prentice again told him what he had told Master, that he could not personally support anyone openly, but that he did think Lindzey was a good candidate and would do what he could.

On the afternoon of March 23, Prentice stopped in to see Troy, and Troy confirmed Prentice's suspicions of a month before. Neither Tally nor the other old resident from the Republican Club, who Troy had thought would support Becker's candidacy, was supporting him. Troy was very angry about this and also about the fact that Becker was not working to be elected. Prentice again suggested that Becker withdraw in favor of Lindzey. Troy and Prentice both agreed that at present both of the candidates whom Troy and Prentice had backed would have a tough time winning, and that probably Lindzey would have a better chance if Becker withdrew.

Special Board Meeting March 23, 1961: Lindzey Works Hard, Gains Ground. Bids were opened and approved for construction at the Bluffview and Elm Grove schools. Approval was also given to waiting four days, as the law allows, to reorganize the board after the election.

On Saturday March 26, Prentice attended a meeting of the Lakeside Businessmen's Association. All candidates and board members had been invited. Only Farley and Lindzey of the five candidates were present, and Prentice was the only board member present. Farley attacked everything from board members, teachers, and administrators to the noncertified staff. Lindzey, while contending that progress could be made, supported the tax levy and the teachers of the district. Prentice made a plea for support of the tax levy and the meeting adjourned.

On Sunday March 27, a coffee was given for Lindzey at the home of the Masters in Bluffview. Prentice's wife attended and openly supported Lindzey, as did the Bluffview Elementary PTA president. Prentice's wife thought Lindzey made an excellent impression on those in attendance. Wilke called in the afternoon and questioned why Becker was still not working. He and Prentice agreed that Lindzey's filing would hurt both Clubb and Becker. Both thought it would be better if Becker withdrew.

Later that day Prentice again suggested to Troy that Becker should withdraw. Troy said that both members of the Lakeside Council from Bluffview agreed and that Troy had spoken to Becker, but Becker refused to withdraw. Late in the afternoon a meeting was held, attended by Prentice, Troy, Becker, and a member of the Lakeside Council, not from Bluffview. This other council member dominated the meeting and Prentice remarked to his wife after the meeting that he felt he had been "sold a bill of goods" on Becker. Prentice argued that Becker should withdraw but barring that must get out literature saying he supported excellent public schools and what he wanted to do to get them. The council member insisted that Becker appeal to taxpayers without children who wanted to keep taxes down. Prentice was even more unhappy with Becker than before.

Early in the morning hours of the twenty-eighth, Prentice was stricken with appendicitis and taken to the hospital. He remained there until the afternoon of the board reorganization on April 7. With two exceptions, he had no interactions with school district members during that period. Most of the information received during the next few days came from his wife.

Before the election Lindzey distributed a circular over most of the district. The Masters painted and put up about a dozen signs supporting Lindzey. Just before the election, a building ordinance was invoked forcing all signs to be removed until permits were paid for. This ordinance had never been invoked before, and it is interesting to note that the building commissioner was backing Becker. The signs were replaced after the payment of a dollar for each sign.

Becker attended his only PTA meeting of the campaign on April 3, 1961, the day before the election. He put out the circular the day before the election following the suggestions of the Lakeside Council, appealing to citizens without children.

On this same day Lindzey discovered that Becker was not a graduate of any college, and his comment "I went to Casper University" meant he had attended that university for a short period of time. Lindzey jumped at this opportunity and put out circulars to that effect all through Bluffview. Becker now had no chance in Bluffview either.

On April 4 the elections were held. Turnout was heavy. Usher, after three previous attempts, was elected, as was Farley; the tax levy failed.

Becker ran last at every polling place. Later, at the board meeting that evening, Wilke made a motion, seconded by Scott and unanimously passed, to resubmit the levy to the district on April 19, 1961.

Comments and Postscript

Prentice left the hospital and went directly to the board meeting, which recorded the votes for the election of board members and the tax levy. It was not the best homecoming for a school politician. Both of the candidates he had supported lost. Lindzey, the candidate he preferred but did not openly support due to his tardy entry into the race, had also lost (by only forty votes). Surely Prentice could have influenced that many voters by (outward) support. The tax election had lost. Worse yet, Farley, a ward politician of the worst type, had won. Farley was a democratic-machine ward heeler in every sense of the word. He had little formal education and little regard for it. He and Prentice clashed many times. Had Prentice been a better "politician of the possible," willing to give a little to get a lot, he would have had an easier time. The other winner, Usher, became a nonentity on the board. He had wanted to win and he had. That was enough. He was easily handled. Given that the "old guard" had no place to go but to Farley, they generally went along with Prentice's leadership.

During the next two years Prentice served as president and no incumbent was reelected to the Robertsdale board. As Prentice had predicted, taxes had to be raised a significant amount due to the previous year's reduction. Those were approved by a vote of the people but only after three attempts, resulting in the largest voter turnout in the district's history. The board annexed the Mid Meadows district four months before Prentice's term ended. He knew he was leaving the state to accept a new position and therefore resigned his position with the following agreement in place: The president of the Mid Meadows board would be appointed to the Robertsdale board to replace him and Joyce's resignation was submitted (in writing) prior to Prentice's resignation. Today Robertsdale is one of the largest and best tax supported school districts in Mid West County.

The Dissatisfaction Theory of Democracy describes the relationship of an elected board, and subsequently the board's appointees, to the electorate, based on values and the ability to tolerate differences in values. The theory is based on the hypothesis that the school board and the superintendent become a closed decision-making system that becomes, with increasing stability, unaware of or unresponsive to the demands of a changing community. The name Dissatisfaction Theory comes from the dissatisfaction that occurs among community members when their values and the policies of the school become incompatible. In the Robertsdale case, Prentice was recruited to board service by new segments of the community who had strong opinions about the education of their children. The old board recognized the political threat from the new group and did everything in their power to maintain control. Robertsdale is a good example of the difficulty caused by at-large elections; board candidates had to campaign districtwide, not just in their own neighborhood. This system strongly favors incumbents with name recognition and those with sufficient resources, including time and energy to carry out widely based campaigns. Prentice's efforts to open up the political process, even expanding the mailing list for the school newsletter, were not well received. The old board knew that their power lay in maintaining tight control over participation; thus they opposed annexation of new areas, limited public discussion whenever possible, limited committee participation, and even limited distribution of the board minutes, though the minutes were carefully constructed to appear harmonious and low-key. Prentice's power increased as he began to attract constituents other than the citizens of the new communities; when he spoke up for the teachers and attracted that constituency, his power was secure.

Dissatisfaction Theory, as originally conceived, focused on a series of four events: (1) community dissatisfaction, (2) incumbent defeat, (3) superintendent turnover, and (4) outsider succession. Later elaborations of the theory looked beyond the events to the underlying values of the community in the series of events and described four related factors: (1) community member values, (2) citizen participation in school board elections, (3) school board member values, and (4) school policies. In the theory, these are related in a causal chain: Change in community values leads to a change in citizen participation in school board elections, which in turn leads to a change in school board member values, which in turn leads to a change in school policies. According to the Dissatisfaction Theory, the periods of electoral quiescence that led others to conclude that school boards are not representative of the electorate in general are periods in which the community is not dissatisfied with school governance and hence simply chooses not to participate in the electoral process.

INDICATORS OF DISSATISFACTION

Following the publication of the Robertsdale case, the attention of researchers became focused on incumbent defeat and increased political activity as the harbinger of community change and ultimate turnover in leadership. Students of Iannaccone and Lutz completed a series of studies of community change, developing indicators at each step of the cycle.

Each of these indicators has become important in refining the theory because they represented the way researchers thought about the theory and in some cases became confused with the underlying concept they were originally chosen to represent. An examination of the development of indicators will show the development of the theory and give a basis for examining the validity of contributing studies.

Changes in community values have been measured by demographic and economic changes in the community. In his studies done in rapidly growing communities in southern California in the 1960s, Kirkendall (1966) found that districts experiencing major political upheaval had recent histories of change in assessed valuation of property, population, and average daily attendance in the schools. These indicators are clearly linked to community changes of in-migration, growth, or patterns of land use such as major industrial or commercial developments. Using the same indicators, LeDoux (1971) studied communities experiencing out-migration and found that such changes were not related to political upheaval in the same way. Garberina (1975) conducted another study in Massachusetts and found that the theory predicted well in cases of decline when he factored in a measure of tax rate adjustment. This finding added considerably to the theory because it substantiated the concept that incumbent defeat occurred when the board had become closed to community demands. Garberina concluded that even when communities change through economic decline, they will not be likely to experience drastic political changes if the board responds appropriately to the changing demands. This piece of research verified the theory with regard to congruence of values and added the interesting possibility that growing communities were more difficult to manage than declining communities; growing communities bring in new, unknown values, whereas declining communities are left with a value structure that is similar to the previous values, even if only a subset of it.

These studies were helpful in confirming the connection between demographic and economic change in communities and political conflict. They also developed a number of numerical indicators of change and conflict that have been helpful in later work. In general these indicators are number of candidates filing for election, voter turnout, and distribution of votes, that is, the consensus or lack of consensus among the electorate. Mitchell and Thorsted (1976) developed the Thorsted Conflict Index (TCI), which was roughly based on the Minar Conflict Index (MCI). The MCI (Minar, 1966), based on a very different theory of political participation, measures the strength of consensus among the electorate by a simple ratio of votes for losing candidate to votes for all candidates; a high MCI showed a divergence of opinion in the community.

Minar Conflict Index

The Minar Conflict Index was the first attempt to use election results as a measure of community conflict, and is mentioned here for its historic role rather than its current usefulness as a measure of conflict. This conflict index is simply the ratio of votes cast for losing candidates to total votes:

$$\text{MCI} = \frac{\text{votes for losing candidates}}{\text{total votes}} \times 100$$

Mitchell and Thorsted (1976) discuss the MCI in deriving their own conflict index, stating that the Minar Conflict Index is favored by those who subscribe to the Continuous Participation Theory of Democracy, described by Zeigler and Jennings (1974), rather than the Dissatisfaction Theory of Democracy, which Mitchell and Thorsted were developing.

The MCI is a measure of the level of consensus among the electorate, not a measure of dissatisfaction with current policy and demand for change. With the MCI, overwhelming support for an incumbent would indicate the same level of conflict as overwhelming support for a challenger. Conflict with this formula measures the extent to which opinion and hence values are divided among the electorate. According to the Continuous Participation Theory of Democracy, an elected body represents the electorate to the extent that the electorate participates in the electoral process. Zeigler and Jennings saw little participation and came to the conclusion that elected boards represent only an elite portion of the population who choose, or know how, to participate. The MCI has been largely abandoned in favor of the TCI in research based on the Dissatisfaction Theory of Democracy.

Thorsted Conflict Index

The Thorsted Conflict Index was developed in the 1970s, based on the Dissatisfaction Theory of Democracy and the concept that citizens participate in the electoral process to the extent that they are dissatisfied with current governance:

$$\text{TCI} = 100\% - 100 \times \frac{\text{votes for all incumbents/number of incumbents running}}{\text{total votes/number of seats being filled}}$$

The TCI considers a ratio of average votes for incumbents to average votes for all candidates. This factor is a measure of support for incumbents and the inverse of this factor is the measure of conflict, or dissatisfaction with incumbents. Number of incumbents running, voter turnout, and distribution of vote are essential elements in the calculation of the TCI.

This index has several problems practically and conceptually. From a practical point of view the TCI requires actual vote counts for each candidate. These are difficult to obtain: Newspaper accounts are frequently incomplete, school districts often fail to keep complete records, and county official counts do not identify incumbents and can only be obtained in some cases by on-site visits to auditors' offices. Regarding the conceptual problems, the index has difficulty when incumbents choose not to stand for election again. If no incumbents run, this leads to an undefined quantity in the numerator of the formula in that the ratio requires dividing by zero.

Another problem arises if when two positions are open, one incumbent chooses to run and the other chooses not to run. If both are unopposed, as frequently happens in school board elections, the incumbent usually receives more votes due to name recognition. In practice, these are low-conflict situations; there is usually little interest in the election, as demonstrated by few candidates and usually low voter turnout. In this case the formula leads to a negative conflict index because the ratio of votes for incumbents is greater than the votes for all candidates.

Incumbent retirement has proven to be a challenge theoretically as well as computationally. Mitchell and Thorsted (1976) originally discussed only the case in which all incumbents retire and suggested that this be considered a case of incumbent defeat. This assumes that incumbents, sensing high electoral opposition, simply choose not to put themselves through the rigors of a campaign to face probable defeat. Hunt (1980) suggested a retirement adjustment to be factored into his calculation to increase the power to predict incumbent defeat. Later Lutz and Wang (1987) suggested that the retirement adjustment be proportionally weighted. In each case the suggested adjustment was to be added to the number of incumbents winning to represent the case as it might have been had more incumbents run. Neither adjustment helps modify the TCI to assess a level of conflict more accurately. In cases in which incumbents choose not to run, the TCI values must be considered as special cases varying over special ranges. They should not be compared with the more usual TCI values (Merz-Hosman, 1989).

POL Index

Recently Lutz and Wang (1987) have attempted to devise better ways of measuring electoral conflict and predicting election outcomes. One in-

teresting index they called POL, the ratio of votes cast against incumbents/
total votes. If votes cast against incumbents are defined as votes for any
candidate who is not an incumbent, whether or not they oppose an incumbent, then this formula yields the same value as the Thorsted Conflict
Index. This distinction is important in districts where candidates run by
position even when voting is at-large. Moreover, POL has the advantage of
continuing to yield consistent and comparable values when incumbents
choose not to run. Thus POL is really an improved TCI, reflecting the
same theoretical base and yielding a very differentiated range of scores,
but without the complications in special cases. Incumbent defeat yields
high-conflict scores in the POL index as in the TCI. POL has the same
practical problems as the TCI regarding collection of actual vote count for
each candidate.

DISSAT

The major focus of Lutz and Wang's work (1987) was not the POL
index, but a new formula based on different factors to measure voter
dissatisfaction. They called their new measure DISSAT:

$$\text{DISSAT} = 1 - \frac{\text{number of seats available}}{\text{incumbents running} + \text{new challengers}}$$

This formula uses information that is readily available and does not
depend on vote counts, a great advantage to researchers and others interested in calculating these values. The theoretical assumption on which
DISSAT is based is that candidates run for office when they sense political
support. Therefore, the number of candidates seeking office measures the
support for change without having to measure voter turnout or distribution of votes. Several interesting aspects of this assumption should be noted. First, an unchallenged new candidate carries the same value in the
formula as an unchallenged incumbent, an indicator of little dissatisfaction. Second, all challengers carry the same value, regardless of how many
votes they ultimately attract.

When applied to a great number of cases, the DISSAT formula, ranging between 0 and 1, falls into fewer values than the TCI or the POL. The
TCI and the POL have large numbers of possible values because of the
range of values possible for each factor. In states with primaries, only two
candidates may run in the general election; thus the DISSAT is limited to
$1 - x/2x$ in which x is the number of seats available or .5 as maximum
value. The primary election must be considered to know how many candidates originally sought election. Incumbent defeat shows up as no special

situation in DISSAT scores since election results do not enter into the formula. The DISSAT score is similar to the "smart market" theory of stock prices, which states that the market price of a stock incorporates all the relevant variables and further analysis of factors affecting the future of the stock is redundant. The efficiency of this line of thinking has great appeal. The single situation that causes some question of the DISSAT index is the case of very small, persistent minorities such as splinter political parties or small religious groups; these groups will frequently run candidates who gain little general support. The presence of these candidates raises the DISSAT scores but constitutes little threat to the existing administration.

Predictive Value

Whether the conflict is better measured by the challenge to an incumbent or the voter turnout remains an interesting question that may be best answered through studies of the predictive value of the indices.

Predictive value of the indices was examined in a longitudinal study in the state of Washington, where groups of school districts were identified as having a high conflict level by each index and were targeted to be watched closely in the next reporting period. Target districts having increasing conflict scores are assumed to be in early states of a conflict cycle, and if accurately identified, would have a higher than average number of incumbent defeats in subsequent elections. In the 1987 elections in Washington State there were 53 incumbent defeats among 213 districts reporting. Thus by chance alone a district would have a 25 percent probability of experiencing incumbent defeat. None of the target groups alone predicted incumbent defeat better than chance. All target groups when combined to identify a group of districts with a high level of conflict by all measures predicted incumbent defeat in the next election with only a 29 percent accuracy. Thus the indices appear to be good descriptive tools, but not very effective predictive tools.

The lack of successful prediction may be due to an interpretation of the theory that is too narrow and literal. It may also be due to a confusion of indicators in which community change indicators are political events themselves; thus correlations become trivial. This search for correlations has in many instances hindered the development of theory to support other patterns of community change in that it focused on voter behavior to the exclusion of the issues being considered. In many ways the research considered itself to be content-neutral. Another line of research since the publication of the Robertsdale case is the systematic study of content — whether campaign issues, attention in the press, or board testimony and debate — that surrounds major cases of dissatisfaction.

Examining the Issues of Conflict

There have been several studies that examined the content of conflict events. These studies combine qualitative methods with the quantitative election analysis, described above, to present a more complete picture of conflict episodes and the process linking citizen demands and policy change. In her study of conflict over a fifty-year period in Santa Barbara, California, Danis (1981) suggested that turning-point elections differed qualitatively from other elections. In turning-point elections candidates tended to run on platforms that focused on issues and articulated alternatives to present policy rather than running for office simply out of civic duty. Weninger and Stout's study (1989) of Scottsdale, which appears here in Chapter 6, further utilized the turning-point election concept and identified the issues of conflict by analyzing campaign rhetoric, newspaper accounts, and school district policy documents in addition to the quantitative demographic and electoral data. Analyses of school board discussions and patterns of board votes have extended the research on the content of conflict. Weninger and Stout, and Rada (1984) have looked at patterns of split votes among board members as one step in the cycle of policy change. Rada identified periods of intense conflict by examining requests from citizens to boards in letters, petitions, and appearances at board meetings as well as numbers of newspaper editorials or letters to the newspaper advocating policy change.

Research into the issues surrounding a period of conflict is fraught with problems. Often a problem is solved only to reappear soon, or solving one problem reveals numerous other problems that were not previously apparent. Numerous small problems, each insignificant or easily solved by itself, can coalesce into a major conflict episode. March and Olsen (1979), in their work on ambiguous organizations, write that the majority of problems simply go away, often with no identifiable solution, or the problem is apparently resolved rationally, only to reappear in a new form. The organization, a school district in this case, may simply fail to "recognize" the resolution of a problem because it does not meet the needs of the organization at the time. Perhaps the wrong people were participating. Perhaps the organization needs a conflict episode to relieve deeper, underlying inconsistencies in values and control structures that have developed as the community changed.

An examination of the issues is an important addition to the picture of community conflict given by electoral behavior, but considered alone, the issues can be very misleading. The extent of community conflict must be assessed through quantitative measures of citizen participation. Power in a democracy depends on having a majority of votes and this is ultimately a quantitative event. No matter how virtuous or eloquent a policy position may be, if it is not shared by a majority of those casting votes, it will not be accepted.

Varying Patterns of Community Change

A number of case studies have been done since the Robertsdale case, advancing and refining the Dissatisfaction Theory. Several of these will be examined in Chapter 6. The clear implication of the Robertsdale case is that political turbulence is due to community change and incumbent defeat is one step in the establishment of a new value system and a new political equilibrium. The causal chain of events in the Dissatisfaction Theory has been considered to be an unvarying pattern: Changes in community values lead to dissatisfaction with school governance, which leads to increased political activity, which leads in turn to incumbent defeat, which leads finally to superintendent turnover and outside succession. Attempts at predicting incumbent defeat and superintendent turnover have all been based on this pattern and have been, for the most part, unsuccessful. While this model is accurate in the original case, it is too narrow or has been too narrowly perceived. It requires broader interpretation in order to adequately explain variations in the patterns of events seen in a variety of cases. Cases in which superintendents are fired before incumbents are defeated or without incumbent defeat and cases in which incumbents are defeated without superintendent turnover will be presented later. These cases are important for an understanding of a more generalized theory of representational school governance. It is possible that political conflict is occurring, or perhaps always has occurred, in a variety of patterns. Researchers need to look at the possibility of a less tightly linked series of events. A more fruitful line of thought may proceed if schools are considered to be ambiguous organizations, with unclear goals, participation, and processes as defined by March and Olsen (1979). Then it would not be surprising to find varying, less predictable patterns of events that nevertheless show theoretical consistency.

6

Case Studies in Local Dissatisfaction

The Dissatisfaction Theory of Democracy has been developed largely through examination of case studies of school district politics. While statistical modeling can contribute explanations and greater depth to our understanding of the political processes, we must turn to actual cases and the drama of community events in order to appreciate the relationship of a community to its elected representatives and policy. Community change and dissatisfaction play out differently in each community. The setting, the players, and their relationships lead to major variations in the events of community conflict. Four cases are presented here to illustrate these relationships in a variety of communities. The first three cases show communities undergoing change that leads to political conflict in order to bring about policy change. In contrast, the final case shows a community that is largely unchanged, exploring how similar events can have different consequences under different circumstances. In only one case, the Scottsdale case, are real geographic names used; in all other cases the names of people and places are pseudonymous.

THE THOMPSONVILLE CASE:
A CHANGING COMMUNITY DEFINES ITS VALUES THROUGH
SUPERINTENDENT SELECTION AND DISMISSAL

Political theory suggests that communities elect school board members who will set educational policy that is consistent with the values of the community and further that the board will select a superintendent who will administer the schools according to the intentions of the board, at least most of the time. How can it happen that a board selects a superintendent with a very different value system? Can this kind of mismatch be foreseen? How does a community repeatedly reelect school board members who represent values very different from those held by a majority of the electorate? The present case involves a school board that, perhaps unwittingly, hires a superintendent who has values very different from their own. Trouble becomes apparent immediately, but just as quickly he becomes very popular with a powerful part of the community. Fully aware that action against the superintendent will result in their own political demise, the board members choose to dismiss him. Analysis and discussion of this case will attempt to answer several serious questions about superintendent selection and democratic control in American schools and lay the groundwork for consideration of the most critical issue—namely, can a serious conflict episode of this nature be avoided?

The selection of a school superintendent can be a complex decision involving preferences, styles, and beliefs based on community values, values of individual board members, and the organizational values of the school system. March and Olsen (1979) look at choices in ambiguous organizations as opportunities to discover, define, or create values. They note that participants vary, and the roles they play vary, within the context of each choice. They further note that often the process of making the choice can be prolonged as relationships and goals are defined or discovered. Often the final decision is relatively unimportant and can even fail to be implemented. The selection of a school superintendent can be considered a choice in March and Olsen's terms. Participation in the choice is relatively fluid; the process is nominally established by the school board when it makes an initial set of decisions, such as how widely to advertise the job and how much to involve community members. From then on the process is unpredictable. Board members choose to participate to varying degrees; community members participate to varying degrees; the role of the press varies widely. In their analysis of a university dean, March and Olsen describe a selection process that changes several times; decisions are made and then changed and participation of many individuals changes over the course of the decision-making process before a final decision is made. In some cases the choice of a superintendent can be an analogously tortuous situation; in other cases the selection can be made quickly with little participation beyond the board.

March and Olsen (1979), discussing decision-making styles of organizations, describe one style as "artifactual," where there is no conflict to be resolved. Such decisions are automatic and represent no particular conscious choice. Such seemed to be the case in Thompsonville in 1979 when a local school superintendent was selected. There were new elements in the community, but the school board and community leadership who selected the superintendent carried out the process as they had for years. This routine decisionmaking precluded community participation and the opportunity to explain or define their values, thus leaving a residual conflict to be resolved later. It appears that a major conflict was lying dormant in the community; participants were only vaguely aware of differences that had developed and the selection of a new superintendent was the catalyst for a surprisingly strong reaction.

The Thompsonville case is an analysis of artifacts and interviews surrounding the brief tenure of a newly selected superintendent, Mr. Johnson. The events took place in a rural southern community over a period of years beginning in 1979. The situation first came to light through an interview with Johnson. Artifacts were collected for analysis including newspaper articles, school board minutes, memos, and correspondence pertaining to the events. Interviews were conducted with key participants in the events — the superintendent and three board members, one who had been the chairperson of the board and Johnson's only supporter and the two women who opposed Johnson most actively. The interviews were conducted with board members seven years after the main incidents of the case and no doubt have been influenced by subsequent events and the passage of time. As such they represent a no less valid impression of the community and may give some additional dimensions to the case in noting the intensity of feeling years after the events, a difference in memories of participants perhaps indicating what each felt was important, and finally a certain objectivity about a tumultuous period in the political life of the school district gained by recalling that time from a vantage point of known outcome.

The events of this case took place in Thompsonville as it underwent economic and social change. Located on a large lake, the established community was made up of dairy and beef ranchers who believed in traditional family roles and values and liked to limit the use of the local recreational resources to themselves. The community experienced a change as younger generations went away to college, served in Vietnam, or in other ways came to accept values different from those with which they had been raised. The established community also felt the impact of outsiders coming south to live in condominium developments as vacationers or retirees. The first group of people who moved in were retirees from the Midwest who liked the weather and the recreation and preferred living in a small town, much like those they had left. Later a more diverse group of people arrived, including urban northerners. A large power plant was built about ten miles away, bringing in another group of people, who commuted from the small town to work at the power plant. School board elections had been uncontested in recent history; board meetings began with a prayer and were uneventful and consensual. When a rare board vacancy occurred, members of the board recruited a friend to fill the position.

Then the man who had been a popular superintendent of Thompsonville schools for a long time took a job in another state. It became necessary to hire a superintendent for the local school system, and thus began a series of events in which the community became aware of the new plurality of values among various segments of its population. The board chairperson was the only person who thought there was any hint of conflict in the time preceding the selection of the new superintendent. He assessed these problems to be board problems, stemming from the personalities of board members, not school or community problems. He advised a local administrator, Bobbie-Mack Knowles, who later served as acting superintendent, not to get "caught in the meat grinder" by applying for the position of superintendent.

The new superintendent selection process was uneventful as recorded in the newspapers and board minutes. An interview with Johnson revealed that he had received his degree from a northern urban university. He had had collegial relationships with the teachers' union in his previous administrative positions. His wife was completing her doctorate and the new position required the family to live apart a good portion of the time in order for her to complete her education. Two of their four daughters, one in college and the other finishing high school, also remained in their former community. When they moved to Thompsonville they lived in a condominium.

The description of the superintendent appearing in the newspaper at the time of his appointment described him much differently from the way he described himself. "New superintendent a fisherman and family man" read the headline, and the article described Johnson's love of fishing and hunting. Johnson and his wife were described as high school sweethearts and she was reported to be looking for a teaching job in a local elementary school. They were both described as attaining long-standing goals by finishing university programs in the coming year. His past achievements were listed as "coming up through the ranks" as teacher, principal, and superintendent. The article referred to a brief stint as a factory worker and quoted Johnson as saying "It's no sin to work with your hands" and as expressing support for vocational education. The description appeared to be highly slanted toward the traditional values of the established population.

At the same time, Johnson described his family situation to the school board and explained his wife's absence. He told the board that she would be seeking an administrative position on completion of her program and therefore would not be applying for a job in the Thompsonville schools. Perceiving a possible problem in having two careers some distance apart, Johnson told the board that he would sacrifice his career before he would ask his wife to give up a goal she had worked so hard to accomplish. The board appears not to have perceived this as a problem. They raised no questions; all references to his wife's studies and career came from Johnson himself. The board seemed not to have heard what Johnson said, although his statements were recorded in board minutes. Today memories differ regarding Ms. Johnson's returning to her studies. One board member recalls that she signed a contract to teach in a neighboring school district and then broke the contract to complete her residency at her university in the North.

These were descriptions of highly disparate value systems. The one reported in the newspaper was typical of the rural, older South, valuing traditional gender roles. The other, characterized in Johnson's statement to the board, was more typical of suburban and urban roles in the North. While there is a great diversity of communities in both northern and southern states, the informants in this case used regional descriptions of themselves and others. Regional identity appears to be an important part of their values and their self-concept. It would appear that while all the facts were available about their new superintendent, the community leaders simply chose to see in him the characteristics they valued most. Not realizing that the urban characteristics might align him with new segments of the community, the leaders simply saw these characteristics as irrelevant and chose to ignore them.

When asked in retrospect why they hired Johnson, Wilson, his only supporter, said they liked Johnson's openness. He seemed like an up-and-coming young man with whom they could work. They knew he was inexperienced but he seemed to have good judgment. James, who had been on the board over ten years, said that he was not her first choice or even her second, but they needed someone and had to hire him. She pointed out that the board voted unanimously to hire Johnson "to give whoever came in a chance." Other board members cannot remember her strongly opposing Johnson's hiring. James and Buck, who were relatively new to the board when Johnson was hired, both remembered another candidate who was then superintendent in a nearby county but had different recollections of why he was not hired in Thompsonville. James said that the other man was offered more money in the other job and Buck said that the Thompsonville board felt he was too closely tied to the other county to do a good job for them. The minutes record that James made the motion to offer the job to Johnson and Buck seconded the motion, which passed unanimously.

By January of the first year, conflict was apparent. Late in February, Johnson privately handed his resignation to Wilson, chairperson of the board and the one member of the board who consistently supported him. A full agenda of complaints had emerged. James complained that Johnson was away from the district too much. The minutes show that, after delivering the opening prayer, James would begin a series of complaints backed up by Buck. She took issue with just about everything Johnson said. There were conflicts over hiring a supervisor for a construction project, how to provide food for a teacher recognition dinner, various phone bills, and the days principals were required to work. Major points of conflict emerged about Johnson's open dealings with the teachers' union and his differences with the principals. Soon the conflict had reached proportions that warranted coverage in the newspaper of a nearby city.

In retrospect, James and Buck talk about the superintendent's inappropriate personal behavior and say they knew many things at the time but never mentioned them publicly. Buck says they were advised by the board's attorney not to discuss the personal allegations in public and James says they did not speak up out of consideration for the superintendent's family and children. Wilson said that Johnson and his wife did not conduct themselves in the way the community expected; he claimed never to have known of any real transgressions or specific charges but made a vague reference to a community expectation of "fidelity in marriage."

James and Buck were convinced that Johnson was guilty of personal indiscretions and saw that as the "only explanation" for his travels and phone calls. James said in an interview that Johnson received many private phone calls, "things that shouldn't happen on work time." She remembered that he made many private calls and wanted them to get a WATS line but they would not. She recalled his attending conventions where they could not reach him. He was remodeling a small office for his private use — she thought this was so he could receive personal phone calls. At the time Johnson explained that he wanted the small office so he could work on his doctoral dissertation on weekends without air-conditioning the entire building. Finally, Johnson instituted a newsletter directly to teachers following each board meeting. Board members felt this was presumptuous and that he presented board matters in a biased fashion, favorable to the superintendent.

Johnson's letter of resignation did not become public until the end of March. Board members do not remember why it took a month for them to put it on the agenda. In the letter, Johnson resigned effective fifteen months later, at the end of his two-year contract. Four of the board members told the press that they wanted him to leave earlier. Newspaper accounts of the board meeting at which Johnson submitted his resignation reveal that the board room was packed with seventy-five teachers and community members who supported him. During that meeting Johnson responded to complaints from board members that had appeared in the local press about his being away from the district too many days. He distributed a record of absences citing twenty-four days away, including thirteen days on board business with board members, and comparing his record with that of his predecessor. He also attempted to deal with criticism from principals who complained that he had required them to work through Christmas vacation when he himself was away. He provided records of principal absences and indicated that he had required someone to be in each school to answer phones during the vacation period. After Johnson finished there were many statements from the audience in support of him and protesting his resignation. Teachers talked about Johnson's visibility and openness in the schools. Lengthy personal testimony in the board minutes suggest certain values of the citizens of the town. The following excerpts from the board minutes show how people responded to Johnson's open and warm style. The style of the minutes also reveals the informal, highly personal nature of the board meetings:

> Mrs. Betty Hill stated that she did not know Mr. Johnson, but her husband had met him. She said she called the school board two years ago and tried to talk to the (previous) superintendent, Mr. Knowles. Mr. Knowles didn't see fit to return her phone call. She said that she did get someone else on the phone that was not too bright. She was calling about children jumping off the roof of a church at a bus stop and she was told by Mr. Knowles' secretary to call the mayor. The mayor couldn't do any more than she could. Her husband called Mr. Johnson about a problem and within two hours was in his office. She said she would send a letter to the State Board of Education and a letter to this school board about a problem that exists at the bus garage.

> Mrs. Bertha Green, a retired teacher, stated that when the superintendent was passing out the newspaper articles, his bottom line was to get back to taking an interest in children. She said if any board member wanted to indicate that this was bad — God pity them.

> Annie Duncan, an elementary teacher, has been here seven years. The board members, families, and parents in the community have made her feel at home. She came because of what she read in the paper over the weekend and she went to her pastor and asked him to pray with her. She read something that put sadness in her heart. She had met Mr. Johnson at open house at her school. Some teachers only had two or three parent visits that night. Mr. Johnson has been an open, democratic person. He was there and let himself be seen and known in every room on her floor. At parents' day at school when parents come to have lunch with their children, he was there shaking children's hands and talking to them throughout the lunch room. He wasn't just with his child, he was with all the children. He appears to be very interested in the children and has impressed her as a very fine person. All of

us have skeletons in the closet and differences at home. (Board minutes, March 25, 1980)

Citizens and teachers uniformly praised Johnson's openness and ability to reach out to them, yet the traditional value set held by the community is clear in their religious references and personal incidents. The last speaker even expressed some tolerance for personal error on the part of the superintendent although no accusations were made against him. Three newspapers reported the meeting. One reported, "When pressed further by the crowd as to whether Johnson had satisfied her with his response to the charges, James said, 'He gave an explanation. I'm not [going to give an explanation]. I'm not going to get into an argument with all these people. If you would like to come to my house I'll be glad to discuss it.'" This unwillingness to discuss the charges in public was criticized heavily over the next few years. When asked now why there was not more criticism from community members at those meetings, board members said that some citizens did not want to get involved and make public charges. Instead they talk to the board members in private and then rely on those board members to act on their concerns. One board member, in a later interview, said the principals were very upset with Johnson, saying that he was putting pressure on them and made them fear for their jobs, but they could not speak out in public.

It appears that the people speaking in Johnson's behalf were largely teachers and newcomers to the community. The board saw themselves representing influential school principals and a silent constituency of citizens who did not want to get involved. The board accepted Johnson's resignation at the next meeting, in April, and announced a negotiated settlement that would allow him to leave at the end of the month to return to a northern university, where he could finish his doctoral studies. Specific charges were never publicly announced, despite requests from the press and members of the community. Johnson's contract allowed termination for "just cause" but the board chose to pay him the remainder of the contract, rather than attempting to establish a case for just cause. The attorney for the board said:

> Board members had philosophical differences with Johnson on how a school should be run. Johnson lets the administrative staff set its own goals and holds it accountable for not reaching those goals. In the past the superintendent set those goals. You can look on it as weakness or utilizing the strength of the employees. It all depends on how you look at it.

Wilson, Johnson's one supporter on the board, said that the description of the differences between Johnson and the board "is all news to me." The newspapers each make a point of describing Johnson's support among parents and teachers. Johnson's biggest critic on the board, James, said:

> I am willing to admit we made a mistake when we hired him and I just want to correct it. I have never had so many calls from people complaining about our schools as I have since he came here. I told him when we hired him that I thought he had the experience to grasp the system here in sixty days. He hasn't been in the county long enough to do that though.

A review of newspaper accounts and public testimony at the board meetings failed to reveal any citizen complaints. One paper stated that "no citizen at the meeting criticized Johnson." When asked if she would change her mind if 90 percent of the citizens said they wanted the superintendent to stay, James said she had done her homework and would not change her mind. Buck said she had heard from many more citizens than were at the meeting, and would not change her mind. Wilson accused his fellow board members of making subjective decisions based on rumor and innuendo, some pertaining to Johnson's personal life. He lamented the decision saying, "It's a shame, just a shame. . . . we must be open and democratic and do our jobs according to the law and with respect for the constituency that pays for this school system."

The board's acceptance of Johnson's resignation brought heavy criticism and pleas for open process from the press. Their treatment of the situation indicates a change in values from their earlier position when Johnson was hired: Then the press had described him as he had been seen by the board. The press now viewed the situation from the vantage point of other community values. A newspaper editorial summed up the situation:

> From the start Mr. Johnson was different from his Southern reared and educated predecessors. An experienced Illinois superintendent selected from 60 applicants, Johnson — as many of Thompsonville's newest residents — is northern-educated and city oriented. That he doesn't respond to situations the same way his predecessors did should have surprised none of Thompsonville's many natives . . . but there is ample proof of his commitment to the community and the schools.

Knowles, who had been acting superintendent when Johnson was hired, resumed duties as acting superintendent. When asked about the cost of another superintendent search so soon, James stated that there were several good local candidates and that they should be considered. She made it clear that any candidate should have a local background "so they can fit in here." When asked why the board had not simply hired Knowles previously, James said, "He's just a good old boy who tries to get along with everyone; he's not superintendent material, can't make the tough decisions." In acknowledging the need to make tough decisions, James indicates that she was aware, perhaps not consciously, of some level of conflict in the community. Her rejection of Knowles as a possible superintendent shows that she saw the job as more than simply a task of presiding over a placid system.

The following September, two incumbents were defeated in the school board election. One of the incumbents, Buck, had been very prominent in the superintendent dismissal episode and the campaign focused heavily on that issue. The challenger was quoted as saying that he ran for the board to provide a change from the old leadership and he accused the old board of being a clique. Nevertheless, when asked about hiring a new superintendent, he stated that he would prefer to have "someone from our own state who would understand this part of the country and the people better than one from the North." Defeated incumbents reflected with sadness on the changing community and talked about the role of the teachers' union in the election, noting that the fired superintendent had been a union leader earlier in his career. But Johnson's supporters were not done yet. One wrote to Johnson, who was back at the university completing his studies:

> Having been born and raised in the north and a graduate of the university where you are studying, I found your forced resignation most disturbing, especially considering the fine job that you did while you were here. Nevertheless something positive has resulted from this. Believe it or not the town is changing. The voters haven't forgotten you. We did not like what the board said, or should I say, didn't say. It wasn't easy but we ousted two incumbents and replaced them with two most promising and capable individuals. It has given me much satisfaction although nothing could ever erase what they did. I hope you and your family are doing well. I just hope that we can find someone who could do as much and care as much as you did about our school system, but I doubt it.

Selection of a new superintendent had become complicated. At first the old board had offered the job to the man who had been an alternative choice when they hired Johnson. He was a high school principal in a nearby county. During negotiations regarding salary and release from other contractual obligations, he withdrew his name from consideration. The board voted to open the position to other candidates in the state. Thus, Knowles was still acting superintendent when the two new board members took office. Ultimately a man from a northern county within the state agreed to take the job and served about two years. While he had been an outstanding principal in his previous location, board members recall that he "wasn't very good at being superintendent." They recall that he got the staff "riled," not taking time to build relationships or gain the confidence of the people, as is necessary in a small town. His departure was much less eventful than Johnson's and he took a position as principal in a high school in another part of the state.

The clean sweep of board members was completed two years later in the next election when two other incumbents were defeated including the vociferous James, who had become the president of the state school boards association. Campaigns focused heavily again on the firing of the former superintendent. At the same time, Wilson, who had been Superintendent Johnson's only supporter on the old board, resigned. Thus an entirely new board was formed. Shortly after this election the board had the opportunity to select another superintendent and chose a local man who had served as Johnson's assistant. He has had a relatively long and peaceful tenure in the district and elections have become uneventful again.

Buck now teaches in Thompsonville and thinks the current superintendent is doing a good job. She says he came up through the ranks in the county and has always had an undercurrent of support. She says the community has changed a lot and no one ever really speaks of those times. James sells real estate and still speaks bitterly of the conflict. She says that if she were on the board she would not have hired the current superintendent. When asked if he were a local person she said, "For a long time maybe, but not born and raised, he's from [a border state] or somewhere." Both James and Buck think that the board suffered publicly for refusing to speak about private aspects of Johnson's life. It is a matter of honor for them and James says, "You don't laundry [sic] a man's dirty linen in public."

Thus the newer segment of the community succeeded in defeating several traditional board members and placing people with new values on the board. This new board then replaced the interim superintendent with one who was, in some ways, very like the one who precipitated the conflict episode.

Analysis

In this case, superintendent turnover precedes incumbent defeat, the opposite of the usual pattern of community dissatisfaction. Most cases in the Dissatisfaction Theory begin during a period of stability in which the board and superintendent have achieved a closed relationship that excludes the demands from a changing community. Inattention to demands builds a high level of dissatisfaction, precipitating political action, resulting in the removal of one or more incumbent board members. The new board, at odds with the incumbent administration, replaces the superintendent with another, often from outside the district. Nevertheless the theory explains this case satisfactorily if one adds the "low participation" concept, typically described in the Zeigler and Jennings work (1974), which allowed the original board to continue in power without being challenged by a segment of the community that held new and different values. In this case, while there were early indications of dissatisfaction with the previous administration, demands had not accumulated to the point of sufficient dissatisfaction to cause electoral problems for board members. Thus the board members were largely unaware of, and therefore unconcerned with, the demands of the community. The board had achieved a stable relationship among themselves. March and Olsen (1979) suggest that organizations can carry out a pattern of behavior that does not represent a conscious choice of participants. In such situations the participants might choose other responses if they were to make conscious choices, but they fail to see the choice situation through selective participation in and perception of events. In the Thompsonville case, the board was apparently unaware of the diversity of values in the community and the potential for conflict if a superintendent were selected whose style differed from their own. Yet to have done that may only have postponed, not prevented, the conflict.

The most unusual aspect of this case is that the board hired a superintendent whose values seemed to match those of the majority of the community, not their own. This was apparently an accident, but it is possible that he was attracted to the community by the same characteristics that were attracting other newcomers, characteristics associated with values that were anathema to the board. When asked in retrospect why they had hired him, one board member said that they liked his open style. To some degree they may have personally desired that style with the board, but not the community. They may even have been aware of some need to open up the school decision-making process, the closed nature of which was to cause them so much trouble, but they seem to have far overshot their mark on the need for openness, given their own closed nature, and failed to maintain a local policy decision-making style as well. The fact that they had a low awareness of changing community values led the traditional board to hire a superintendent who did not match their values. Value differences were not apparent to them.

It was never clear whether the old board really thought that they represented a majority of the community, as they seemed to indicate as they referred to the many private phone calls they received, or whether they were simply willing to commit political suicide for the values they held so strongly. Perhaps it was a bit of both. It would appear that when confronted with protesting citizens, their value system simply would not let them see the evidence of a changed community, in much the same way their value system had not let them see the differences in Johnson's style, which seemed so readily apparent at the time of his hiring. At least they were, within their value system, unable to respond to it. In that fashion they were similar to the Robertsdale board.

The Dissatisfaction Theory of Democracy has proposed that community values and choices proceed in a sequential manner. Community values change, then participation changes, then representation changes, and finally policies change. Similarly, March and Olsen's (1979) theory of choice in organizations would suggest that the change in participation would follow awareness of the need to participate, which would happen when opportunity arose to define a difference in values, that is, an opportunity to become "dissatisfied." The selection of a superintendent is, in this scenario, one of many possible policy decisions, any of which could have precipitated the conflict episode. Given a board that cannot adjust, the script seems to be the same.

Each community seems to have its own tolerance for the pace of change. One of the new board members in Thompsonville voiced a preference for a local superintendent even after the first election when two incumbents had been defeated. The first superintendent after Johnson was a local. He did not live up to the board's expectations and lasted only two years. His "local" qualities alone were not enough; the board knew by this time that a superintendent with a more open style was necessary and were able to find a man that combined an open style with local characteristics, the apparent formula for success in Thompsonville in the early 1980s. The old board knew they needed a superintendent with qualities other than a local orientation; otherwise they could have tried to hire Knowles, who was available from the beginning and served as acting superintendent for a period. Exactly what the other qualities were, and what the balance should be among the qualities, became defined and increasingly different for each segment of the community through the events of the period. It is interesting that the board chairperson, seeing impending conflict, advised Knowles not to apply for the job and later resigned from his board position rather than run for reelection. Perhaps all of the old board was subconsciously aware of community conflict and wanted an outsider to provide the catalyst event to bring resolution. It is a dreadful, but not necessarily unique, possibility that the community may have needed an outsider to be a scapegoat for resolving internal tensions.

Another set of conflicting values emerges in interviews with board members and when reading firsthand accounts of the incident. Some board members perceived Johnson as a philanderer and saw this as reason to remove him as superintendent. One board member said, "The superintendent should be someone everyone can look up to, someone who is beyond reproach." It was a strong point of local honor that they would buy out his contract rather than allow such accusations to become public and perhaps "taint" their community. To this day those board members feel that the school district sacrificed financially and politically to preserve public silence on this "sacred" issue. It was an equally strong point of honor with the other, "secular" segment of the community that someone should not be removed from his job without a chance to respond to accusations against him. Johnson's supporters thought that the board was trumping up the charges of immorality against Johnson and, given a chance to answer accusations, he could have been exonerated. Moreover, they felt that the behaviors to which the board objected were simply unimportant and were far overshadowed by his responsive, open management style.

SCOTTSDALE, ARIZONA:
POLICY CHANGE AS A FUNCTION OF SCHOOL BOARD
MEMBER–SUPERINTENDENT TURNOVER

Central to the Dissatisfaction Theory is the notion that change occurs when citizens become sufficiently dissatisfied with policy to elect new representatives who will implement changed policy. The study of Scottsdale, Arizona, by Weninger and Stout (1989), the only study in this collection in which the real name of the location is used, makes an important contribution to the understanding of the Dissatisfaction Theory in two ways. First, it traces the policy aspects of the conflict episode, showing that dissatisfaction was related to major issues. Second, it shows a prolonged conflict episode that was not resolved simply by changing the leadership, but continued until certain policies were instituted. The study traces the history of the community from 1896 to 1986, with particular attention to the 1956–1986 period in which major change occurred.

The researchers gathered ten major categories of information, which allowed analysis of demographics and issues: enrollment data from 1896 to 1986; assessed valuation from 1922 to 1986; school board election data, including numbers of votes for each candidate in every recorded school board election; listings of all superintendents and acting superintendents, with their years of service; campaign rhetoric for all modern school board elections; school board policy documents; records of school board votes in modern times; school district bond and budget election results; listings of school board members and their terms of office; and newspaper accounts of elections, election rhetoric, school board meetings, and general school district issues.

Data sources included materials provided by the Scottsdale Unified School District, the Maricopa County Office of Superintendent of Schools, the *Scottsdale Progress*, the *Phoenix Gazette*, the *Tempe Daily News*, the Maricopa County Assessor, two published histories of the community, and the Arizona Department of Education. Semistructured interviews were held with four former superintendents of the district, two education reporters, two charter members of the Scottsdale Historical Society, and the current, long-term mayor of the city.

Scottsdale was founded in 1894 as a marketing center for citrus growers and as a resort for winter visitors. Until World War I, the community was small (about 200 residents), rural, and, on occasion, isolated from the greater Phoenix area by floods. During World War I, cotton farms were added to the citrus groves, but the community remained small, suffering the general effects of the Great Depression. By 1940, the population had grown to only 740. During World War II, Scottsdale served as a commercial and retail center for a nearby military air base and a prisoner-of-war internment center. After the war, Scottsdale returned to its small size and modest growth, showing a population of about 2,000 people in 1950. The community incorporated as a town in 1951.

In 1957, Motorola, Inc., established its Military Electronics Division for Aerospace Technology and opened its first plant with 1,250 employees in Scottsdale. By 1958 the community had 4,000 citizens. From that year, growth accelerated, reporting a population of 10,000 by 1960. Growth did not come without turmoil in city government. As a result, city officials formed the Scottsdale Town Enrichment Program (STEP) to develop a master plan. By 1965, the community's population was 55,000; by 1975, 79,000; and by 1985, over 150,000. The economic infrastructure is diverse (six major business parks, electronics manufacturing, forty retail shopping centers, two master-planned residential communities, more than thirty major resort hotels and about as many "championship" gold courses, and an emerging financial district). In sum, Scottsdale is now a major suburb of Phoenix with an image of expensive houses, chic shops, very expensive winter resort facilities, culture, and a bit of southwestern flair.

The growth and development of the Scottsdale Unified School District has paralleled that of the community. Organized in 1896 with nine students, the school district enrolled 826 students in 1940 and 1,083 in 1950. In 1958, about 8,000 students attended, and in 1960 there were 14,746. That figure grew to about 25,000 in 1965 and 27,000 in 1975. Between 1975 and 1985, while the city continued its prodigious growth, the school district enrollment declined to about 19,000 students. Enrollment has grown slightly since 1985. Assessed valuation in the school district has outstripped student population growth, rising from about $1,800,000 in 1940 to $1,230,413,000 in 1985. In most respects, the city and the school district encompass one of the wealthiest communities in the Southwest.

The early history of Scottsdale revealed that a Turning Point Election Period (TPEP), as defined by Iannaccone (1983), occurred between 1930 and 1943. Consistent with the Dissatisfaction Theory, the ratio of student enrollment to assessed value changed, the district experienced modest growth, as did the community, and the city suffered through the depression, finally losing its one bank and seeing tourist volume diminish. Dissatisfaction Theory would suggest that school board members would be defeated and that the superintendent would be replaced. All incumbent school board members were, in fact, defeated in 1937, 1938, and 1939, with two new superintendents hired between 1939 and 1943. This is interpreted as political realignment in view of the fact that incumbent school board members were routinely reelected beginning in 1942 and that the superintendent appointed in 1943 served until his retirement in 1953. Policy data from the period were too sketchy to determine if significant changes in policy directions followed the realignment.

The period 1956 to 1986 provides a rich analytic environment for examining the Dissatisfaction Theory. The entire period can be viewed as a Turning Point Election Period encompassing all of the theoretical phases described by Iannaccone (1983), including rising voter dissatisfaction, election of a new board majority, realignment of policy system, and final test election. The study presents data for examining the changes in policy that accompanied the political processes of rising voter discontent and realignment. The first indication of major dissatisfaction was the defeat of incumbent school board members. From 1953 until 1986, forty-two board seats were filled through election. During that same period, only ten incumbents were reelected; five were defeated, and the others had not sought reelection, further signaling a shifting political system. From 1960 until 1974, a time of intense conflict, no incumbent was reelected. During the thirty-year interval, 140 persons ran for election to the school board. On average, the ratio of candidates to contested seats was about 3 : 1 and at times was as high as 6 : 1.

A second indicator of rising voter discontent was voter rejection of bond and tax override elections. From 1909 until 1956, voters approved all nine bond and budget requests. From 1957 until 1966, twelve of sixteen were approved. However from 1967 until 1986, eight of nine were defeated. Although the pattern of approval and disapproval mirrors the extremes in national trends, this was a community in which student growth was explosive during the period 1957–1976. As will be seen, the issue during the TPEP was not whether the district needed the money but whether the projected uses of the money were congruent with citizen demands for planning and programs.

A third indicator of dissatisfaction is the rate of involuntary superintendent turnover. Involuntary turnover is thought to follow a general political realignment or to accompany attempts by the incipient majority to gain control of the policy agenda. As such, it represents another indicator of political struggle. From 1942 until 1961, three superintendents served the district, again following rather closely the Robertsdale story after Prentice left (Iannaccone and Lutz, 1970). Between 1961 (when the prior superintendent was fired) and 1986, the district had twelve superintendents or acting superintendents, one of whom served an extraordinarily long term of eight years.

The period from 1956 until 1986 is a TPEP, in which rising voter discontent prompted a continuing struggle for political control. Incumbent school board members were routinely defeated to be replaced by others who could not build a new policy agenda. In their attempts to retain control and forge new political mandates, school board members routinely fired superintendents and sought to appoint persons of their own persuasions.

The point of Dissatisfaction Theory is that this political and administrative turmoil generally produces a significant change in policy, that democracy prevails if the policy shifts are politically responsive to a dissatisfied electorate. Without shifts in policy, voter discontent will continue, as will political turmoil, until a board is elected that can articulate and implement the new political mandate. During this TPEP we trace the inception of what came to be a new political mandate in Scottsdale, demonstrating how the political system worked to forge it, and how it led ultimately to a period of political quiet.

Policy and Its Redirection

According to Dissatisfaction Theory, an important indicator of the struggle by an emerging majority to impose a new political mandate is the level of acrimonious debate among school board members. In effect, a school board changes from an elite council to an arena council, in which the old consensus gives way to public dispute over policy direction. During the period of interest, the first recorded public vote split was April 1953. Only five split votes were recorded in the next thirteen years. However, from 1966 forward the board meetings showed arena council behavior. The issues over which the school board disagreed were not trivial. For example:

December 1970	3–1 to cancel budget referendum
February 1971	3–2 new board member casts tie-breaker vote seven times
March 1971	3–1 to fire six principals
July 1971	3–2 to hire new superintendent
February 1972	3–1 to distribute Gideon Bibles
April 1972	3–2 to extend superintendent's contract
May 1972	3–2 to approve budget
October 1972	3–2 to shelve extended-year plan
April 1976	3–2 to cancel budget referendum
April 1978	3–2 to hire additional teachers
June 1978	4–1 to change attendance zones
March 1982	4–1 to approve a new curriculum
April 1982	3–1 to sell an empty school
January 1983	3–2 to close a high school
January 1983	3–1 to hire new superintendent
October 1983	3–2 to send students to a conference
May 1984	3–1 to approve teacher contracts
July 1985	4–1 to reorganize top administrative echelons

In the late 1970s, the *Scottsdale Progress* asserted editorially that the 3–2 vote had become a school board tradition.

Four major policy issues can be tracked and analyzed over the period of the study: acceptance of federal aid, school organization, the teaching of controversial subjects, and school closures. Although perhaps hundreds of issues surfaced and were resolved during the period under review, these four issues had some special characteristics. They persisted in one guise or another. They continued to be controversial. The local newspaper covered them and wrote editorials about them. Informants identified them as the "hot ones" in the community. In short, these four issues refused to go away, continuing to simmer from election to election and from superintendent to superintendent. These issues represent instances of basic disagreement in the community over expectations for students and teachers, the nature and scope of community involvement in school matters, and long-range planning. In a larger sense, the school district was buffeted by citizen disagreement over questions of political participation and educational values.

The triggering election occurred in 1960, presaging the political turmoil to follow. This was the first election since 1953 in which an incumbent was not returned to office. It was the first election ever to feature large-scale advertising by candidates, endorsements by community activists, detailed platforms, sponsored debates, and implicit slates. Nine candidates entered the race for one seat, again a high DISSAT factor. The incumbent withdrew from the race, as did another candidate who endorsed the eventual winner. All of this activity, including a fivefold increase in the number of votes cast compared with the election in 1959 (3,482 to 751), is consistent with a triggering election as defined by Danis (1981) and consistent with the basic Dissatisfaction Theory. The winning candidate's platform included a demand for sound, practical, long-range planning with realistic demands on the district taxpayers, adequate teacher salaries to encourage professional competence, and an improved curriculum.

In 1961, another long-term incumbent was defeated, and in a personal interview (February 1987) explained his defeat: "The balance of power had shifted north with the new Scottsdale residents wanting a change." This too is consistent with designating 1960 as the year of the triggering election and a statement by the "Old Guard" board members in Robertsdale.

The decision to accept federal aid occupied the public agenda from 1961 until 1973. In 1961, all candidates and all sitting school board members publicly opposed accepting federal aid for school programs, arguing a loss of local control, although the school district did receive subsidies for the school lunch program. At the time, it was the only school district in Arizona that had not received other forms of federal aid. In 1962, an opponent of federal aid was elected to the school board. In 1963, the local newspaper reported that in its poll of citizens, proponents of accepting federal aid outstripped opponents by a 5–1 margin. A total of 300 persons attended an April 1963 board meeting, and their public comments were assessed to be about 2–1 against federal aid. In 1964, the winning candidate opposed federal aid, finishing 1,000 votes ahead of the pro–federal aid candidate. In 1964 the board had three staunch opponents of federal aid and two who were perceived as moderate opponents, willing to be influenced by public opinion. In 1965, a pro–federal aid candidate was elected by 26 votes (1,994–1,968). In February 1966, the board refused to apply for federal funds to assist in the purchase of library books. One week later, the board voted 3–2 to submit the application. The superintendent was quoted as saying, however, "An application is not a commitment to use them [the funds]" (*Scottsdale Progress*, February 8, 1967).

In 1967, a pro–federal aid candidate was elected by 1,000 votes over his nearest rival in a six-candidate field. In the 1969 campaign, the winning candidate favored receipt of federal funds. In the 1970 election, receipt of federal funds was not an issue. In the period from 1967 to 1970, the district had applied for and received several grants and a Director of Supplemental Funding had been appointed. In the July 31, 1970, issue of the

Scottsdale Progress, the editorial writer asserted that "ten years ago to accept federal aid was considered communistic and proposals for innovation were condemned." At the August 27, 1973, meeting, the school board for the first time requested to hear an "outline of all federal funding to date" (*Scottsdale Progress*, August 28, 1973). By 1973, receipt of federal funding was an accepted practice, and all five school board members supported the concept. None of the five had been board members in 1965, and all incumbents opposing receipt had been defeated.

The second major issue, school organization, stayed on the agenda from 1965 until 1977. In 1965, overcrowding in schools prompted the school board to ask the superintendent for alternatives to the K–8 and 9–12 school organization structures then being used. He suggested a number of alternatives, but no action was taken. In 1966, the winning candidate had campaigned on a platform that included the accusation that the district had failed to anticipate enrollment growth. In 1967, several public meetings were held to discuss district needs, and a university consulting team recommended converting to a K–6, 7–9, and 10–12 configuration. A citizens' committee recommended a 6–2–4 configuration, with a 6–3–3 configuration in the future. In September 1967 a $13 million bond election was defeated under criticism from the "Citizens for a Sane Fiscal Policy" for its proposed conversion to a middle school (grades 7–8). The winning candidate in 1967 opposed the creation of middle schools. A 1969 bond issue was passed after the superintendent announced that the middle-school concept had been shelved as a result of the Citizen's [bond election] Steering Committee.

After subsiding for three years, the issue surfaced again in 1972 and the board voted 3–2 to retain the K–8/9–12 configuration. The winning candidate in 1972 subsequently campaigned in opposition to middle schools. In 1973 the administration, again in search of solutions to overcrowding, made two attempts to establish middle schools in new developments. Both were abandoned after citizen protest.

Between 1973 and 1976, two district-sponsored committees deliberated, two districtwide opinion polls were taken, several well-attended public meetings were held, and two citizen groups opposed to middle schools emerged. In the 1976 school board election, all winning candidates favored a careful and slow implementation of the middle-school concept. By then, however, the rationale was not for relief from overcrowding but making efficient use of buildings, given declining enrollment. In 1977 the district opened the first middle school, where things "went smoothly" according to local press reports. Subsequent board decisions continued to create middle schools and abandon the K–8 structure. Of the eighteen schools in the district that enroll children in grades K–8, only one is of the traditional K–8 configuration. All the others are K–5, K–6, 6–8, or 7–8 configurations. Once again the school board's policy direction had been completely reversed.

The third issue, how to deal with controversial subjects in the classroom, first emerged in 1972. The school board adopted a policy requiring that all curriculum materials receive prior board approval. After homosexuals had been invited to speak to an elective class in the high school, the board enacted further restrictive policies in 1975 and 1976. Later in 1976, the board tightened the policy again but softened it after complaints from the teacher association. In 1977, responding to complaints about offensive books used in a high school elective literature course, the board appointed a citizens' review committee and charged its members with reviewing the 1,800 books on the course reading list. In all, 13 of the 1,800 were forwarded to the school board for further review and 12 were approved, with the stipulation that the thirteenth not be "disapproved" but only withdrawn from the list. In September 1977, the review committee requested that the board disband the committee. The board did so in October 1977 and directed the superintendent to develop administrative procedures to handle the issue. It immediately dropped from the policy agenda.

School closure, the fourth issue, was explosive. Our informants called the decision to close Scottsdale High School the most controversial decision ever made in the district. Discussions of school closures began as early as 1972. Several elementary schools were closed in the late 1970s and early 1980s. However, the suggestion of closing a high school lay dormant until February 1981, when the administration submitted a plan to the board for school closures and boundary changes. The plan exempted all high schools, and the board rejected the plan.

Board discussion focused on closing Scottsdale High School. Immediately, citizen groups formed to protest the possibility. A subsequent study indicated that the cost per student at Scottsdale High School was lower than that at Arcadia High School. Board discussion then turned to closing Arcadia High School. Citizen groups immediately formed to protest that possibility. Public discussion was heated. Parents of Arcadia students threatened to secede from the district, and state legislators representing the Arcadia attendance district hinted at legislative reprisals against the district and the city if the school were closed. In September 1982, the superintendent resigned and was replaced with an interim superintendent. On November 30, 1982, the board voted 3–2 to "delay the decision to close Arcadia until January 18, 1983 in order for the community to provide added information" (*Scottsdale Progress*, December 1, 1982). Public debate intensified. The newspaper argued to keep all high schools open. The superintendent argued that keeping high-cost schools open was unfair to other schools. Arcadia parents argued that the projected enrollment decline of Scottsdale High School and the higher value of the property it occupied made it a better choice for closure. On January 18, 1983, the board voted 3–2 to close Scottsdale High School. On January 25, 1983, the interim superintendent was named superintendent.

The New Mandate

In June 1983, a newly elected board majority approved four district goals by a unanimous vote. They included, first, an instructional program based on expectations that all students would master certain competencies; second, a system of employee recognition and reward for good performance; third, a long-range plan for resource use; and fourth, a system that ensures effective participation by citizens and staff in evaluation and planning. The goals are important for two reasons. The first is that they became, for the first time in history, official district policy. The second is that each one of the issues can be traced to platforms of board candidates as early as 1960.

From 1962 until 1982, every winning candidate had a platform favoring increased citizen involvement in the school district policymaking. Again, similar to Prentice in Robertsdale, board members attempted a number of schemes to involve citizens but abandoned all of them, falling back on their historic reliance on ad hoc groups in times of crisis. Although thousands of citizens were involved in the four issues analyzed, none of the groups endured as a planning or advisory group.

From 1960 until 1982, all but five winning candidates had campaigned with a platform that included a demand that the board engage in long-range planning. Although the district was not devoid of facility planning committees during those years and had consultant reports on facility needs, the community perception was that the district lurched from crisis to crisis. One of the community informants said, when interviewed, that the community was "disenchanted with the long range plans of the district" (*Education Reporter*, March 1987). In establishing the goals, the board took a major step, for the first time in district history, to articulate a mandate that had its roots in the early 1960s, which had proponents in almost every election in the period but had not been made a formal policy direction.

The Mandate Implemented

Following adoption of the goals, the board charged the administration with developing an implementation strategy. It did so by creating Citizens for Effective Schools, the process of creating the organization involved almost 1,000 citizens and all major district administrators. The committees that evolved identified ninety-six key issues, of which twelve were deemed of highest priority. The board directed the administrative staff to develop action plans for resolving those twelve issues. Each issue was identified with one of the four goals.

For each goal, elaborate action, monitoring, and reporting procedures were adopted. For example, the board established standards of student performance and behavior that cut across almost all aspects of school life, monitored the indices, and reported them by school in public meetings. A teacher and administrator merit pay system was implemented. The Facility Master Plan was presented and adopted, as was a policy called Facility Consolidation and/or Boundary Changes, which included the criteria to be used in future decisionmaking and the procedures by which citizens were to be allowed to participate. The Citizens' Development Committee was established, as was the Office of Educational Partnership. In short, the newly appointed superintendent accepted the mandate and implemented it with apparent vigor.

Community Affirmation

In February 1986, the community approved a $55 million bond and tax override election and approved the lease of Scottsdale High School to developers. In February 1988, citizens approved a $126 million bond election. Four of the members of the board at the time of the study in 1988 had been reelected since 1982. A new superintendent had been appointed from inside the district without an external search. All of the informants interviewed agree that the district has entered a period of political quiet, although most warned that some long-standing disputes between old-timers and the newer residents may continue to simmer. Our evidence is that the community has accepted and approved the new mandate.

THE CASES OF HAMILTON AND RIVERTON: TWO COMMUNITIES STRUGGLING WITH CHANGING DEMOGRAPHICS AND MINORITY ISSUES

Growth is a perplexing event in communities, as has been amply demonstrated in the cases of Robertsdale, Thompsonville, and Scottsdale. Newcomers to the community bring new expectations, often similar to expectations of small groups preexisting in the community. This combined and enlarged group places demands on existing political structures, straining existing balances of power. These issues can become further complicated when old relationships are thrown out of balance through social trends and external demands such as civil rights movements and desegregation orders. The effect of growth also seems to be determined to some extent by the relationships of the growing segment of the community to the established community, as well as the propensity and tradition of political activity among the new citizens. A study of two communities experiencing growth and shifting power among ethnic communities sheds some light on these issues. In many ways the communities, known here as Hamilton and Riverton, are similar. They cover approximately the same geographic area; both are a combination of rural, small town, and new subdivision commuter communities. They are both experiencing growth and had important ethnic minority communities. The demographic indicators of change in population, school enrollment, and assessed valuation would look very similar, but they are different in many other ways. Hamilton is within commuting distance of a rapidly developing metropolitan area; it is an amalgamation of previously independent communities. Growth in Hamilton is caused primarily by the development of subdivisions, which range from low to moderately high cost. Riverton is in a relatively isolated agricultural area where the outlying farm land is dependent on the town economically and culturally, with some new subdivisions for local business people or people who commute to neighboring towns. Growth in the population of Riverton is primarily from the Hispanic population.

Hamilton:
A Crazy-quilt Landscape of Suburban and Rural Communities

The Hamilton school district covered 230 square miles of suburban, small town, and rural areas previously served by several small school districts that had been consolidated thirty-seven years earlier. At the time of the study, the district had a relative short history as an entity. The consolidated enrollment was about 10,000 students, housed in two high schools, three junior highs, and ten elementary schools. The district was located in one of the fastest growing sections of the state, adjacent to the largest urban area in the state, with a population of two million people. Hamilton was near several large military bases and a university. Most of the community economy was built on small businesses and farms, but as land became expensive in the urban areas, Hamilton had become one of the few places where land was available and moderately priced. At the time of the study the assessed valuation was one of the lowest in the state; there was no major industrial tax base. One segment of the population could be described as transient due to military transfers. Another segment was composed of long-time residents and a third was composed of individuals buying homes in new subdivisions. School news of great importance was covered by the daily newspaper in an adjacent city, but since there were many school districts served by the same paper, much school news went unreported except in community weekly papers serving small segments of the district. The five school board members were elected to represent specific geographic areas in which they lived; however, voters from all areas could vote for all positions.

Early interviews revealed that this district had a history of frequent board member turnover with many resignations filled by appointments. There was a history of electoral challenge and two incumbent defeats prior to the current superintendent. The previous two superintendents had been fired. The current superintendent had been a superintendent for fifteen years in three different communities of increasing complexity. He had left his previous district while experiencing a good deal of board criticism. His style was described by the long-time residents as brash, active, and folksy.

One board member was relentless in her challenges to the superintendent. Tape recordings of board meetings and newspaper accounts suggest that she considered herself a watchdog for overspending. She had also begun to criticize other board members and had brought her own attorney to some board meetings when the division on the board grew to major proportions.

The four other board members were usually supportive of the superintendent, yet each occasionally took issue with some particular item. One board member was on the faculty of the school of library science at a private college located in the district; she was very concerned about school library issues and academic standards. She exerted frequent pressure on the superintendent and while they agreed on many issues, the superintendent saw her as meddlesome. The other three board members were small business owners. One was a member of a long-standing influential family in the community; the superintendent described him as "my best board member." This board member had unseated an incumbent at a previous election and had several relatives working for the schools in classified positions. He was very concerned with administrative attitudes toward classified employees.

In the last two elections, candidates had been challenged by outspoken members of the African-American community. The challenger had received sizable votes, but had not been successful in unseating the incumbents. The superintendent saw himself as working successfully with minority groups in communities in the district where he previously had been superintendent. He soon created a special council to deal with minority issues and instituted a curricular program of multicultural education. At the following election, no member of the African-American community ran for election.

During an annual retreat that the watchdog board member did not attend, the other board members began talking about finding someone to run against her. They decided to solicit the candidacy of a woman who had been on the board previously. She agreed to run and defeated the troublesome incumbent. Board meetings were at once less eventful and more harmonious.

The incumbent defeat, in which the watchdog board member was defeated, was not followed by superintendent dismissal. In this case the incumbent campaigned heavily on idiosyncratic missions and representational issues. She was strongly opposed to most policies of the school district. The campaign qualifies as a turning point campaign by Danis's (1981, 1984) definition but the incumbent was in the minority as indicated by the election returns. This is an important example of an incumbent defeat that marks a correction, by community members, of a previous election mistake. In the previous election the candidate was elected by a minority of the registered voters, as most school board members are. The majority of those did not understand the candidate's view in her first election, probably because of community apathy and low-profile campaigning strategies. When her views became well enough known through her board activities, which received extensive coverage in the press, a larger group of citizens chose to vote and elected another candidate who better represented their views. Her failure to represent the views of a sizable constituency was verified in yet another election when that same defeated school board incumbent made a bid for a seat on the county council and received little support.

A second change in board membership occurred when the superintendent resigned from a local library board. Seeing an opportunity to rid himself of a constant source of conflict, he recommended the library instructor as his replacement on the library board. She was pleased and preferred serving on the library board to serving on the school board. The school board, in appointing her replacement, actively recruited and appointed a black candidate at the suggestion of the superintendent. The new board member was a corporate manager in the large city to which he commuted. While his family was active in school and church activities, he was not particularly active in local minority causes. The superintendent talked privately about the importance of his intervening in board appointments. He thought it part of a superintendent's responsibility.

Since that time there have been many changes on the board. An African-American activist who was originally unsuccessful in his bid for a seat on the board was finally elected, which provided two African-American members of the school board. Two members moved out of the district and were replaced by others, with little opposition. One of the new appointees represented an interesting combination of constituencies. He had formerly been a school principal in a nearby school district and there were reports of his leaving the district under unhappy circumstances. He was reported to be an opponent of centralized district authority. When he retired from professional life, he devoted his time to a small farm in a distant part of the school district, and came to represent frugal, rural interests in the community. The board member whom the superintendent described as his best board member withstood an electoral challenge successfully and remained a staunch supporter of the superintendent.

During the early period of study, the district had harmonious labor relations, passed a large bond issue for new schools, and received a number of awards. Relations with the minority community were relatively peaceful; an African-American teacher was president of the education association. But the sequence of community change was not over. The board member who was a civil rights activist became president of a regional minority organization and began to receive attention from the press. The reporter who covered the school news for the city newspaper was active in the minority community and hence was particularly interested in minority issues. A division began to form between the two African-American members of the board, one supporting the superintendent and the other continually raising minority issues. Two members of the board began to raise financial issues and accuse the administration of waste. Audits were ordered but turned up no wrongdoing. The business manager resigned, despite the lack of proof regarding the allegations, but board investigation continued. Leadership had changed in the teachers' association and a controversial president was chosen in an election in which there were charges of fraud. The new president proclaimed a goal of getting the superintendent fired. Parents at an elementary school became unhappy with their principal and picketed to have him removed. The pickets received considerable coverage in the newspaper. The district arrived at a private settlement with the principal but did not announce the settlement to the public. The picketing continued. Neither the superintendent, nor the board, nor any other party involved leaked this information to the press. After months of leaks, this single piece of information was well guarded. It was as if everyone concerned wanted to keep the level of conflict high. The superintendent's relationship with the press began to break down. The conflict in the district was receiving a lot of attention and the education reporter called the superintendent at his home and office frequently. The superintendent began to get testy in these phone conversations.

During the time of the picketing and audits, the board began the annual process of superintendent evaluation. After two months of meetings, many of which were cancelled due to board member absences the board voted 3–1 to ask for the superintendent's resignation. On the night of the final vote, the long-time board member who had supported the superintendent and withstood electoral challenge was absent. His absences had plagued the process for several months. It is possible that he saw the sentiment of the community and was caught between his desire to support the superintendent and his equally strong desire to represent the community. He may have seen his absence as the only way to avoid making a painful choice. Recall a Robertsdale board member leaving a board meeting to break a tie vote rather than changing his position.

A board election was held shortly after the superintendent resigned. The two incumbents who were up for election were returned to office. The African-American activist was not challenged and the other incumbent was challenged by a candidate who supported the ousted superintendent. That challenger received very few votes. A month later the African-American activist resigned to move to another state.

Riverton:
A Community of Groups Historically Linked to Each Other

The Riverton school district presented an interesting contrast to Hamilton. Riverton encompassed an agricultural area and a town of about 20,000 people. There were about 6,000 students in the schools, about 30 percent of whom were Hispanic, and 10 percent African-American and Asian. There were eight elementary schools, two junior highs, and one high school. The assessed valuation of this district was well below the state average, with most of the local industry being farming or farm related. Considerable division existed between farmers and townspeople. Some of the newer people in the community were professionals working at a nuclear power and research facility located in a town nearby, outside the district.

The district had experienced rapid growth, mostly in the Hispanic segment of the population as former migrant workers settled in response to changing agricultural patterns that afforded more year-round employment. While comprising a large segment of the population, the Hispanics were still a minority and were rather inactive in the political and business aspects of Riverton. Few had registered to vote or attended board meetings. No Hispanic had run for, or held, a political office. On the other hand, the African-American community was very active politically. Organized around a group of churches on the east side of town, African-

American citizens attended school board meetings, political caucuses, and city council meetings and ran for office. Riverton had an African-American mayor at the time of the study. The town had a history of racial tensions between the black community and the white community. The conflict had been particularly harsh during the 1960s, but as the African-American citizens had acquired more wealth, education, and political sophistication, a balance had been struck and they had become part of the town's power structure. School news was covered in great detail by a local daily paper. The paper served several neighboring communities and had one reporter who covered education news exclusively. All school board members ran at-large.

The school board in Riverton had a history of turmoil. After a series of short-term superintendents fifteen years earlier, a young superintendent had been hired from outside the community. During the height of the racial tensions he attempted many drastic changes, including closing the only school in the outlying farm area and firing a popular high school principal. The entire board had been recalled at that time and the superintendent was fired. Since then, there had been three superintendents serving six, three, and five years respectively. There were almost always challenges in elections and incumbents had been defeated.

At the time of the study, the board consisted of a woman from the farm community, the former high school principal who had been fired fifteen years earlier, a professional man from the nearby nuclear research industry, and two women who had professional positions at local colleges. The male professional was African-American; all other board members were white. The farmer had run for the board in a previous election and failed to unseat one of the incumbents by only a few votes. She was successful in her bid at the next election. Considerable tension existed between her and the board member she had previously tried to unseat. Despite electoral conflict, there had been relatively little board turnover. Candidates had run for the board from evangelical Christian organizations and splinter political groups, but at the time of the study these had not been serious challenges.

The Riverton board historically functioned as an arena council. There were many split votes at the board meetings. At the time of the study, the board member from the farm community and the former high school principal showed a strong orientation to represent their constituents in the community. The other three board members tended to support the superintendent.

At the beginning of the study the superintendent had served in Riverton for six years, following one year as assistant superintendent. He was in constant conflict with some principals and was unpopular with the farm population, but was active with the community leadership in town. The superintendent had appointed a strong and controversial principal to the district's single high school. While the principal received a lot of criticism, his tough administrative style was always popular with the community. He was openly critical of the superintendent on occasion but privately they seemed to have struck an agreement that allowed them to coexist. During the years of the study there were many difficult times for the board and the superintendent. Various professional activities required that he spend a good deal of time away from the district. During this time, his staff carried out administrative duties. He remained as superintendent much longer than had any of his predecessors.

During the second year of the study, a period of intense conflict resulted while the board considered the location of a new school. Community meetings were held and citizens advocated various locations. At the first meeting, some Hispanics were present; one spoke with the assistance of a translator. No Hispanics were present at subsequent meetings. Many members of the African-American community spoke at each meeting advocating placing the school on the east side to help them build a family neighborhood. There had been a very old school on the east side of town that had been closed twenty years earlier. Many community members expressed the belief that some previous board had promised to rebuild a school on that location. There still existed an alliance between the farm community, the east-side African-American population, and the fired high school principal (now board member) over the board recall issue from fifteen years ago. A few west-side citizens spoke, expressing fear of drug dealers, prostitutes, and violent crime on the east side. The board proposed an east-side location and the community narrowly defeated the bond issue to build the school.

The district had been under a mandate from the state to balance the racial composition of its schools. Boundaries were changed every few years in an attempt to achieve racial balance, but patterns of housing repeatedly resegregated the schools. Each time boundaries were changed great numbers of citizens flocked to the board meetings to make their opinions known. These people were generally members of established community groups, white or African-American, but almost never Hispanic, despite the fact that the most racially imbalanced schools were overwhelmingly Hispanic. Rapid growth in the Hispanic sections of town meant that these schools were overcrowded and children often had to be bused to other schools across town where there was sufficient space. Hispanic parents complained to principals about their children being bused, but rarely appeared at a board meeting to present a case for attendance areas that would serve their families better.

After long study, the superintendent's staff presented a plan to the board that would revise all attendance areas and require that all children in the district participate in busing to the same degree. The plan established "paired schools," in which certain schools were for primary grades and others were for intermediate grades. All children would have had to be bused for half of their school years. After numerous community meetings and repeated board debate, the board voted against the paired-schools plan; therefore, the need for frequent boundary adjustments to achieve racial balance continued. One group that made frequent and vocal appearances at the board meetings consisted of citizens living in the newer sections of town. They were parents of the children who would have been transferred to schools across town if the proposed plan had gone into effect. It was interesting to note that these residents of the new "suburbs" were generally not newcomers to the community, but the offspring of long-established families in the town. The vote to abandon the plan was a victory for the established community, which was able to influence every boundary change proposed. Hispanic children continued to be bused disproportionately.

Board members talked of not running in the next election, but privately they and their friends talked about political enemies who might get their board positions if they did not run. There had been relatively few resignations from the board, and therefore few opportunities to change board membership other than by challenging incumbents. District administrators were reluctant to get involved in board membership changes for fear of recriminations from political factions. Board members accepted the fact that they would be challenged at every election, with the exception of the former high school principal, who has become an institution on the board and has not been challenged in many years. Thus amidst uneasy alliances and political turmoil, the established community continued to hold power and the superintendent continued his tenure.

Analysis

Both Hamilton and Riverton were changing and experiencing new racial, social, and economic composition. The African-American community had established a strong political position in both districts. In Riverton, the African-American community appeared to wield power in school district decisions greater than their numbers indicated and ultimately greater than their votes were able to support at the polls. In each district one African-American board member tended to represent the upper-middle-class professional segment of the community as much as or more than the traditional African-American community. The Hispanic community was the largest unrepresented group in Riverton, and it was the portion of the community experiencing the most rapid growth. The new sections of the area were largely inhabited by children of the old power families in town and hence functioned as a conservative force in the balance of community power. At the conclusion of the study, the established power structure seemed unthreatened in Riverton; it remains to be seen how the community will adjust if the Hispanic community becomes politically active. It may go through another period of conflict as it did in 1970 when the African-American community became a powerful political force.

Hamilton sustained rapid growth throughout the period of the study and anticipated the same growth for the future. The newcomers to the community were politically active and sought change, in contrast with the growing segments of Riverton. Cultural differences may account for the differences in political activity. The school board experienced high turnover. By the end of the study only one board member remained who had been on the board at the beginning of the study. Some positions had turned over several times and board records confirmed that this had been the pattern for years. In Riverton four board members remained throughout the study, despite constant challenge; one resigned when his job took him to another state.

The superintendents in the two districts studied approached their boards very differently. The superintendent in Hamilton was experienced at political manipulation and thought that it was his responsibility to intervene in the political processes of board membership. He appears to have attempted to establish an elite board but was unsuccessful in doing so. The community was fragmented and this fragmentation continued to characterize the board. Recognizing the need for minority representation, the superintendent established a citizens' committee and a multicultural educational program and later assisted in appointing an African-American board member. The board member was supportive of the superintendent but not a representative of the minority community that had raised issues previously. The attempt to coopt the opposition through a board appointment was unsuccessful. Other board members had idiosyncratic concerns, which were not necessarily widely held but became focal points for a generally dissatisfied, growing community.

Riverton had long-standing community roles with alliances going back two decades; these are not easily subject to manipulation. There was also a strong traditional prohibition against administrative involvement in board politics. The superintendent recognized that fact and kept a low profile in community politics. The Riverton superintendent also had a very controversial staff, which received a lot of attention in the community; thus attention was often focused on the board or the staff rather than the superintendent.

School news was reported in great detail to the entire community, so events were subject to constant public scrutiny and speculation in Riverton. In Hamilton there was little contact among the separate communities and school business became the focus of intense public interest only sporadically. The alliance that formed between a reporter and a board member was unfortunate for the superintendent in Hamilton.

Despite its many conflicts, Riverton remains a tightly connected community with predictable relationships. Hamilton is struggling as it moves from rural to suburban communities linked by little except the schools. New subdivisions and old farms coexist across the district and new schools become crowded as soon as they open. Newcomers have little interest in past achievements of the schools and see only the conditions resulting from growth getting worse. Establishing a relationship with a new and growing community remains a continuous challenge for the new administration.

BLOOMDALE INDEPENDENT SCHOOL DISTRICT: SUPERINTENDENT TURNOVER WITHOUT INCUMBENT DEFEAT

The Dissatisfaction Theory continues to be employed in tracing the episodic upheavals in the life of a school district, chronicling the events that lead to incumbent defeat, superintendent turnover, and policy change. But there is another story that is played out each year in the sociopolitical drama of superintendent/board relations. That is the sometimes "gut-wrenching" struggle of superintendent contract renewal or nonrenewal, often totally unrelated to incumbent defeat. This event has gone largely unnoticed by the Dissatisfaction theorists, but certainly not by the superintendents and their families, who face severe consequences. The case of Bloomdale tells the story of a school superintendent who came to a district where three superintendents had been fired in the previous three years without incumbent defeat (Moore, 1988).

The first post office was established in Bloomdale, Texas, in 1871 and the railroad arrived between 1881 and 1887. The town incorporated in 1890 and the names of some of its first elected officials are still to be seen on the mailboxes of present-day Bloomdale residents. From its beginning, Bloomdale was an agricultural community relying largely on cotton farming, ginning, and selling. When "cotton was king," Bloomdale had four operating gins and several independent cotton brokers, two lumber yards, mule barns, blacksmith shops, several grocery stores, three drug stores, several cafes, meat markets, a number of churches, a newspaper, five physicians, and a bank, and operated a large community fair.

Education has always been important in Bloomdale. Since 1869 Bloomdale has operated its own school and in the early 1900s even had a private college within the town limits. Its first public school opened in 1890. The depression of the 1930s all but closed Bloomdale. Banks failed, shops closed, farmers went bankrupt, and gins shut down. By 1977 Bloomdale had recovered somewhat. It had 800 residents, still had a newspaper, one strong bank, and four churches, and pride in public schools. Many new residents sought the rural atmosphere in Bloomdale but worked in urban areas within commuting distance. To some extent Bloomdale had become a suburb of neighboring urban areas, but it retained several strong and important community elements. These included a consolidated school system, one large industrial employer, a strong local bank, a local newspaper, and four churches, each of which could boast of more than one hundred years of continuous service in the community.

Bloomdale Independent School District: 1980–1985

Hinch, superintendent of nearby Mud-Flat, was in his office talking with his high school principal, Deacon. Twenty years earlier Hinch had been superintendent in Bloomdale and retained many of his contacts with leaders there. On this day he received a call from one of these friends asking him to consider returning to Bloomdale as superintendent. Three years earlier, a superintendent who had served for seven years had become involved with his secretary and was dismissed. The board at that time brought in an outsider from a larger district. It was said that person "never unpacked." While opening up the system, he antagonized the staff. It was said that he was an alcoholic. He publicly maintained that image by disposal of numerous alcoholic beverage containers around his rented property. Again, without incumbent defeat, this second superintendent was removed.

The next time the board went for an "insider" whom they could trust. They selected a man who had been high school principal in Bloomdale for years. Perhaps because of being too close, too well known, too much "one of the boys," he could not assume the role of superintendent. He never achieved the confidence or respect of the community in that role. Before the year was out he was attacked by an irate parent in his own home, and resigned as of the year's end. This led to the phone call to Hinch. Hinch refused the offer but said he had a good man for them sitting in his office.

Within two weeks Hinch accompanied Deacon to Bloomdale so that Deacon could personally apply for the position and Hinch could introduce him to "the right people."

Their first stop was to meet a long-time friend of Hinch, a farmer who had two relatives presently serving on the school board. During the conversation, Hinch lauded Deacon's ability and integrity. The farmer noted that Deacon's old, beat-up pickup, in which he and Hinch had arrived, was the same model and in the same condition as the one the farmer drove. That apparently was taken as a symbol of Deacon's frugal and conservative stewardship. The visit continued in this positive manner. At the next board meeting Douglas Deacon was unanimously awarded a one-year contract as Bloomdale's school superintendent.

On his first day in office, Deacon contacted and had an interview with the editor of the local newspaper. The previous superintendent had thrown this editor off the school campus. A complimentary article immediately appeared in the paper, beginning a five-year period of growing respect and support. Deacon found the school buildings in deplorable condition. After meeting with the board on August 7, he hired two workmen and worked with them, putting in 12–18 hour days repairing leaky roofs, painting walls, and sanding floors, in preparation for the opening of school.

The first major incident occurred at the regular board meeting August 14. The high school principal had failed to complete his required certification. Additionally, he had divorced his wife and married a high school senior from a neighboring district. Deacon recommended, and the board accepted, his resignation. Deacon clearly demonstrated that his moral standards matched those of the community. All votes at the August 14 meeting were unanimous for the first time in four years. Five days later a special board meeting was called in which Deacon proposed a tax increase to ease the rapidly declining financial condition of the schools. The board unanimously supported an 18.34 percent tax increase. This pattern of unanimous voting was to continue throughout the next five years.

As the school year began, Deacon served as both superintendent and high school principal, as no replacement was immediately found for the released principal. He served in that capacity for three months and things were running smoothly. But a high school principal was needed and an interesting opportunity presented itself. Hinch, who had been superintendent in Bloomdale twenty years before, who had been superintendent where Deacon was high school principal, and who had recommended Deacon to Bloomdale, was suddenly widowed. He had been reassigned lesser duties in his school district, and with the loss of his wife, had no need to stay in Mud-Flat. Deacon called Hinch and asked if he would like to come back to Bloomdale as high school principal. Hinch accepted and at the November 18 board meeting Hinch was unanimously appointed Bloomdale's high school principal.

As was evident from Hinch's influence in helping Deacon get the superintendency, Hinch had maintained close ties with the Bloomdale community. Hinch settled into a daily routine. After school was dismissed he would walk down to the local gas station and sit on the bench talking to the locals who would drop by. Then he would move to the local cafe or grocery store. Hinch knew and was trusted by the powerful local citizens. He knew how to give them information about what needed to be done without telling them what to do. Thus, he was to privately plant the seeds of change that Deacon would publicly initiate.

Deacon continued to talk to the board about the need for new facilities and curriculum change. In December he gave the board a set of superintendent evaluation forms and asked that each evaluate his work to date. This pleased the board and they were quite enthusiastic in their appraisal of him. Also in December, Deacon recommended a new head football coach, a close friend, who was unanimously appointed. The team won the district championship three years later.

In January, Deacon was given a new three-year contract with a $2,500 raise. In February, Hinch decided he would not continue for another year and the board accepted Deacon's recommendation for a replacement. All Deacon's professional recommendations were unanimously accepted by the board during his tenure. At Deacon's recommendation, a system of board training and policy development was begun.

Early in the 1981-1982 school year architects were hired to do a facility survey. In November the state education agency notified the district of current facility deficiencies and gave the district until June to indicate how they planned to rectify the conditions. This came as no surprise to the board, as Deacon had initiated a system of almost daily contact with each board member. The board had unanimously supported a bond election to accomplish some of the needed building. That election had passed by a 3-1 margin, with the endorsement of the newspaper.

By April Deacon's contract was again extended with another raise and both board incumbents had been reelected. Deacon had carefully monitored the elections and moved to assure continued support wherever he could. He obtained an additional voting box in a critical area of the district and appointed supportive election officials.

During the summer, Deacon negotiated a grant to further assist in plant improvement, the board approved plans for the new building, furniture for the building was purchased, new football stands approved, and a new high school principal was employed, along with his wife as a teacher.

The son-in-law of the bank president was appointed to replace a board member who had resigned to take a job that required him to move from the district.

During the 1982–1983 year the new building was dedicated and occupied. Deacon made several moves to boost faculty morale. Unable to provide a salary raise for teachers, he won approval for teachers to eat lunch free of charge in the cafeteria. He sponsored a teacher appreciation banquet. There were rumors, however, that Deacon might leave and the board extended his contract again, with a sizable raise. The high school principal's contract was extended with the intention that he might succeed Deacon if Deacon left.

Things did not move quickly enough in 1983–1984 for the principal's wife. She initiated a campaign, largely through her friends in the Baptist church, to have Deacon removed. Deacon was a member of the same church and had not been inattentive to those contacts. The move backfired as the principal's wife submitted her resignation as a teacher in an attempt to precipitate the situation. Her resignation was unanimously accepted in August and by October her husband resigned as well.

In January 1985 Deacon received his fifth straight raise and contract extension, but in April he submitted his resignation in order to accept a better position in a larger district. During his five years as superintendent there had *never* been a nonunanimous vote on the board, a $250,000 grant had been procured, he had encouraged the board to establish a $20,000 recruiting fund to attract math and science teachers, a bond issue had passed, a new high school building had been built, and the curriculum was modified and upgraded. He had made 104 speeches to various community groups and received five unanimous contract extensions and raises — this following a three-year period of many nonunanimous votes, facility and curriculum stagnation, three superintendent firings, and considerable school board controversy. How was this accomplished and what meaning does it have for the Dissatisfaction Theory of Democracy?

Analysis

Bloomdale had experienced relatively little change over the past one hundred years. It had begun as a rural community, dependent on agriculture. It was a religious community with a large number of churches. It had traditional values that included an interest in and respect for education. In 1980, Bloomdale remained largely in that same image, with minor changes. Highways had replaced the railroad, and sorghum and cattle had largely replaced cotton. More people worked in neighboring urban communities, returning to Bloomdale in the evening to enjoy the less hectic life.

But all was not tranquil in Bloomdale. After a seven-year tenure the school superintendent had violated the sexual mores of the community and was fired. The next superintendent drank too much and almost made a fetish of littering his property with the evidence. He too was fired. The third superintendent, although having lived in the community, just could not make the transition to superintendent. He also was fired. During those three years, and the six preceding, the necessary work of running the school district had received little attention. The buildings had deteriorated, the curriculum had not been revised, the tax rate lagged behind the fiscal needs of the district. No one seemed to care. The overt breaking of community norms cost three successive superintendents their jobs without incumbent defeat.

Then Deacon came on the scene, young, novice superintendent, outsider, with ideas about how the public schools in Bloomdale needed to be improved. How likely was it that Deacon would become superintendent in Bloomdale, much less be able to keep the job if he got it?

In current research utilizing the Dissatisfaction Theory of Democracy, superintendent turnover is usually paired with incumbent defeat. Bloomdale, however, had experienced superintendent turnover three times without a single incumbent defeat. It was expected that this research would result in a major modification of the theory, but this turned out not to be so. Several things are different:

1. Apparently the community did not change and was not looking for major change. Actually the community appeared content and allowed education to remain static, as facilities deteriorated and curriculum fell behind. No changes occurred and no one was apparently very dissatisfied.
2. It was a change in the behavior of the person in the superintendent's role that created the value conflict and the dissatisfaction. The superintendent(s) changed.
3. The board stayed aligned with the community values, *not* the superintendent's values.
4. The board took action to realign the situation (firing the superintendent three separate times) until the three power sources of school policy (community/board/superintendent) were again in congruity.

Using this explanation, the theory remains essentially a good explanation of a democratic process of school governance. When the community is dissatisfied enough it will take action. In this case, the board acted for the community it represented in firing the three superintendents and, thus, avoided incumbent defeat.

Here the board and the community remain together. When the superintendent gets too far out of line, the community signals the board. Perhaps they simply make a phone call, as in the Thompsonville case. Perhaps no signal is necessary. If the board is truly congruous with the community, and a very homogeneous community in this case, members may act for the community simply because they share the same standards. The board takes action for the community and a new superintendent, presumably in line with community/board values, is employed. If the new superintendent fails to demonstrate those values, the board will act again and again until a satisfactory "fit" is achieved.

But how was it that Deacon succeeded? The odds were surely against his making so many changes in the schools without creating friction with the board and a community that had seemed content with the status quo. Deacon had a strong and important ally in Hinch. He showed acceptance of traditional community values and operated in a style the community liked. The fact that Bloomdale was a homogeneous community allowed Deacon to proceed. He knew the power structure and the values of the community, thanks to Hinch.

Deacon's situation is an interesting contrast to that of Johnson in the Thompsonville case. Johnson was faced with a community that was sharply divided in terms of values even though it seemed united on the surface. Johnson had no mentor to help him deal with the community power structure or to help him find a style that would have pleased them. In pleasing the board, Deacon pleased the community; in pleasing the community, Johnson displeased the board. In Thompsonville the board and the community were seeking realignment and the superintendent was caught in the middle. Deacon was not faced with the predicament that Thompsonville's superintendent was. Different "plays" require different actors and different roles.

WHAT WAS LEARNED? A SUMMARY OF CASES

1. While each of the four cases discussed here presents a different configuration of elements, it is clear that the generalized Dissatisfaction Theory finds a way to encompass each of them. That configuration depicts periods of local school politics when there is very little conflict and almost no incumbent defeat or involuntary turnover.
2. The apparent requirement for such a condition is that community values, board policy behavior, and superintendent administration of policy be congruent.
3. The notion that the sequence leading to conflict and change in school district policy must proceed unfailing from community changed values

to incumbent board defeat to superintendent turnover to policy change is exploded. Different conditions precipitate varying patterns, but in the same fashion the elements are mixed and remixed until a new alignment is complete and an equilibrium achieved.

4. New elements such as Turning Point Election Periods and "affirmation elections," in which an incumbent defeat merely affirms the current policy direction and superintendent's administration, or "correction elections," in which the community corrects a previous election mistake, provide new and helpful conditions that explain local school politics and make the superintendent's job more manageable.

7

Site Politics and the Dissatisfaction Theory

In both political science literature and popular fiction, the nature of big-city machines and the reforms that took corruption out of politics has been frequently explored. The reform movement always strengthened the bureaucratic aspects of the political system in some fashion and put the allocation of resources, including influence, in the hands of a "supra-oligarchy" composed of well-trained professional and socioeconomic elites. It was contended that such individuals could not be corrupted as they were not poor nor were they without influence. Therefore, specific rewards could not be used to corrupt them. That argument breaks down, however, at both the theoretical and empirical levels. Theoretically and in empirical fact, reform governments can be and have been corrupted. They are also exclusive, leaving "the people" a step away from power. Reform government tends to consider the people a "great beast," as legend suggests Alexander Hamilton stated. In such a condition the people are incapable of rational action in their own behalf. In this chapter the *machine* political process of government will be considered as an alternative to reform government and used to examine the role of local site politics, control, and responsibility in public education.

It could be said that small rural schools provide a "natural" environment for the sacred, gemeinschaft politics of schools. In rural America, everyone knows most everyone else, what they are capable of and what they are doing, their faults, needs, potential, and resources. In the gemeinschaft school-community, if Tom is having difficulty passing biology it is likely that Tom will receive whatever help he needs to pass. This occurs because everyone knows Tom's parents and grandparents. "They are a good family, and can be counted on to support the school." Likewise, of course, everybody knows Harry, whose siblings, mother, and father were "always no account and not worth wasting your time on." Thus, treatment of individual students is governed not only by a universal set of rules, as in a secular bureaucracy, but at least as much by a gemeinschaft process that depends on a sacred way of knowing. This is not to say that all small schools and school districts are sacred and gemeinschaft or that only metropolitan schools and districts are secular and gesellschaft. Each of those community types are "ideal-typical" constructs and as such provide a continuum and promote, even invite, elements from each contrasting description to be present within the same organization or social system.

However, urban schools as a group are different from rural schools. They tend to be more secular and impersonal. Usually the governance of urban schools developed, for the last sixty years at least, toward a reform-secular type. Urban schools lead the way in school reform. There are a few recent examples useful to explore.

The mid-1960s New York City model of community control can be viewed as an aborted effort to move New York City school governance away from the secular and toward the sacred, away from reform and toward the people. That is probably why it was abandoned. Those at the top of the secular power structure would have lost significant power if community control had succeeded. Additionally, the recent 1989 "experiment" in Chicago attempting to restructure the city's public schools appears to take this same direction, but apparently without carefully examining the reasons for the New York failure. Nevertheless, the Chicago reform was a move to place more power in the hands of the people and to force the system, for better or worse, to respond to wants and aspirations of the people whose children attend Chicago's schools. In doing so it provided a meaningful role for community members, and attempted to be responsive to the people at the grassroots level of the public schools, the site level. Finally, the 1990 Texas Senate Bill #1 also seems to move toward allowing teachers and parents a large role in local school governance on a statewide basis. It is this general phenomenon of allowing the people to participate in meaningful ways in educational decisions that is examined in this chapter.

MACHINE–REFORM POLITICS

At the turn of the century there were two important movements effecting changes in public education, particularly big city public education. These worked together to influence the superintendent/board and the school/community relationships. The first was the movement toward scientific management in both industry and public education. That movement fostered the image of the superintendent as a school executive, and ushered in the era of the "cult of efficiency," described by Callahan as an "American tragedy" (Callahan, 1962, p. 240). That process has already been documented. Hand in hand, and driven in part by the same mentality, was the effort to reform politics, particularly big city and public school politics. Woodrow Wilson was in the forefront of that movement.

As a prominent professor of political science and then as president of Princeton University, Wilson promoted the notion of professional managers of public policy. His solution to government inefficiency and corruption was to create a two-layer process in public policy. One involved legislative politics, where elected officials enacted laws. The other level was where government was administered—highly trained professional bureaucrats administered government free of the political pressures that too often corrupted the political process (Wilson, 1941). This played well with the notion of the school executive and was seen as a lifesaver for the beleaguered "vulnerable" superintendent.

The reform movement took two directions as it affected the superintendent/board relationship. First, the superintendent became the school executive. Occasionally, but not always, this resulted in dual administration of schools, again most often in the large cities. In such cases there was an instructional superintendent, who operated the educational organization free of politics, and a business manager–administrator, who reported directly to the board about fiscal matters, maintenance, contracts, and purchases. This organizational scheme permitted, if not encouraged, the continuance of certain kinds of "machine rewards" to be disseminated should the board be of that mind. Still, it avoided a direct "corrupting" effect on the educational aspects of the school district operation. The second trend was the reduction of the size of school boards, the removal of the system of electing board members by wards and substituting at-large general elections or even appointing rather than electing boards. This not only reduced the politics on the board but quickly ended the practice of dual administration. The executive school-expert superintendent was now clearly in the saddle. Cronin (1973, pp. 90–122) vividly documents this trend, at least in urban superintendent/board relationships. He concludes:

> After 1920, the number and kinds of school board reorganizations diminished. Controversy over the relationship of city schools to city government, and of school superintendents to boards, continued, and several of the larger cities continued to search for a system which would insulate the schools even further from what was felt to be the sordid side-effects of city politics. (p. 116)

The fact is that not only the school politics machine, but the city machine itself, was on the way out, as described by Banfield and Wilson (1963). Yet if the people want the machine and are willing to tolerate corruption in order to get the rewards they cannot get in other ways, both machine and corruption will persist.

Banfield and Wilson make a point that the machine depends heavily on "specific and material rewards" (1963, p. 115). *Specific* describes the particular individual's needs. Thus, a particular reward is given to one but not necessarily the other. The reward is concrete — money, food, fuel, a job. Banfield and Wilson point out that the objective of the specific material reward process is to control votes, stay in power, and thus control the political process. Further, they point out that free-enterprise businesses are the same type of machine process "in that they rely largely on specific, material incentives (such as salaries) to secure dependable, close control over their employees" (p. 115). Although in most cases employees have no direct control, such as a ballot box, over the tenure of the management, the analogy is well taken and leads to an obvious conclusion: While it is clear that some businesses have operated in a corrupt, illegal fashion, it is also clear that such a condition is the exception, not the rule. Most businesses are machines, according to Banfield and Wilson, and operate in not only a legal but a moral fashion as well. Thus it seems reasonable that corruption is not a necessary condition of the machine organization. This idea is essential in order to understand the machine process as an acceptable method of operating the politics of local education.

Several other points about the machine, made by Banfield and Wilson (1963), are essential to our argument here. Although it was said that the machine depended heavily on material rewards, Banfield and Wilson emphatically state that the machine did not use only specific and material rewards.

> The voter, however, is the one contributor to the machine's system of activity who is usually given non-material inducements, especially "friendship." . . . people will exchange their votes for "friendship" more readily than for cash or other material benefits; and the machine cannot afford to pay cash for many of the votes it needs. (p. 117)

Even the material things the machine gave to people were more "symbols of friendship" for the voter than anything else. Thus it was friendship and not material rewards that kept the machine in power. It was in spite of corruption and not because of it that the machine stayed in power.

Another point made by Banfield and Wilson (1963) is that it was almost always people from the underclass, the poor, the minorities, and the new immigrants who supported the machine because it was the only way they found to get the help they needed. The machine provided a way into the "system." It is interesting to speculate whether some of the alienation felt by certain minorities today may, in some fashion, be linked to the disappearance of the machine from the political scene. The removal of one of the major ways minorities had of moving up in the American political system, replaced only by "welfare," may leave people politically apathetic, if not alienated.

> Even though in the abstract one may prefer a government that gets its influence from reasonable discussion about the common good rather than from giving jobs, favors, and friendship; even though in the abstract he may prefer government by middle-class to government by lower-class standards, and even though in the abstract he may prefer the rule of professional administrators to that of politicians, he may nevertheless favor the machine in some particular concrete situation. (p. 127)

Certainly Banfield and Wilson were aware of Merton's (1968) concept of latent and manifest functions and unanticipated consequences, as *Social Theory and Social Structure* was first published in 1949. In the 1968 edition Merton identifies the political machine as his example of a latent function. He compares the function of uncorrupt-government and corrupt-government to legitimate and illegitimate business. He uses that comparison to illustrate the concepts of latent and manifest functions explaining that not every function that persists in a society benefits equally every segment of that society and that some functions have both latent and unanticipated consequences (pp. 124–136). The arguments offered here about machine government as a model for site-based management of schools follows and is based in part on those ideas.

The machine was replaced by "reform" government, both in city government and in the public schools. Election of school board members moved from the wards to at-large or even to "blue-ribbon" appointed boards. Boards appointed by blue-ribbon panels selected from among the city's economic-social elite are not likely to come from nor represent well the lower classes or minorities. Neither are the lower classes nor the minorities likely to feel represented by those boards. Given this reform trend, Banfield and Wilson (1963) posit two reasons why the professional administrators of the reform system naturally move into a position of power that is itself political. First, they have a virtual monopoly on technical and other detailed information. Recall our earlier discussion of the superintendent as the sole source of information for the board. Second, board members are part-time amateurs while the superintendent is a full-time, well-trained professional. This gives the superintendent a great advantage and considerable control. Consider also the matter of the superintendent's agenda control (Schattschneider, 1960) and add to that the fact that often it is to the advantage of elected officials to allow the "civil service bureaucrat" to at least appear to have initiated a proposal that may become a "lightning-rod" for community discontent, and the role of the superintendent in the reform superintendent/board relationship begins to clearly take shape. We see an elite board, appointed, or at least elected from the social-economic elite upper-middle and upper classes, acting as trustee for a public and a parent group whose values they probably do not hold. We see superintendents who, if they did not have socioeconomic origins above the societal mean, now with their education, salary, and housing (the three clearest indicators of socioeconomic status), are essentially in the upper-middle class. They tend to meld into the culture of the board and act as trustees for their boards. In such a manner it could be suggested that every step along the machine-reform continuum, toward the reform end, removes education further from the politics of the people and, more particularly, away from those whose children attend the public schools. What can we imagine will occur, finally, to school/community relations as this happens?

Within the professional bureaucracy a new machine inevitably replaces the deposed old political machine. This machine is not at the disposal of the voters nor required to provide specific rewards to the people, but is at the disposal of and required to provide specific rewards to the professional bureaucracy. This machine has been particularly visible in the largest, most urban school districts. Thus the cities, where the corruption of the old political machine cried loudest for reform, became the places where the new bureaucratic machine became the most insidious (Rogers, 1968, pp. 212–213). Rogers notes that school boards operate with considerable privacy. Although somewhat affected by "sunshine laws," enacted in the last two decades, they still retain and use the privilege of executive sessions and other means to establish consensus, later to be enacted in public. Rogers adds, when speaking of the superintendent/board relationship in New York City during the mid-1960s, "The independence from party politics should have lead to more professionalism, it has not. Under the guise of professionalism, a number of protectionist practices that are distinctly non-professional have begun to affect the system. . . . A new form of 'educational politics has evolved'" (p. 213). This is the politics of the new machine, which rewards long-time bureaucratic insiders in order to obtain their support. Without that support no big city school district can function if structured in traditional fashion. Nor can any superintendent long hope to survive opposed by that machine. Large, complex, bureaucratic urban school districts have not changed significantly in the past twenty-five years. Neither has the nature of a bureaucracy, nor has the "iron law of oligarchies" (Michels, 1966) been amended or repealed.

If the machine process might better serve the needs of the parents whose children attend the public schools, if the machine process in government need not mean corruption, if the reform does not end corruption in politics or public school governance, if the reform creates another type of machine government replacing the old and not subject to the will of the people—then perhaps it is time to think the "unthinkable." Perhaps it is time to consider how the machine process in local school governance could well serve the people in order to provide quality public education.

APPLYING MACHINE PROCESS TO THE POLITICS OF LOCAL SCHOOLS

Attendance Areas as Wards and Precincts

In the education machine process model presented here, the superintendent relies on the principal of each school to behave as a "ward boss." In such a role the principal is responsible for knowing what is going on in the ward (the attendance area), who is important, who has influence, who needs what, what is rewarding to whom. The principal is responsible for seeing that those who must be counted on for support receive the specific rewards necessary to assure that support. Everyone has at least the influence of one vote. Political machines cannot wait to ask for it after they need it. A basic premise in this model is that no one thing is rewarding to everyone and that no one educational decision is good or correct for every child. Further, the model assumes that parents have a right to help determine what is best for their children and suggest some sort of "individually prescribed educational program" (a specific and material reward) for their children and, therefore, for themselves. Each teacher is the equivalent of a precinct captain, knowing intimately each child and parent, their wants and needs, and seeing to it that the rewards are distributed.

Perhaps a word about wants and needs is required here. Goodenough (1963) has distinguished between the wants and needs of an organization or society undergoing change. He stresses that a change agent must recognize these differences. People tend to identify a set of wants that they believe will satisfy them. On the other hand, there is a set of needs necessary to accomplish those wants, which the change agent must identify. A successful change agent is able to synthesize the wants and needs into a set of activities and outcomes that at once satisfy both wants and needs. The ability to accomplish that merger is the job of the machine, if the machine wants to stay in power. If the school district wishes to avoid getting the people dissatisfied enough to turn out the incumbent board and superintendent, the wants of the people must be considered when identifying needs.

The teacher (the precinct captain) and the principal (the ward boss, who is responsible for a group of precinct captains) are together responsible to the superintendent (the machine boss) for keeping the voters in the wards and precincts if not satisfied, at least not dissatisfied enough to get out and vote against the policies, the taxes, the school bonds, and the incumbent board members who establish or propose them. When voters vote against the incumbent board they tend to be voting against the incumbent superintendent as well. When incumbent board members are losing at the polls or refusing to run for reelection it is likely that the incumbent superintendent is also in trouble. When the machine is not doing its job, the machine boss will probably be put out of office along with the "party."

In order to keep the machine properly oiled and functioning, the machine boss must find sufficient resources to distribute, on ward and precinct bases, to keep the voters from becoming too dissatisfied. But the machine boss does not make all the decisions, or a single centralized decision, about the distribution of those resources. The boss monitors the decisions made by ward bosses and precinct captains and makes sure that the voters know that it is the machine boss that is to be thanked, and kept in office, if the voters are to assure that these gifts of friendship will be continued. If a precinct captain is not doing the job, get a new precinct captain. If a ward boss is not doing the job, get a new ward boss. That is the way a machine process works.

It is important to note that not every want of every voter can or must be satisfied every time. There simply are not enough resources at the disposal of the machine to do that. The machine makes friends. The voters realize they have a friend in the machine. It is the *friendship* that is sought, not just the specific rewards. Specific rewards are but the symbols of the friendship. Friendship is an element of the gemeinschaft society needed and sought by everyone and difficult to find in our increasingly gesellschaft society. Local schools can provide that sense of gemeinschaft through a machine process of operation. To the extent they do, they will make lasting friends who will support them in times of trouble.

In the machine process the term for a ward that can be counted on for unflinching support is *delivery ward*. The term is descriptive of the process. A delivery ward can be "delivered" when and where the machine needs support, either at the polls or at a political rally. Juxtaposed to delivery wards are the "newspaper" wards. A social reality that tended to perpetrate the "old" machine politics was the fact that poor and immigrant people of the cities needed *verbal* instructions about what was needed to get things done (i.e., how to fill out a job application, how to mark a ballot, etc.). They either had difficulty reading and understanding the written word or could not read English at all. In the newspaper wards, however, people could read. They had jobs and could get their information from the newspaper—thus the term *newspaper wards*. Specific and material rewards were not very important to them; therefore, a ward boss could not guarantee a newspaper ward.

What is suggested in this education machine process model of local school/community relations is that the principals and the teachers turn their school attendance areas and classrooms, respectively, into delivery wards. Such attendance areas would support excellence in education because people knew that their children were receiving a quality education in *their* schools. When the superintendent and board needed several busloads of supporters for a proposal at a board meeting or votes in a bond election they could call a ward boss who would deliver the bus loads on time and with proper enthusiasm. Almost any attendance area can be turned into a delivery ward because the people need the education machine. Parents know that they *want* their children to receive a good education, to be able to go to college, to get a good job, to succeed. They usually do not know what is needed to obtain that want. Professional educators do, or should, know what is needed. They can use that ability to establish delivery wards if they choose. Or they can retreat into the new machine, the professional bureaucracy, and ignore the people. They can "hide" for a while, but not for long. American public education is governed democratically. When the people are dissatisfied enough they will get what they want. They will vote.

Some Experiments in Community Control

One can recognize certain similarities between what we have called the education machine process and what has been called community control or site management. Community control of public schools is not a new concept, as recent literature of site-based management might have one believe. Public education began in colonial America as site-based, community controlled schools. No colonist could have imagined it otherwise. The establishment of education as a state rather than local function began the gradual erosion of community control. The decision to "reform" education and end the corruption of the machine further removed the control of education from the common people, as education was seen as too important to leave to the dirty business of politics. Reform placed public education in the hands of at-large elected, or appointed, elite councils of trustees to be run in businesslike fashion by well-trained, civil-service-like school executives. As the community began to feel more and more left out of the decisionmaking, and less apt to support school bonds and taxes, the school executives and their elite boards became more and more concerned about managing a school/community relations program that would "sell" the schools, which they run for the people, to the people. In many cases, that procedure has not been very successful. In the last thirty years, three major political efforts attempted to put the governance of public education closer to the hands of the people again.

The New York City schools had been well "reformed" by the early 1960s. The reform board had been corrupted and removed and a new blue-ribbon board had replaced it. As the civil rights movement gathered momentum in the 1960s and "white flight" from America's cities left New York schools without sufficient white students to desegregate the schools, even if anyone had been serious about doing that, the parents of the African-American students who actually attended New York City schools moved politically to seize control of the public schools from the white board. No one on that board had children in the schools. Marilyn Gittell (1967) documents the conditions that led to this attempt to seize community control of the schools. The attempt, if successful, would have resulted in largely African-American control of the schools. The attempt was aided by the Ford Foundation (Fantini & Gittell, 1970) and liberal scholars often funded by that foundation.

In the end, the effort to gain community control failed. It failed at the state legislative level because neither the Ford Foundation, the liberal scholars, nor the indigenous parents knew how to play the legislative political game in New York State. The professional bureaucracies, the American Federation of Teachers, and the state labor council did. That process is excellently documented by Iannaccone (1970). In place of real community control, a five-borough system utilizing a confederation of thirty-one "local" decentralized districts was instituted under the city board and the commissioner. The new arrangement was heavily influenced by a liberal scholar who had presumably championed the effort for real community control (Gittell, 1967). That new system effectively removed any threat of real community control and left the professional bureaucracy largely in control. The New York City effort to seize community control was a bold experiment and those who witnessed it will not forget it. The experiment was chronicled in almost every lay and professional journal in the nation (Alsworth and Woock, 1969; Baratta, 1970; Calhoun, 1969; Lisser, 1970; New York Civil Liberties Union, 1969). In its January 1969 issue, the official organ of the National School Board Association defended the New York City School Board's inability to respond to demands for community control by attempting to shift the blame to school administrators, teacher organizations, labor, political parties, and even the civil service system. Surely there was plenty of blame to go around, including well-meaning liberal educationists and researchers and the New York City School Board itself.

Kirst (1989) called the most recent community control attempt, the Chicago community control legislation, the most radical education reform in a century. At least the Chicago plan was enacted at the legislative "nodules of power," described by Summerfield (1974) as those changing coalitions that make legislation possible. Community control in Chicago is now the law in the state of Illinois. Whether that law will succeed in putting the education of Chicago's children in the hands of the community remains to be seen. The professional bureaucracy of administrators, although greatly reduced, has already been to court to block total implementation of the law.

The Chicago school system was called the worst school system in the United States by then U.S. Secretary of Education William Bennett (Walberg et al., 1989). This infamous distinction would be as difficult to prove as it will be to escape. That charge undoubtedly helped precipitate the legislation and its implementation. The Chicago reform law immediately shifted formal power from the country's largest educational bureaucracy to "parents and community people at each of the city's 504 schools" (Wilkerson, 1989). The Chicago reform was different from the earlier New York reform in several significant ways. The legislative battle was guided by the powerful as opposed to the powerless. That is, it was the legislature itself, not the indigenous poor of the inner city, that devised the reform and guided its passage over a two-year period. It was originally devised by Senator Keith Snyder, chair of the Elementary and Secondary Education Committee of the Illinois Senate. It came into being as legislators sensed the frustration of the people and acted before dissatisfaction was sufficient to turn them out of the legislature. The legislative action turned out the bureaucratic machine that had been running the schools, replacing it with a type of site-based management similar to the machine governance process described above. The people and the parents now hold the majority of the vote on the local school councils. They run budgets and hire staff. It remains to be seen if they can produce better schools. In any case the people were heard.

A third piece of state legislation follows the trend toward what is presently termed site-based management and is intended to encourage the participation of new individuals in the public education decision-making process. In one of Texas's several special 1990 legislative sessions, a law was passed mandating that every school in the state demonstrate that they utilize both teacher and parent participation in school decisionmaking.

That law would seem to require that some type of machine process would occur, at least to some extent, in every school in Texas, but the Texas Association of School Boards in concert with the State Board of Education has already issued an interpretation that makes it unlikely that much of the grassroots process suggested in the legislation will occur. The law was not the result of popular demand but was enacted by the legislature as part of a financial bill. Perhaps it was part of the state legislature's attempt not to be left behind in the "race to reform." It seems likely that grassroots participation occurs most effectively when it is initiated because of the dissatisfaction of the people.

These three situations are not the only examples of current movement toward community participation in school policy. Kunesh and Bakker (1990) note this trend in *Policy Briefs*, followed by a recitation of five North Central states that are doing something to obtain more community participation. Valesky, Smith, and Fitzgerald (1990) cite numerous policy initiations across the nation including Dade County, Florida, California, Minnesota, and New York, and conclude with a detailed description of what Tennessee is doing.

A word of warning, or unhappy prophecy, may be in order. Earlier efforts to involve citizens and community in public school policymaking often resulted in little more than the formal listing of citizens' committees necessary to meet federal regulations. It is to be hoped the present trend produces more in the way of positive school/community relationships.

QUELLING DISSATISFACTION IN THE WARDS

The result of citizen dissatisfaction can occasionally be harmful to the operation of the public school. This occurs when small groups of people disrupt school board meetings or, by voting against incumbent board members, turn the board into an arena board, resulting finally in a change in the superintendency without clear specification and articulation of needed policy change. While "voting out" incumbents may seem very democratic, there are some potential problems with the procedure. It can leave political scars. Occasionally, because of the usual low voter turnout, small groups of "single-issue" voters can control an election, remove an incumbent, create dissension on the board, and get inordinate media attention without actually representing even a large minority of the community.

In other cases a rather large coalition of voters dissatisfied enough to defeat an incumbent manages to agree about nothing except their discontent with the board and superintendent. They represent a coalition so fragile that it does not last beyond the election victory. Thus, the newly elected board member, lacking a power base, is powerless. In such cases the school district is disrupted without redeeming virtue. Worse still is that such a result from discontent will likely repeat itself until a new power base is established that can support and stabilize policy change. This process of continuing dissatisfaction and incumbent defeat is documented by Weninger (1987), and a synopsis of that case is reported in Chapter 6 of this book. Constant political turmoil serves no good purpose in public education.

Of course there is the case when the Dissatisfaction Theory does describe the uniquely American process of the people's becoming dissatisfied enough to take political action and elect officials who will represent their interests and develop policies that provide for the needs and wants of the society. That process in local school districts not only serves the cause of public education, but also serves as a grassroots model of American democracy. It demonstrates to the people that the American democratic system does work and that voters can change the system.

Another way to get the system to work, other than throwing the incumbents out, is to get the incumbents to respond, at least in part, to the demands, the needs, and the wants of the electorate. That response can be made in terms of "voter hygienes" and can be done, perhaps, relatively easily. McGehee (1990) demonstrated that there are things that function in school districts in a fashion similar to what Herzberg (1959) called "hygienes." According to Herzberg, hygienes operate so as to keep employees from becoming dissatisfied and unhappy with their work. They do not motivate the worker, they simply avoid worker dissatisfaction. McGehee found that there are, apparently, similar things operating in a school district that avoid the dissatisfaction, described in the Dissatisfaction Theory, that sends voters to the polls to disestablish the status quo. Voters who think that schools are safe places, that they have a friend on the board or employed by the school district, or that their schools are doing well compared with those of other states tend not to vote in school board or school bond elections. They apparently have what might be called "voter hygienes." Other voters, who have a set of what might be called "voter motivators," tend to vote in such elections. They vote for incumbents and for school bonds. Those who lack both hygienes and motivators vote against incumbents and bond issues. Based on McGehee's research it appears that it could be relatively easy to provide hygienes for voters but perhaps more difficult to supply motivators. It should be relatively easy to convince the public that the schools are safe and that they have a friend somewhere in the system, someone who will listen and someone who will help if they need it. That is, after all, the job of the machine, to provide at least friendship if not always material rewards. Teachers and principals should work at that job as part of their role in a good school/community public relations program. No public relations program is going to work for long if the schools are not safe and doing a reasonably good job of teaching children, and there is not someone in the system who cares enough to listen when a parent has a problem.

CONCLUSION

People who are dissatisfied *enough* to oppose the present policy and governance of the local school are often united only by their dissatisfaction. One small special-interest group may be dissatisfied about the special education program; another small group about the gifted program; another about the athletic program; another the band; another the science/math offerings. Each individual in each group has some *special* interest in that activity or area for a reason *special* to that person. One potential voter may be a former school star quarterback who never went to college and has no children in the schools. Another may be unathletic and a "Walter Mitty" type with a son who made the team. Both are dissatisfied with the cut in the athletic budget. Still another person, whose child is in special education, has approached the principal about obtaining more materials and a paraprofessional to assist such students, only to be told there are no funds. Having approached board members she was referred to the superintendent who said (five years ago) that he would consider it and was sympathetic. An ally of this woman, opposing the present policy-making structure, is the head of the chemistry department at the local university. His daughter was unable to engage in enough laboratory work because no new equipment has been purchased for the last seven years. These last two individuals actually oppose each other in terms of budget priorities, but they are united in their opposition to what they see as an uncaring school board and administration.

All of these people are members of small groups, dissatisfied about something. These groups, potential combatants on a pluralistic political field for resource allocation, are united in their dissatisfaction with a policy structure, the superintendent and school board, who see them as special-interest groups to be shunned because they do not care about the best interest of "all the kids."

But there is no best interest of *all* of the children. Children are too different. Parents are too different. Resources are too limited, viewpoints too narrow. Homans (1960) shows that social justice is operationally a matter of putting the "just" interest and needs of others after our own "self" needs and interests. Easton (1965) has defined politics as the authoritative allocation of values — but *whose* values becomes an important issue. Merging Easton and Homans one might expect that justice in politics involves putting the justified needs and wants of others just after the satisfaction of the needs and wants of the ruling oligarchy.

How long can people be turned away? How long will they tolerate being given no real evidence that their special interest is of concern to the policymakers who are supposed to represent them? How long can those in power neglect special-interest groups without creating a plurality of people "dissatisfied enough" to vote against the incumbents, the taxes they levy, and the bond issues they propose? The purpose of a good school/community relations program is to avoid extended dissatisfaction. Such a program requires answers to the above questions. It is not necessary to "satisfy" each group (active and potential) making demands for resources. It *is* necessary to prevent things from becoming dissatisfying enough to disrupt the normal function of schools.

8

Putting Dissatisfaction to Work

It is the position of those who propose the Dissatisfaction Theory of Democracy that dissatisfaction fuels the engine of the American democratic process. It is during times of citizen contentment that the American voter becomes apathetic, not concerned enough about the problems nor dissatisfied enough with the current solutions to go to the polls and vote. This lethargy allows the wheels of American democracy to rust from disuse. It allows the politicians and professional managers of public bureaucracies and agencies to become complacent and, too often, neglectful of the changing society. The period of Calvin Coolidge and the first year of the Herbert Hoover presidency, just prior to the Great Depression (1923–1929), is an example.

The question, therefore, addressed in this chapter is not how to eliminate conflict and discontent but, rather, how to put dissatisfaction to work for the public schools. Previous chapters have addressed various mechanisms applicable to conflict management in the governance of local school districts. Most of the "reform" mechanisms in education have moved government away from the people toward an elite of professional government managers who are protected from the people and toward a form of government in which the people do not have direct access to those who govern. Their demands are, therefore, less likely to receive a tangible government response. Resisting public demands is one method of managing conflict; it tends to hide conflict under the rug. Another strategy is conflict management, which kicks up the dirt rather than hiding it. In general, if conflict is handled early, a district can avoid dissatisfaction that becomes great enough to cause major episodic political upheaval. Coupled with the conflict-management movement is a trend toward what is presently being touted as "site-based management" and presented as a new idea. Such a system, together with community site boards, operationalizes the "machine" of government, bringing both the formal and informal politics to the equivalent of the ward level, that is, to the individual building and neighborhood level.

In an attempt to manage conflict, school boards might move away from elite council behavior and toward arena council behavior, so that each segment of the people might see their values represented and hope that their demands would some time be attended to. Such a move, coupled with a "politico" superintendent who not only is able to act as an expert educational leader but also is capable of occasionally operating as a representative of the people and their board, would go a long way toward managing conflict rather than submerging it until it erupted like a pent-up volcano. Finally, understanding that while Zeigler, Kehoe, and Reisman (1985) may have generalized beyond their very small sample and failed to recognize the very broad spectrum of services operated in most school districts and managed by superintendents, it probably remains true that school superintendents are badly served by the attitude that they are the prime decisionmakers in the district and that the board that does not trust their superintendent to make decisions alone has the wrong superintendent. Conflict is a real part of managing any complex organization, particularly a political organization. School districts are political organizations. Conflict will occur. The question is when, to what degree, and how it will be handled. Any notion that consensus and harmony comprise the natural state of a dynamic, changing, and heterogeneous political system like a school district harbors the seeds of unrealistic expectations and is sure to spawn discontent and disappointment.

INDICATORS OF DISSATISFACTION IN LOCAL DISTRICTS

Almost from the beginning, a major thrust of the Dissatisfaction Theory has been the attempt to predict in some useful fashion the degree of community dissatisfaction that disrupts school districts, dismantles boards, and disposes of superintendents. It has been the assumption of the originators of the theory that the episodic change that characterizes the Dissatisfaction Theory does not serve public education well and that more gradual change, in response to public demands, would better serve the cause of democracy as well as the cause of public education. Therefore, in addition to suggesting structures that might be able to manage the conflict and dissatisfaction in a gradual rather than episodic manner, we have sought to identify indicators and predictors of dissatisfaction and possible voter revolt prior to its occurrence.

Social-Economic-Political Indicators

The first efforts to discover indicators of dissatisfaction were those of Freeborn (1966), Kirkendall (1966), and Waldon (1966). As a result of those studies a set of social-economic-political indicators was identified that discriminated between school districts that had experienced superintendent turnover and those that had not. The set included generic indicators such as change in average daily attendance (ADA) — a sociological indicator; change in district tax evaluation — an economic indicator; and change in voter turnout — a political indicator. Of particular consequence, these studies established not only that there were economic-political-social indicators related to school board incumbent defeat but that involuntary superintendent turnover followed incumbent defeat within three years at a significance beyond the 0.001 level. Not only were these findings relevant under the usual nonpartisan elections of "reform" politics, but Moen (1971) established the fact that they held true for politically partisan school board elections as well. The first effort to determine the degree to which incumbent defeat and superintendent turnover might be predicted was made by Garberina (1975). Stimulated by a study done by LeDoux (1971), which challenged the ability of the Dissatisfaction Theory to account for incumbent defeat/superintendent turnover, particularly in school districts in which the indicators were turning down rather than up, Garberina found that a combination of socio-economic-political indicators could account for a significant amount of the variance in incumbent defeat at the 0.005 level. That study, using for the first time multiple regression techniques, was still deductive rather than inductive inasmuch as the question asked was not whether an election could be predicted but, rather, would some of these indicators account for significant variance in an election that had taken place. While this seemed a reasonable step, it still fell short of prediction. The data did not "test" the hypothesis — they described a condition.

In 1980 Hunt attempted to actually predict a school board election using a regression equation developed from Garberina's data and data from a set of school districts in Ohio. The prediction attempt failed. Yet some of the same generic indicators were again able to account, after the fact, for significant amounts of the election results. In an attempt to explain this perplexing phenomenon the authors suggested that election predictions, like weather predictions, were only possible based on data that were very near the actual event predicted. Thus, like tomorrow's weather, tomorrow's election can be predicted but, like next year's weather, next year's election is impossible to predict accurately. Still it is the same set of predictors that will be useful over time. Without knowing it, they set the same propositions that were being formulated by the chaos researchers (Gleick, 1987).

Based on that idea, additional work was undertaken. The DISSAT factor was found to have stability and to be near enough the predicted election results to have been able to predict the Ohio districts used by

Hunt. Later Wang and Lutz (1989) reported that this DISSAT factor was able to predict a set of school elections in Texas. The DISSAT factor is simply one minus the quotient of the number of board seats up for election, divided by the number of candidates running for those seats in the election being predicted. This DISSAT factor has now been shown to be a significant variable in the prediction of school bond elections (Foerch, 1989) and has been quite stable across three sets of data.

While the DISSAT factor seems a good predictor and is useful in supporting the theory, it is less helpful to the practitioner as it is available only a few months before the election being predicted. An incumbent needs more notice than that. What these findings tell us is that the political world behaves much like the physicists tell us the physical world behaves— chaotically. That is, events cannot safely be predicted in linear fashion or over very long periods. The events are orderly but variables are unstable and interactive. Each influences the other so that, as one chaos researcher has shown, a butterfly flying in South America can influence the weather in New York (Gleick, 1987).

What can be done with relative ease, however, is to watch the indicators that have continuously proven to foreshadow incumbent defeat, that is, changes in average daily attendance, assessed evaluation divided by ADA, voter turn out, and challengers running. These indicators foretell a discontent that often precedes incumbent defeat and superintendent turnover. If they are perceived early enough, concerned school board members and superintendents have time to work out strategies that will avert the sufficient discontent that episodically grips local school districts resulting in the disruption of the orderly governance of the local public schools.

THE PRACTICAL POLITICS OF INCUMBENT DEFEAT

There are other factors that have been shown to be related to this dissatisfaction process. Edgren (1976) showed that communities have a political culture that blurs the distinction between types of local government and that citizen satisfaction is related to participation in that governance at the level desired by the citizen. Further, he found that citizens are more willing to give superintendents more decision-making latitude than they will give to city managers but, although citizens are given the right to be heard, citizen opinion makes little difference in the board's decisions. In similar fashion Cistone (1970) demonstrated that there were strikingly similar values held by voters leading to their preference for a city-manager form of government and their willingness to allow the superintendent of schools to make educational decisions. Two additional studies, Danis (1981) and Emminghan and Rawson (1985), confirm the notion of political culture's role in triggering the episodic events described in the Dissatisfaction Theory, including both state and national events. Kerchner, Mitchell, Pryor, and Erck (1981) and Chichura (1977) demonstrated that major new education legislation can stimulate local district dissatisfaction and become the catalyst for political action. Boyd and Johnson (1985) reported general confirmation of the Dissatisfaction Theory process, highlighting that the plurality of dissatisfied voters have little in common except their dissatisfaction. Their data questioned an eight- to ten-year period of episodic change, as does the Weninger (1987) study. However, Thorsted (1974), Mitchell and Thorsted (1976) and Criswell and Mitchell (1980) seem to strongly suggest an eight- to ten-year episodic period is the most general type.

The above data provide the basis for a set of political conclusions offered by Lutz and Iannaccone (1978) as a blueprint for the regular and episodic political events that intervene in the history of local school district politics.

1. Communities change; they grow or decline in population. Blue-collar factories close and high-tech ones open. Neighborhoods change — ethnically, racially, and socioeconomically.
2. Such changes are usually accompanied by value changes including citizen aspirations and expectations, beliefs about family and religion. Such belief changes impact the local schools. Parents expect different things from and for their children. This leads to different demands on the schools.
3. Over time school boards and their superintendent tend to become closed systems and elite systems, representative of the community that once elected them but that no longer exists. They tend to ignore and resist the demand of the newer special-interest groups as they fail to share their values.
4. These special-interest groups first attempt to get the superintendent and the board to respond to their needs. At this point they do not even think of these needs as political "demands." But elite boards are reluctant to deal with special-interest groups. They perceive these groups as disinterested in what is good for all children and they underestimate the collective power of such groups.
5. In addition to local and special interests that exhibit dissatisfaction there are troughs of political satisfaction and waves of political discontent at both national and state levels that can influence local dissatisfaction and make local issues more or less salient to the local voters.
6. Dissatisfied voters and groups have little in common other than their

dissatisfaction. They represent unlikely and unusual coalitions. Under certain circumstances, however, these groups will unite to form a plurality of the voting electorate. In addition to personal "gripes," these conditions include but are not limited to the current tide of state or national discontent and the recognition by several of these discontented groups that each, albeit for a different reason, is discontented enough with the present administration (the board and the superintendent) to become politically active and change it.

7. Before a coalition of discontent is well formed it is likely that one could observe the social-economic indicators changing and therefore have an opportunity to respond. As the new coalition grows, however, one will observe that voter turnouts in school elections will begin to increase, as will the number of challengers for school board seats.

8. Some incumbents, unhappy with increasing community demands and factional politics (arena politics in our terms), will refuse to run for reelection. Often the refusal of a sitting board member to run for reelection can be taken as the same political event as an incumbent being defeated at the polls.

9. Incumbent school board member defeat, accompanied by a political rhetoric calling for new education policy and programs and followed by another "reconfirming election," is very often followed (within three years) by involuntary superintendent turnover.

10. A new board will, after getting rid of the incumbent superintendent, hire an outside superintendent who shares its value system. This "new administration" will develop new policy and hire new staff to carry out that policy, and new programs will be operationalized that better satisfy the political-social system of the existing community.

If a school administration is to use this blueprint as a guide for avoiding the disruptive affects of episodic and revolutionary upheavals, that administration must become familiar with and responsive to the political realities described in the Dissatisfaction Theory. It must consistently monitor the community power system and the social-economic-political indicators that suggest the possibility of growing community dissatisfaction. Superintendents and school boards should be consistently aware of the shifting coalitions forming the power system of their community. Personal bias and perception are likely to cloud even the most astute observer's view of reality. As noted in step 7 of the blueprint, the indicators of citizen dissatisfaction precede the political events of step 4 and beyond. Certainly by step 4 the superintendent should be aware of a political storm on the horizon. Evidence of possible change demands should be shared with the school board.

All school boards will not greet the news of pending political problems with enthusiasm. A politico superintendent will have prepared the board by providing regularly scheduled reports on the nature of the school community and on the changes and their probable effect on community demands coupled with possible policy responses. The news that the "enemy" is now at our gates with a large and hostile force can get the messenger killed, especially when it comes as a surprise. By the time the district reaches step 6, particularly if state and national waves of dissatisfaction are also present, the board is in trouble and the messenger is almost sure to be blamed.

Superintendents must consistently work at this process of school/community relationships, governed by the precepts of the Dissatisfaction Theory, if they are to survive long enough to successfully play the role of education statesperson.

By the time the political situation reaches step 8 or 9, the solidarity of the incumbent elite board is shattered, the politics of the board has surely changed from elite to arena. It is unlikely that the new arena board will have developed new norms for governing such behavior. Then the superintendent as well as the school district is in trouble. A superintendent who manages to survive three years of such conflict has a good chance of continued survival, but the likelihood of survival for that length of time is not high (Wang, 1989).

There are strategies for superintendent survival following incumbent defeat. However, they may be difficult for a superintendent to adopt after years of being tied closely to an elite board. Now challenged by insurgents who have defeated members of the old elite board, the superintendent must try to adapt. One strategy, not recommended but occasionally successful, is to "stonewall" the insurgents and attempt to co-opt at least some of the insurgent board members. Such a strategy assumes that the old power structure still exists sufficiently to be mobilized and reelect some representatives of that structure. This strategy is most likely to work before a reconfirming election occurs and when the superintendent has a contract continuing for two or three years.

A different strategy, more to be recommended, is for the superintendent to move away from a role as "part of the board" and toward a role as administrator of board decisions, providing several policy alternatives for the board to enact (probably by split vote) and then administrating whichever policy is enacted by majority vote. At the same time, the superintendent must begin to assist the board in working out and adopting a new set of group norms that allows for or even encourages disagreement about policy alternatives and open debate of value differences. If new norms cannot be developed, the board itself will become "anomic" and self-destruct.

ation resulting in low voter turnout.

Once step 10 has been reached, the new superintendent has no choice but to adopt the latter strategy, probably working with a split board until a new power structure is forged. In their original work on the theory of citizen dissatisfaction, Iannaccone and Lutz (1970) noted the difficulty of obtaining this new power stability, naming the chapter on this subject "I Shall Overturn, Overturn, and Overturn. . . . "

WINNING SCHOOL BOND ELECTIONS

A word about school bond elections and the Dissatisfaction Theory seems appropriate. Relatively little work on school bond elections has been done by Dissatisfaction theorists. McGehee (1990) has been previously cited in Chapter 7 as identifying a set of hygienes and motivators capable of distinguishing those who vote from those who do not, and those who vote for a bond issue as eligible voters from those who vote against it. Previous to McGehee's work, Foerch (1989) demonstrated that incumbent defeat and superintendent turnover were both related to the results of school bond elections. Districts with considerable incumbent defeat or superintendent turnover were significantly more likely to lose a bond election compared with those with little such defeat or turnover. As incumbent defeat and superintendent turnover are themselves significantly related, superintendent turnover was alone a sufficient predictor of bond election failure. After the variance accounted for by superintendent turnover was removed from the election results, incumbent defeat and the DISSAT factor were still able to account for 13 percent of the variance in the bond election results. The more incumbent defeat in the year of the bond election, the more likely the election was to lose.

Another thing Foerch (1989) found was that there was a slight but not significant relationship between voter turnout and the defeat of the bond election. In general, nonsignificant relationships are not worth reporting. Yet much is still made of Carter and Savard's (1961) finding that as voter turnout increased so did the likelihood of losing the bond election. Often omitted from those findings is the fact that when voter turnout reached very high levels the bond issues again began to pass. However, Hamilton and Cohen (1974) found that higher voter turnout tended to increase the number of voters likely to oppose increased local government spending. Such findings tend, on the surface, to discourage school boards and superintendents from "getting out the vote," unless through a highly "selective" encouragement resulting in low voter turnout.

When democracy is assumed to mean the full and continuous participation of voters, then such school board and superintendent behavior in school elections appears antidemocratic. Some "best-practice" beliefs have tended to suggest that this "keep the issue quiet" and get out only the vote you can count on, essentially parents of public school students, is still commonly practiced in many school districts. Returning to the work of McGehee (1990), we know that people with political hygienes, who then lack sufficient dissatisfaction, are less likely to vote in either school bond or school board elections. While hygienes may vary from district to district, it appears that they are relatively inexpensive to provide. They include such things as citizens' perception that the school is a safe place for children and that their district is providing reasonably good academic and athletic programs *compared* with other districts in the state. People who perceive these minimum things are not sufficiently dissatisfied to vote against bond issues or school board members. According to the recent Gallup polls on education, most people do believe that "their" school is better than the average school and a safe place for children (Elam, 1989). Therefore, according to the theory, most voters will not bother to vote. Empirically this is correct; most voters do not vote in school elections. Of those motivated enough to vote, a set of motivators can be established that discriminates between those who vote for versus those who vote against bond issues and incumbents. It therefore should be possible to determine clusters of voters more predisposed to vote against the bond issue and then work to supply them with relatively inexpensive hygienes. One should also be able to identify those voters most supportive of the bond issues and work to motivate them to go to the polls and vote their predisposition. In voter behavior theory this process is called the use of crosspressure.

Spinner (1967) made an interesting finding that appears to have been little noticed. He found that in bond elections that failed in New York State during the late 1950s and early 1960s, the total yes votes had not changed significantly from those recorded in the last election, when the bond issue had passed. (i.e., In 1958 a bond issue had passed 553 yes–349 no. In 1962 a similar bond issue failed 548 yes–640 no.) Such data suggest that the district had not lost its strong supporters — they seem to have again voted for the 1962 bond issue. Studying the bond elections that had lost and then been proposed again, without changing the dollars requested, Spinner found that the no votes remained stable in subsequent elections — they tended not to change — but the yes votes steadily increased in each resubmission until the bond issue finally passed. (i.e., After losing in 1962 548 yes–640 no, it finally passed six months later 710 yes–638 no.) This pattern suggests that the relationship between turnout and lost elections observed by Carter and Savard (1961) is correct but is curvilinear. When bond elections fail, the voter turnout is higher than when they last passed. But as the issue is resubmitted turnout continues to increase, and bond issues finally pass. This is consistent with what the Dissatisfaction and crosspressure theories would suggest.

Nunnery and Kimbrough (1971) explain that the more a voter feels crosspressure, the more likely he or she is not to vote or to decide late about how to vote. Lutz (1980), applying the notion of crosspressure to school bond elections, suggests that most Americans are "predisposed" in favor of public education in spite of specific grievances they may have. As crosspressure and cognitive dissonance theory suggest, individuals seek to reaffirm their already held values and ideals. Therefore, it should be to the advantage of school politicians to reinforce their belief in that value of public education so as to, at the same time, decrease the crosspressure on predisposed yes voters, getting them out to vote, and increase the crosspressure on predisposed no voters, getting them to change their minds late in the campaign or to stay at home and not vote. This phenomenon of increasing crosspressure would appear to account rather well for Spinner's (1967) findings. If the predisposed no voters, in Spinner's elections, were left alone by the school politicians in the lost election, but identified by the leaders opposed to the bond election, their crosspressure would have been relieved and they would have turned out to vote against the bonds. The same number of yes voters had voted but were overwhelmed by the "new" no voters, who had not bothered to vote before. The total voter turnout significantly increased but new voters were not proportionally representative of the total electorate. Following the loss, Spinner's school districts proposed the same bond issue but abandoned the "keep a low profile" strategy and went to the total electorate. They did not do much to convince the predisposed no voters to change their minds. Having already defeated the proposition, they are reinforced and vote again. What the school district *can* do is to relieve crosspressure in potential yes voters who had not voted in the last election, convincing them that their votes count and are needed. These voters now go to the polls and vote their predisposition, for public education, and the bond issue passes without decreasing the number of no votes that had defeated the bond issue in the first place. Of considerable interest, and commensurate with what the Dissatisfaction Theory would predict, after the bond election passes, which sometimes takes more than one attempt, the election turnout usually returns to the original pattern of reduced participation and regular success for bond elections.

BLOCK VOTERS IN SCHOOL ELECTIONS

Recent data indicate that the American voter is becoming less of a block voter. More and more voters, and politicians for that matter, are changing parties, or at least voting occasionally for someone from another party.

This may indicate a lack of platform differences between parties, a lack of clear issues, or a lack of voter choice among candidates, or it may in fact indicate more voter independence. While certain group predispositions still exist (i.e., Republicans still tend to vote for Republican candidates and those with more education tend to vote in favor of school bond issues), the distinctions are not as clear or as rigid as once thought. They still should prove helpful to school politicians, however.

Three studies have recently been completed by the Center for Policy Studies in Elementary and Secondary Education at East Texas State University. As this is a state policy center, the data are limited to that state but the findings provide reasonable notions about voters in school bond elections. Smith (1989) studied voters over fifty-five years of age. Reihl (1991) studied Catholic voters, and Lutz and Mize (1990) studied a random group of metropolitan voters in school bond elections. The majority of all of these voters, regardless of group, reported that they vote in school bond elections and that they vote in favor of the bonds. These data raise some questions. Few bond elections get a voter turnout of over 50 percent. Next, all bond elections do not pass. If the respondents were truthful and representative of the population the data would be different. What is the explanation and what use can be made of it? First, it is likely that there was some tendency for those individuals most opposed to public schools not to respond. Yet there was an effort to interview nonrespondents in each study and those nonrespondents looked very much like the respondents. It is probable, however, that people antagonistic to public school are more likely to be hidden among the nonrespondents. On the brighter side, Americans tend to believe that they ought to exercise their right to vote and tend to say that they do, even if they often do not. Most Americans also believe in free public education and may be reluctant to admit that they failed to support it and, in fact, voted against a school bond issue. To the extent that this explanation is tenable, school politicians have an advantage if they choose to use it. If people tend to say they vote and vote for school bond issues when they do not, they must feel somewhat "guilty" about their behavior. It could be that they are acting against their predispositions because of crosspressure. Thus, it could be that the notion of "keeping the election quiet" may be losing these potential yes voters who find themselves in sufficient crosspressure to avoid voting.

Another interesting fact emerging from these studies is that neither older voters nor Catholic voters can be called block voters. They report that they vote much as the general population votes. One cannot predict voter behavior in school bond elections based on whether the voter is over fifty-five or whether the voter is Catholic. This finding debunks two long-standing myths in public education. The reality seems to be that older and retired voters do not oppose public education or refuse to pay for it. Nor do Catholic voters, who may be paying for a parochial education for their own children, oppose public education or uniformly refuse to pay for it.

In general, voters are more likely to vote as their education level and income increase. Also, as education and income increase voters tend to more supportive of bond elections, except those voters at the highest levels of education and income. Then support decreases for some reason, but never falls below a majority. Two other findings differed from the preconceptions of the researchers: Older voters having grandchildren in the school district did not vote for the bond issue more often than those without grandchildren in the schools, and voters living in the district longest showed some tendency to be less disposed to vote for the bond issue than those in the middle range.

CONCLUSION

It is not the job of superintendents or school boards to concern themselves with increasing or decreasing the voter turnout as such. Rather, it is their job to know the community, its hopes, aspirations, wants, and needs. It is not their job to eliminate conflict and disagreement but to use them as stimuli to achieve excellence. In a representative government, those who serve the people must represent the people. They may also lead the people. School programs must respond to the various needs and aspirations of the community and its subcultures. Good leaders help shape those needs and aspirations, but they neither ignore nor belittle them, except at their own risk. School leaders must know the politics and indicators of dissatisfaction as well as the technology of public relations and the art of communication.

9

Public Relations and Dissatisfaction

Community relations cannot be separated from school governance. In a democratic society, the public controls the schools to some extent and in one way or another. So far we have looked at the processes of community control of the schools in various communities and at various times. We have seen the gradual strengthening of the bureaucracy as voters choose not to participate. As the schools drift further from the community they serve, we have seen increased voter participation, resulting in a process that can bring the schools back in line with community expectations. We now turn to the processes of community relations and look at some of the options school districts have.

One of the options schools have is to influence community opinion through a program of public relations, a strategy that, not surprisingly, originated with and has often been driven by the public relations of business. While the success of a business is connected to consumer satisfaction and thus to public satisfaction in a larger sense, the relationship to the board of directors and the stockholders is the relationship of control and accountability. The community's relationship to the school is, however, that of both consumer and stockholder. If one is going to model school community relations after a business model, one must look not only at advertising, but also marketing and stockholder relationships. Thus the business model of public relations, while informative, has limited application to the schools.

The school board and superintendent who wish to lead schools, in the democratic contexts that have been described, are faced with the question of assessing the demands of the community. As we have seen, the community as a unitary entity is largely mythical. It is instead a delicately balanced group of subcommunities, each with its own set of values, percep-

Special thanks to Gay Campbell, public relations director for Tacoma (Washington) Public Schools, for her assistance on this chapter.

tions, and demands for public education. Assessing and addressing these demands is made even more difficult by the possibility of a sharply divided or growing community. New subgroups develop; interest in the schools waxes and wanes among groups and is often related to specific issues.

The dissatisfaction research sheds special light on community politics, which must be understood in designing formal and informal programs of public relations. Most of the cases presented earlier have provided examples of boards and superintendents that failed to hear clear messages from their communities until dissatisfaction built to the point where their departure from the district was inevitable. These cases of dissatisfaction were often influenced by old patterns of interaction and power that failed to accommodate new aspects of the community. In other cases, the need for change was recognized but change occurred at a pace impossible for the community to accept. Each community has its own tolerance limits for the rate of change; moving too fast or too slow can result in trouble, as we have seen.

Public relations professionals long have recognized the special needs of diverse communities and have directed programs at various "publics." Dissatisfaction research confirms this approach, but adds a step in which the community is examined continually for newly developing groups. Traditional programs for newcomers to a community have been designed in order to socialize the new residents to existing community values. The present research would suggest that it is equally important to develop avenues in which new groups in the community can express their values and help effect community change.

School leaders must not underestimate the difficulty of opening up their organizations to new segments of the community. It is psychologically difficult because the schools are often running well, according to the norms of the established community leadership. The superintendent and board that reach out may appear to be buying trouble and run the risk of offending long-time supporters. Reaching out to new groups will also increase the diversity of demands from the public and increase conflict in board decisionmaking. Leaders can take these steps only if they realize that by dealing openly with changing demands they are making the schools more responsive to the community. They are dealing with conflict in smaller, more manageable units rather than avoiding it until it becomes overwhelming. It is impossible to avoid conflict. It is possible to manage it.

Public relations professionals have also recognized the need for two-way communication and have utilized surveys, town meetings, and coffee hours to accomplish this end. Although helpful, these efforts are often frustrated by public apathy, and school officials tend to ignore these more open forums in favor of informal conversations in traditional contacts with friends. The research presented in this volume sheds a new light on public apathy. We have seen that conflict occurs in cycles and that in the periods between episodes of conflict, public apathy is a natural condition. Such apathy is confirmation that the community is in a period of quiescence. Apathy is often an indication of little dissatisfaction and, as such, it should be expected. When avenues of expression of public opinion elicit little response, it is likely that the public has no pressing demand at the time. Such avenues should not be abandoned nor long ignored, but should be utilized periodically in slightly different ways to allow public expression.

We will now discuss some specific techniques of community relations based on dissatisfaction research.

TRADITIONAL COMMUNITIES

Superintendents have traditionally been taught to assess the power structure of the community and to build communication links to the powerful people in the community. This works well in traditional communities and is illustrated in the Bloomdale case. Kimbrough (1964) was one of the most influential writers in illustrating the power structure in traditional communities. Relying on a technique called "reputational power," he discovered the powerful players in a community by asking people who influenced community decisions rather than assuming that those people in nominal positions of power were necessarily the real leaders. The mayor and city council members, the newspaper publisher, the ministers, and the bankers may be opinion leaders in the community but they in turn may be strongly influenced by several very powerful leaders who remain relatively invisible in the day-to-day business of the community. Such people often have great economic or social power established over many years or even generations. Alliances struck through earlier community events may lead to relationships that are hard for the newcomer to see or understand.

Vidich and Bensman's *Small Town in Mass Society* (1968) is a clear example of a traditional town in which the major decisions are heavily influenced by a few very powerful individuals. This power structure lies unused a good share of the time, making it even more difficult for the newcomer to the community to see and understand it. Only when an important decision must be made, a decision that affects various segments of the community in different ways, does the power structure operate, usually accomplishing its desired ends quickly.

In Chapter 4 the case of Riverton is a good example of a traditional community with relatively invisible alliances affecting current decisions. The powerful farmers become allied with the leadership of the African-American community in certain circumstances, although they are at odds a good share of the time; this is a confusing situation to one looking for an orderly and predictable pattern of relationships. Both of these groups combined cannot outweigh the power of the town leaders who hold no elected position and who are never quoted in the press but remain firmly in control of decisions regarding school locations and boundaries.

How a school leader can come to understand this kind of power system is well illustrated in the Bloomdale case. The new superintendent had a mentor who brought him into the community and shared his knowledge of the working of the town. In a gemeinschaft community, there is no substitute for this word-of-mouth information. It is revealed only in a relationship of trust. Establishing this kind of relationship in which the deep structure of the community is communicated is the primary task of the school leader. In traditional communities, it comes through affiliation with service clubs, churches, and civic organizations. Patronizing local businesses and taking the time to chat in informal situations are important for school leaders. A danger lies in the fact that such contacts soon become routine and the superintendent can be lulled into thinking that they serve to maintain relationships with the community, when in fact they represent relationships with a small segment of the community, the traditional power system. In changing communities it is highly likely that this kind of community relations will ultimately result in the superintendent's dismissal as the school leadership becomes closely identified with the old power system. The superintendent, talking regularly to the same group of citizens, fails to see the community change and fails to hear the mandate to change until it is too late.

Even in changing communities, however, the traditional power structure must be recognized. The Thompsonville case is such an example. Johnson affiliated quickly with groups who remained on the margin of real power. While the power of the established leaders of the community was fading, they still constituted the school board. His style alienated the traditional power players and his undoing began almost from the day he came to town. Thus a balance must be struck and the superintendent must bear in mind that all segments of the community must be represented, old and new. To avoid becoming identified with one segment or the other requires great diplomacy and skill.

CHANGING COMMUNITIES

Growing communities bring special challenges to school leaders. In the Robertsdale case and subsequent iterations of the Dissatisfaction Theory, the established power structure loses power to newcomers and is gradually ousted, usually accompanied by its appointees. The transition is never a linear one and power tends to reside in the established community long after its members are outnumbered by new players, as in the Robertsdale case. School leaders must develop ways of reaching out to newcomers in the community to build lines of communication. These newcomers bring beliefs and expectations about education from their previous communities that can have a major impact on schools. An effective program for newcomers can provide an avenue for these people to express their ideas about education and allow them ways to begin to influence the schools. Too often we have given lip service to this principle while really providing programs designed to socialize the newcomers to the existing norms of the community.

It is especially important in growing communities to keep good relationships with realtors. Realtors are often a family's first contact in a community. They can communicate strong messages of support or hostility toward the schools. School leaders can meet with realtors' associations, meet realtors in other community settings such as service clubs, or simply visit brokers personally on a regular basis. Personal meetings are probably most helpful and realtors often have valuable information about which areas of the community are receiving the most market attention, thus helping school officials predict growth. Good schools are important factors in real estate sales and realtors usually welcome these contacts. Some districts have found it useful to develop an information packet for realtors and prospective residents; the packet should contain a map of attendance areas, entrance requirements, transportation policies, and telephone numbers for other information. The National School Public Relations Association (NSPRA) (1980, 1986) publishes useful resource tips on working with realtors in public relations efforts.

Openness to new families in the community can be communicated in many small ways. The first and most lasting impression of the school is often formed when parents come to the school to enroll a child. The way they are greeted by the secretary or clerk, the warmth with which they are led through the school's paperwork, and the friendliness with which the child is escorted to class and introduced to the teacher and classmates are key elements in building a good relationship with the newcomer. School-site personnel should receive special training and support in stressful times of rapid growth as a steady stream of newcomers may try the patience of teachers and office staff alike. The sighs that can accompany the news of "one more child" will probably cause negative feelings in parent and child that may never be overcome. The NSPRA makes available kits to help districts conduct workshops for key employee groups such as office staff, transportation staff, and food service workers. These workshops can help these important school employees communicate with the public in a way that will further good relations (NSPRA, 1979).

Schools with declining enrollments face a different set of problems. Out-migration and aging populations leave communities with under-enrolled or overstaffed schools. Ultimately, budget cuts can force teacher layoffs and school closures. These situations bring special challenges to leaders in their relationships to the community. Research cited in Chapter 4 tends to support the notion that communities accept these changes if members are informed and if budget cuts are appropriate in size and scope. But school closings are always potential public relations problems. Communicating budget information requires careful attention because it is detailed and can easily be misunderstood. Mailings are often used because graphs and simplified balance sheets are easier for citizens to understand than verbal reports alone. Community meetings are important in allowing questions and discussions of alternatives. School personnel who tend to get discouraged at low citizen turnout for such meetings should take heart in knowing that a few well-informed citizens can be very effective in spreading the information through the community. Looking back on earlier discussions of key community leaders, the school leader who clearly understands the communication network in the community can use that information to hold special invitational meetings and individual conferences with top community leaders. Understanding where these leaders gather can help the school system target efforts toward certain community service clubs, churches, or ethnic associations. A special word of caution needs to be said here in light of the Dissatisfaction Theory: General community meetings where there are unexpectedly large turnouts often indicate dissatisfaction. These meetings need to be handled particularly carefully. Providing orderly systems for public testimony and clearly indicating a willingness to listen to citizens' concerns are probably more important than any factual communication of budget information. Records of testimony, whether taped or stenographically recorded, will provide important data for analysis and follow-up, allowing the board and the administrative staff to consider which groups in the community are most concerned and what those concerns are.

Closing a school often means dealing with community memories and the symbolic meanings attached to an old building. This sentiment in a community is important and should be honored explicitly. Often community sentiment is a bigger obstacle to a satisfactory resolution than is defining new attendance areas for students. Schools have often become an important part of the way a community defines itself and the loss of the school threatens the existence of the community itself. People worry, justifiably, that a "mothballed" school with windows boarded, walls covered with graffiti, and grounds gone to seed will have a negative effect on property values and become a depressing factor to the community. Some communities are able to sell the building to a new user and old schools have become small shopping centers, condominiums, or public citizens' centers. Razing the building is often more desirable than allowing it to stand empty if new uses can be found for the land. If a building must be razed, various ceremonies can help the community deal with their memories. Open houses honoring former students and teachers, featuring photographs and memorabilia, can be positive events. Retaining a portion of decorative stonework in the new structure or giving small pieces of bricks from the old building to former students, staff, or community members can leave positive memories.

SPECIAL-INTEREST GROUPS

In one sense the community is a composite of special-interest groups. In fact, we have defined the political process as the allocation of resources according to the values of certain segments of the community. That parents want to exert control over the schools in order to provide the best program for their children is a natural phenomenon. Thus families from a certain geographic area, or of an ethnic group, or with children who have special needs band together to become more politically effective in providing the education they want for their children. The term *special-interest group* has come to mean a group that is not only interested in the welfare of a specific group but one whose interest is at the expense of other groups. There is considerable indication that the increasing diversity of communities today is leading to increased demands on schools. Federal involvement in terms of entitlement programs and court decisions has increased expectations for services. With federal cutbacks, strong messages of fiscal restraint at the state level, and limits on local tax participation, funding has not kept up with demands and so there is increasing competition for the limited pool of educational dollars. Special-interest groups other than parents have come into being; the most obvious is teachers, whose associations have become effective political entities. In some areas taxpayers' associations have become special-interest groups to control school spending. In spite of some evidence to the contrary, some board members may fear that increases in the elderly population will mean that the public will be less willing to support schools financially or that services for the elderly will become a higher priority for tax dollars (Institute for Educational Leadership [IEL], 1986). Business has played an increasing role in schools, reminiscent of the role of business in the original reform of the late nineteenth and early twentieth centuries. This role has become so strong that some writers see business as the proper voice of the community in determining the course of education. They fail to see that business is in fact just another special-interest group. While many special-interest groups are most concerned with increasing or limiting educational expenditures, others want to exert control over the curriculum; into this category fall, for example, religious groups, public health and safety groups, patriotic groups, and business.

Some of the cases presented earlier give insight into special-interest groups. While often representing a small number of people, these groups may wield considerable power when they form a coalition with other groups of dissatisfied citizens. These groups need to be heard and it is the wise school leaders who build open relationships with these groups and provide them an avenue for expressing their needs. School boards will frequently have one or two members who represent identified constituencies. Frequently the first such representative will be someone who has played a prominent role as a leader in a special-interest community.

As discussed earlier, special-interest groups can change a board from an elite council to an arena council. Boards must deal with this phenomenon in an open way, airing differences and debating issues. Training for both superintendents and board members, today more than ever, must include training in conflict resolution and the art of group decisionmaking. The classic work of Margaret Parker Follett (1924) is still a prerequisite to being effective in this area. The understanding that segments of the community are competing for limited resources and the fact that one group's gain will often come at the expense of another group are hard realities to face. It is to be hoped that keeping the debate open to public scrutiny will prevent the exclusion of any one group and keep control of the schools from being vested solely in one powerful oligarchy. Sometimes a leadership team can be assembled in the schools with assistant superintendents and directors who have ties to various parts of the community. This was done in the Riverton case described in Chapter 6. The representative and diverse leadership team worked well with the delegate board and provided citizens with several avenues for getting requests to the board. The schools also had several avenues for getting information to citizens. The resultant patterns of relationships were far from harmonious; conflict was frequent and open. To try to eliminate conflict from this community would however be unwise, if not futile.

READING YOUR COMMUNITY

The established power structures in stable communities are best read through the reputational methods described by Kimbrough and discussed earlier. However, as mentioned, these methods give no reading on the changing power system. The main avenues for assessing changing opinion are community surveys and analysis of various expressions of community opinion such as newspaper editorials, letters to the editor, and citizen appearances at school board meetings. School principals who are in touch with citizens in their attendance areas can often see community changes before they become apparent in public forums.

Community surveys have become increasingly popular and increasingly sophisticated in recent years. Mail and telephone surveys are both widely used and each offers advantages that must be weighed in the context of an individual community. Mail surveys allow a more thoughtful response but are easily neglected by the recipient. They tend to work best in communities with a higher level of education and interest in the schools. Telephone surveys have the advantage of a prompt response but usually have to be much shorter than written surveys. Some citizens may find telephone surveys intrusive; others welcome an opportunity for a "chat about the schools." Telephone surveys may be conducted by school personnel, community volunteers, or a professional survey consultant team. Using staff and community volunteers can be cheaper and allow a personal contact that may elicit more information as well as providing an opportunity for positive contact from the school. It can be time-consuming to recruit and train these people and the data collected by volunteers may be less uniform than data collected by a professional team. A professional team may provide greater cost savings in the long run considering district expenditure of time designing the survey, recruiting and training surveyors, and compiling the data. The design of a written survey is an important consideration because it conveys a message as well as eliciting meaningful information for school leaders.

Depending on budgets, districts may seek assistance in designing surveys from public relations firms, various educational consultants, or local university sources. Professional teams usually can modify survey instruments to some extent to meet local needs. They usually have good experience in judging the length of the survey and can save the district money by assuring instruments that promise a better return rate. It is important that people who know the community be involved in the survey design to be sure it is consistent with local norms in terms of content, style, and length. Whether or not outside assistance is sought, it is important for the leaders involved — the superintendent and the board and the site principal and staff — to first think through what kind of information they want to receive. A sample telephone survey is included in Appendix A.

Communities with various non–English speaking groups present special problems to surveyors. Written surveys with English on one side and Spanish on the other can prove helpful if Spanish, for example, is a predominant other language. Bilingual surveys can cause some negative feelings in the traditional power system in communities that have not yet faced up to their bilingual nature. Surveys can be targeted by specific language if recipients can be identified. This also holds some danger of offending citizens because a few misidentifications will inevitably occur. Telephone surveys can be conducted by bilingual interviewers if the native language can be identified and appropriate interviewers found.

The problem of community surveys quickly becomes apparent in communities that are becoming more diverse. A dilemma develops in which one cannot survey the community until one understands the community and one cannot understand the community until one surveys it. The school district must understand the limitations of the survey and realize that they are breaking into the circular problem at one point. In surveying a changing community it is especially important to select and identify responses by geographic subsections of the district.

We should bear in mind that in order to manage schools effectively it is most important to know about community dissatisfaction that is of a magnitude likely to motivate a significant segment of the community to political action. Surveys to which citizens respond passively, such as phone surveys, are apt to uncover expressions of opinions the respondent would not otherwise be motivated enough to express. Do these represent an early reading of the beginning of dissatisfaction or do they simply represent "noise" — background levels of a range of community opinion the schools could never satisfy? Written surveys, to which citizens must devote a little time and energy to complete and return, would appear to have an advantage in reading levels of opinion held strongly enough to motivate political activity. Because of the expense, surveys are usually undertaken only when important fiscal decisions are to be made, but periodic surveys of satisfaction with the school programs and level of funding can be instructive for the ongoing decisions in the schools. Surveys are particularly important when tax issues will be presented to the voters and can provide early readings of citizen support.

TELLING YOUR STORY:
BROCHURES, FACT SHEETS, CALENDARS, AND NEWSLETTERS

Most districts print some kind of informational literature for their patrons. General brochures about schools and programs can be mailed to each household and business and placed in libraries and realtors' offices for people new to the community. These are sometimes done in the form of a corporate annual report but must be designed carefully to suit the norms of a community. Some districts have had beautiful glossy brochures prepared by commercial firms, only to offend the frugal nature of a working-class community that found the expenditure frivolous.

District calendars with important dates are useful to parents. These calendars can include important phone numbers as well as policy information parents need, such as inoculation requirements and inclement weather procedures. These often work better than a district handbook because parents tend to keep them in a central location and know where to find them. Calendars afford good opportunities for photographs of children and can give a message of being child-centered and helpful. Recreational businesses such as theaters, bowling alleys, or skating rinks often appreciate these calendars so they can schedule special events around school vacations.

Newsletters are usually most effective when developed at the school level and will be discussed specifically as a site-based issue. Nevertheless school newsletters usually reach only parents and give brief coverage to district-level issues. There is an important role for district-level newsletters that are mailed to all households and businesses in the district. Districts recognize that this is especially important before tax issues are put before voters. Newsletters are useful on an ongoing basis to communicate information on current programs and services in the district. Tempting as it may be to feature board members and the superintendent, this information should be kept brief and greater space devoted to children and teachers. In communities with long-standing traditions, a short historical segment of what was happening in the schools twenty-five, fifty, or one hundred years ago is often popular. Old board minutes are a rich source of such material. As we have discussed in other contexts, the style of the newsletter is extremely important and can give powerful messages to the community. A small newspaperlike piece on newsprint may get a better reception than a glitzier piece on high-quality paper. Graphics and photography should be professional and carefully selected with the style of the community in mind. Keep in mind special-interest groups and other individuals such as voters without children in schools. Special articles, or even issues, may be helpful in communicating with these groups. The NSPRA publishes a number of helpful resource tips for publications in their kits previously cited.

RELATIONS WITH THE MEDIA

Traditional community relations advice is to build open relationships with the press by being honest and available. Responses to a Phi Delta Kappa survey (Wayson et al., 1988) indicate that about 25 percent of the public received most of their information about the schools from the media, particularly newspapers. According to the survey, public confidence in schools was highly related to positive reports in the media. The media often represent several roles in the community and the superintendent wishing to use them most carefully would do well to sort out the various roles. The management and editorial staff are often part of the traditional power structure of a community. In communities with more than one newspaper or television station, each may cater to a different segment of the community. A good relationship with media management can affect the amount of school news and the kinds of stories reported as well as editorial positions on school issues. Relationships with reporters must be cultivated separately from those with media management. These relationships are especially important since they represent the first line of access into the news. No amount of good relationship with management can correct misinformation that gets into print or on the air because of careless or overly complicated statements in interviews with school personnel.

Reporters vary widely in their understanding of educational issues and their philosophical positions toward these issues. Education reporters are often young, inexperienced, and looking for promotion to positions in larger news organizations. This means that the superintendent is constantly building relationships with these people only to have them move on and be replaced by other neophytes. Reporters tend to like short, straightforward responses and the superintendent or district spokesperson should be aware of the tendency to reduce television or radio quotes to small fragments. The fragments are often used as highlights while the larger story is described and summarized by the reporter. Thus it is wise to jot down a few ideas before beginning and then cull any overly complicated material from the message. This is particularly important if the message could be misconstrued if taken out of context. Some reporters will accept designated comments off the record. Policies vary in this regard and it is important to ask specifically before offering background information that, if quoted, could be damaging. One public relations specialist advises school people to practice giving their message in twenty seconds in twenty different ways prior to the interview, knowing that a twenty-second message is less likely to be edited than a longer one.

A common complaint of board members is that superintendents tend to constantly seek attention from the press (IEL, 1986). Whether superintendents are overly anxious to be in the limelight or whether this statement reflects board members' competition for public attention, districts would be well advised to work out a policy regarding who will speak for the district.

The most popular media stories result from school sites where students, classrooms, and athletic events can be featured. The school district should plan for this and develop policies to guide site managers. Most school districts prefer that potential feature news be reported to the district office where press releases or feature tips are prepared for the media. Principals should be briefed on contacts with the press and given opportunities to practice being interviewed. Districts usually request that any contact initiated by the media be reported to the district office. Principals should be aware of which questions are best answered at the site and which are best referred to a central office. NSPRA resources that are helpful in dealing with the media are found in the *Basic School PR Kit* (1980) and *Building Confidence for Your Schools* (1986).

Joyce has particularly good guidelines for writing news releases in *Written Communications and the School Administrator* (1991). According to Joyce, news releases should be written in newspaper style in which the first paragraph contains the most important information. This style allows an editor or a reader to cut the article without losing the essential material. Paragraphs should be short, containing only two or three sentences, and each paragraph should begin with striking words that will catch the reader's eye. Joyce further suggests that a standard format with an easily recognizable heading will eliminate the need for a cover letter. Each event should be covered in a separate news release and a contact person should be identified for further information.

SITE-BASED COMMUNITY RELATIONS

Site-based community relations are rooted in ward-based political history and as such are a part of the larger counterreform movement that has been growing since the 1960s. In communities prior to the reform government period, members could go to the ward boss, who would act as an advocate for them in the organization. Citizens knew they had an advocate in exchange for their political loyalty. Corruption and caricatures of this system have led to the popular opinion that these systems are to be avoided, but the need for the citizen to have an advocate in the bureaucracy has not diminished nor has the need for the system to have the support of the people diminished. Today's "wards" can be geographic neighborhoods or citizens united by a special interest, but increasingly schools are seeing the importance of uniting the citizens of the district through the schools their children attend. Parents have a natural affinity for their children's schools because someone there knows them and their children's needs. This is not a faceless bureaucracy, but teachers with faces and names who meet their children every day. The Gallup poll has long noted that people tend to rate their own school better than schools in general. Public relations must take this into account.

School districts that have had to move away from neighborhood schools to avoid racial segregation have paid dearly in terms of community isolation. The cost of busing in terms of time and money is immediately apparent, but the cost of separating the schools from their community is a subtler expense of which we are only now becoming aware. Parents of all races want their children to attend a school near their home or work site. Parents will rarely cross town to attend a program or even a conference. The school becomes the faceless bureaucracy with which neither individuals nor the community can identify. There is no friend, no advocate for the family, which increasingly needs help in dealing with the system. Large city schools in their recent decentralization efforts have recognized this phenomenon and attempted to provide a closer connection. This lack of a connection to the schools became apparent long ago in big-city schools, but has also become an increasing phenomenon in smaller districts. Each year school districts across the nation consolidate and close community ties are sacrificed to administrative expediency. Site-based management is one way to reestablish that connection.

In recent decades school managers have attempted to form citizens' committees as a way to involve the community in school governance. In the 1960s and 1970s these efforts were enhanced through federal entitlements, which required Parent Advisory Committees as a condition for receiving funds. Those committees were designed to involve minority parents and parents of handicapped children in school decisions. The very fact that these committees were required was an acknowledgement that school decisionmaking had moved far from the constituents and steps were needed to reinvolve them. These measures have been described in Chapter 8. As citizen committees became popular, they began to be appointed for local purposes and have given rise to a movement that appears to have culminated in site-based management.

Site-based management has become popular in recent years as school managers come more and more to realize the importance of involving the community more immediately in school governance. Some districts have turned most management decisions, including those regarding budgets and hiring, to a site council that includes parents and other community members with site staff. Other districts retain decisions at the superintendent/ board level and assign an advisory role to site councils. Independent site councils operate in many ways as ward-based boards did more than one hundred years ago.

There are potential political and administrative problems inherent in delegating major decisions to the building level. Hiring and budgetary decisions made at the site may not meet legal requirements for equity; processes must be established to provide training and review for basic legal compliance. The political problems inherent in strengthening site-based ties and asking principals to serve as liaisons for their communities, as ward bosses did in machine politics, far outweigh the administrative problems. Principals may become very competitive and will often be selective in the information they pass on to the district leadership. Principals serve in a boundary-spanning role between the site organization and the district organization. They feel strong allegiance to their site and yet they report to district-level administration. Their success with their community depends on their ability to represent the site in district transactions, yet gaining resources and attention for their building often alienates them from the rest of the district and can ultimately backfire. In order to survive the tensions of these relationships, principals quickly learn to become astute politicos. Superintendents recognize this and will sometimes prevent principals from becoming tied to their sites by transferring them regularly. Principals are frequently rewarded for district loyalty by being moved to larger or more prestigious schools. These policies weaken site ties and will need to be reviewed if the local school is to become a meaningful vehicle for community representation. In situations where transfers are not possible, as in districts with a single high school, the high school principal becomes a powerful figure, sometimes more powerful than the superintendent. One only has to review cases of major political turmoil in districts to see the number of times they involve a superintendent being fired for removing a popular high school principal. Superintendents will have to recognize the power that is given to the "ward bosses" and live with it in communities that function as wards. Superintendents should establish clear policy about the relationship of each site to the school board and let principals know how to handle contacts initiated by board members or when, if ever, principals should contact board members directly. Novice principals will often extend a personal invitation to a board member to attend a special event without thinking to clear it with the superintendent's office. Depending on the number of schools and norms of the community, superintendents may want to coordinate such invitations.

Community relations activities carried out at the building level are among the most powerful that the district can undertake. Parents will read newsletters from their neighborhood school when one from a central office is tossed aside unopened. School events such as open houses, programs, and concerts attract an interested and supportive audience. Phone calls home or to a parent's place of work are the kind of connections that need to be tended. Notes home praising special accomplishments are worth the time and are apt to be delivered.

Probably the most effective community relations vehicle is the local school newsletter. District-level public relations departments can assist principals in preparing newsletters by providing training, supplying sample articles, and providing efficient printing services. Principals' associations often provide tip-sheets on good newsletters and experienced principals usually keep files with ideas. The National Association of Elementary School Principals (1984) advises members to consider the needs of their readers, who are usually strong supporters of the schools: They do not need to be convinced; they like information on policies that affect their own children; they like facts; and they like to know about upcoming events.

Newsletters should be written in journalistic style, keeping to "who, what, where, when and why." Keep sentences and paragraphs short, avoiding jargon and abbreviations. Use student art and writing sparingly for maximum effect.

Good newsletters tend to avoid a section called "from the principal's desk"; people seldom read such boring, pompous reflections on "how time flies and here it is January already." In all probability the whole newsletter is from the principal's office — let your message show in the tone and selection of individual entries. Have a purpose in mind for the newsletter and relate the newsletter to other school goals; for example, if a better relationship with bus drivers is part of a school goal to improve student behavior on buses, feature one bus driver in each issue and let families get to know them better, perhaps sharing how they have gone out of their way to help students.

Use upcoming events to offer a little parent education; for example, before conferences include a list of ways to get the most out of a conference or, before standardized tests are given, include a brief article on what such scores mean and how they are used in the district. These topics need to be written with a specific audience in mind in order to achieve the correct level of vocabulary and sophistication (an example is shown in Appendix B).

Send copies of the school newsletter to appropriate district offices and ask if copies should be sent to board members. Superintendents will usually prefer to include building newsletters in a general board packet. Experienced principals exchange newsletters with other schools in the district and encourage liberal borrowing of ideas (do not forget to make any adaptions that might be necessary for each particular site). Keep copies of the school newsletter available on the office counter for families new to the school and send copies to special community contacts such as businesses or senior citizens who are especially interested in the school.

Community surveys that are specific to one school can be included in a newsletter. A very simple survey is included here as an example in Appendix C. Site-based management policies usually require some kind of survey. Generally, simpler surveys will assure more responses. Parents who wish to write lengthier responses will usually do so. Further information on school site surveys is available in *Written Communications and the School Administrator* by Joyce (1991) and the NSPRA kits previously cited (1980, 1986).

CITIZENS' COMMITTEES

While officially the school board represents the community in decisions on school business, and site councils represent specific communities in decisions related to their sites, most districts find broader representation helpful in certain cases. Going back to federal mandates for Parent Advisory Councils, many districts in the 1970s formed standing advisory councils of citizens to listen and give feedback on district matters. Districts that were required by state law to involve citizens' groups in curriculum decisions often formed citizens' advisory committees to meet this requirement. Most districts find it hard to maintain interest and participation on advisory committees, which have general and ongoing assignments, and have moved to task forces convened for specific purposes. Citizens are more apt to agree to serve if their responsibilities are limited to a specific area in which they are interested or have special expertise and if they see their influence in important policy outcomes. There has also been a general trend toward including a few citizens on committees that are otherwise comprised of school personnel. Committees constituted in this way are easier to manage, but there is a danger that representatives will be selected who are in general agreement with district policy. While this type of committee participation serves to incorporate a citizen voice in school decisionmaking, boards and superintendents should not be deluded into thinking this presents a forum for expression of divergent community opinion. Committees with a few citizen friends are similar to the other community relations techniques that work well in traditional, stable communities but fail to alert school leaders to changes in the community or to provide a means of dealing with community conflict. Increasing community diversity will demand that superintendents and boards become aware of groups with conflicting values in the community and develop the skills to bring representatives of these groups into committee debate processes.

Many districts are attempting to establish or maintain close ties to their communities by developing strategic management plans. The first step is to develop a representative citizens' committee that will then establish a mission for the district and set priorities for management. The research cited in this book would indicate that in this process districts are wise to take the time to develop and use representative and interested committees. This is often done by nominations from known special-interest groups and geographically defined groups. If challenges to the committee appointments occur, the district is wise to devise a process in which groups can express opinions and take the time to allow the community to participate in the committee appointments. The purpose is to establish a consensus, and moving ahead rapidly with a committee that lacks important voices can defeat this purpose. Superintendents who at first fear the inclusion of a fringe-group member usually find these fears groundless as the process of consensus-building controls a few radical viewpoints.

Districts interested in undertaking this process typically send a couple of staff members for training in facilitative skills. The group of citizens and staff that has been convened usually goes on a retreat of two or three days during which they begin the process of writing a mission statement for the schools and establishing management priorities. The products of the retreat are then shared with the community and feedback is received by the committee. The statement and plan are modified if necessary. Ideally a strategic plan would assure that schools are managed in a way that is consistent with community values. Unfortunately, the process is limited by the nature of representation in the same way that all representative governing structures are limited. The representatives may not speak for all their constituents, or the community may be changing in such a way that new groups emerge and old groups disappear. The representative committee may be a figurehead for a tightly controlled community power structure. Nevertheless school superintendents and boards that undertake such plans are usually in better positions than those that fail to involve the community in meaningful ways.

CONCLUSION

The task of the board and superintendent who are to survive is not to keep all their constituents satisfied, but rather to keep a majority of the constituents from becoming so dissatisfied as to take political action that opposes them and their policies. A good public relations program is important in accomplishing this in that it provides avenues for communication, helping the schools understand their community and helping the community understand their schools. Thus a public relations program as a communications system within the context of democratic governance, allowing the people to receive important information about schools and to express their opinions in open fashion to policymakers, is perhaps the most important tool for the schools in forestalling devastating political conflict. It can work in this way only so long as it reaches important constituencies in the community and only so long as the schools hear and can respond to the messages from their community.

Appendixes
References
About the Authors
Index

Appendix A: Telephone Survey

1. Do you currently have children attending Fairview Schools?
    2. IF YES, Could you tell me their grade level?
        Do you have any pre-school age children?
    3. IF NO, Have you had children attend Fairview Schools?
        Do you have any preschool age children?
4. How long have you lived in Fairview School District?
    IF LESS THAN 5 YEARS, What single factor most influenced your moving to Fairview?
5. Do you work in Fairview?
    6. IF NO, How far do you drive to work?
7. Have you volunteered at or been involved in Fairview School functions?
8. On a scale of 1–5, with 1 being very little and 5 being very much, how much do you feel you know about Fairview Schools?
9. Using the same scale (1 = very little; 5 = very much), how much do you want to know about the schools?
10. What grade would you give Fairview Schools on the kind of job they are doing educating our children?
11. What would you say is the *primary* source of your information concerning Fairview Schools?
    Probe: If newspaper, which one?
    Probe: If radio or TV station, which one?
12. Which *one issue* do you consider the most important problem facing Fairview Schools?
13. School enrollment in Fairview School District is increasing by about 500 students each year right now. Do you believe school bond funds will be needed to provide the necessary new school buildings?
14. Do you consider yourself a supporter of school issues such as levy and bond elections?

The authors express appreciation to Gary Peterson, professor of communications at the University of Puget Sound, for this survey instrument.

Appendix B: What Do Test Scores Tell Us? (Example of an Article for a Parent Newsletter)

All of our students will be taking the California Test of Basic Skills during the week of October 3–7. Why do we spend a week of instructional time on tests? What kind of information do we get? These are important questions for parents to ask.

Test scores tell us how students performed on certain days on certain tasks. They are a sample of their school behavior. While this test may not be the best measure for any one student, the scores let us compare our students' skills with those of students in other schools in the district, in the state, and in the nation. It is an important way for us to tell you how we are doing. Every year we look at the scores to see what areas we need to improve. This last year we have made improvements in our math program and in our remedial reading program, based in part on test scores.

If a student's scores are low, we look to see how we might help the student. Low scores can mean a child needs a different program; sometimes low scores mean a student does not know how to take tests or is afraid to take tests.

Tests are a big part of today's world and we want our students to have the skills to do well on them. We want our students to try hard and do their best but we know that tests are not the most important part of school. The most important activity in school is learning. What teachers and parents see on a day-to-day basis is always the best measure of how a child is doing in school.

Appendix C: Give Us a Grade (Example of a School Site Survey)

Dear Parents,

We invite you to circle the grade you think our school deserves in each of the following areas:

Instruction	A	B	C	D	F
Discipline	A	B	C	D	F
Availability of Staff	A	B	C	D	F
Student Recognition (Awards)	A	B	C	D	F
Appearance of School	A	B	C	D	F
Friendliness and Helpfulness of Staff	A	B	C	D	F
Communication Between Home and School	A	B	C	D	F
Transportation	A	B	C	D	F

Comments:

References

Alsworth, P. L., & Woock, R. R. (1969, April). Ocean Hill Brownsville: Urban conflict and the schools. *Urban Education, 4*(1), 25–40.

Alvey, D. T., & Underwood, K. E. (1985). When boards and superintendents clash, it's over the balance of school power. *American School Board Journal, 172*(10), 21–25.

Awender, M. A. (1985). The superintendent school board relationship. *Canadian Journal of Education, 10*(2), 176–198.

Bailey, F. G. (1969). Decisions by consensus in councils and committees. In Michael Banton (Ed.), *Political systems and the distribution of power*, pp. 1–20. London: Tavistock Publications.

Banfield, E. C., & Wilson, J. Q. (1963). *City Politics*. New York: Vintage Books.

Baratta, A. N. (1970). Decentralization in urban school districts. In F. W. Lutz (Ed.), *Toward improved urban education*, pp. 81–94. Worthington, OH: Charles A. Jones Publishing Company.

Becker, H. P. (1968). *Through values to social interpretation*. New York: Greenwood Press.

Bender, T. (1978). *Community and social change in America*. New Brunswick, NJ: Rutgers University Press.

Bernard, H. R. (1988). *Research methods in cultural anthropology*. Newbury Park, CA: Sage.

Bisso, J. M. (1988). Board president: Here's how I stay friends with the superintendent. *American School Board Journal, 175*(6), 38–39.

Blumberg, A. (1985). A superintendent must read the board's invisible job description. *American School Board Journal, 172*(9), 44–45.

Boyd, W. (1976). The public, the professionals and educational policy making: Who governs? *Teachers College Record, 77*(4), 547–549.

Boyd, W. L., & Johnson, W. E. (1985). *Rural population trends and school politics: Newcomers, old-timers, and community conflict*. Paper presented at the American Educational Research Association, Chicago.

Braddom, C. L. (1986). Prescription for improvement: Make certain your school board's system of evaluating the superintendent is fair, fast, factual and frequent. *American School Board Journal, 173*(8), 28–29.

189

Brown, R. D., Newman, D. L., & Rivers, L. S. (1985). Does the superintendent's opinion affect schools boards' evaluation information needs? An empirical investigation. *Urban Education, 20*(2), 204–221.

Burnham, W. D. (1970). *Critical elections and the mainsprings of American politics.* New York: W. W. Norton.

Butts, R. F. (1955). *A cultural history of Western education: Its social and intellectual foundations.* New York: McGraw-Hill.

Butts, R. F., & Cremin, L. A. (1953). *A history of education in American culture.* New York: Henry Holt & Co.

Calhoun, L. S. (1969). New York: Schools and power — whose? *Integrated Education, 7*(1), 1–35.

Callahan, R. E. (1960). *An introduction to education in American society.* New York: Knopf.

Callahan, R. E. (1962). *Education and the cult of efficiency.* Chicago: University of Chicago Press.

Carter, R. F., & Savard, W. G. (1961). *Influence of voter turnout on school bond and tax elections.* Washington, D.C.: U.S. Government Printing Office.

Chichura, A. (1977). *Change from strife to accommodation in organizational behavior as affected by collective bargaining.* Unpublished doctoral dissertation, Pennsylvania State University.

Cistone, P. J. (1970). *Formal governmental structures and the school board-superintendent role relationship.* Unpublished doctoral dissertation, Pennsylvania State University.

Cooley, C. H. (1909). *Social organization: A study of the larger mind.* New York: Scribners.

Counts, G. S. (1930). *The American road to culture.* New York: John Day Company.

Counts, G. S. (1952). *Education and American education.* New York: Bureau of Publications, Teachers College, Columbia University.

Cremin, L. (1970). *American education: The colonial experience, 1607–1783.* New York: Harper & Row.

Cremin, L. (1988). *American education: The metropolitan experience, 1876–1980.* New York: Harper & Row.

Criswell, L. W., & Mitchell, D. E. (1980). Episodic instability in school district elections. *Urban Education, 15*(2), 189–213.

Cronbach, J. C. (1988). Playing with chaos. *Educational Researcher, 17*(6), 46–49.

Cronin, J. M. (1973). *The control of urban schools: Perspective on the power of educational reformers.* New York: The Free Press.

Cuban, L. (1986). *Superintendent as leader: The dilemma of autonomy and accountability.* Paper presented at annual meeting of American Educational Research Association, San Francisco.

Cuban, L. (1990). Reforming again, again, and again. *Educational Research, 19*(1), 3–12.

Cubberly, E. (1920). *The history of education.* Cambridge, MA: The Riverside Press.

Cunningham, L. L. (1964). Community power: Implications for education. In R.

S. Cahill and S. P. Henclay (Eds.), *The politics of education in the local community* (pp. 27–50). Danville, IL: Interstate Printers and Publishers.

Dahl, R. A. (1961). *Who governs*. New Haven, CT: Yale University Press.

Danis, R. (1981). *Policy changes in local governance: The dissatisfaction theory of democracy*. Unpublished doctoral dissertation, University of California, Santa Barbara.

Danis, R. (1984). Policy changes in local schools: The dissatisfaction theory of democracy. *Urban Education, 19*(2), 125–144.

Downey, G. W. (1984). Top executive educators: How and why we did it. *ERIC, 6*(2), 15–39.

Durkheim, E. (1933). *The division of labor in society* (G. Simpson, Trans.). New York: The Free Press.

Easton, D. (1965). *A framework for political analysis*. New York: Prentice-Hall.

Edgren, D. J. (1976). *An analysis of community viewpoint on education and municipal issues*. Unpublished doctoral dissertation, Pennsylvania State University.

Elam, S. M. (1989). The 22nd annual Gallup poll of the public's attitude toward the public schools. *Phi Delta Kappan, 72*(1), 41–53.

Emminghan, R., & Rawson, A. (1985). *Applying the dissatisfaction theory to analyze regional political history*. Paper presented at the American Educational Research Association, Chicago.

Fantini, M. D., & Gittell, M. (1970). *Community and the urban school*. New York: Praeger.

Fiedler, F. (1967). *A theory of leader effectiveness*. New York: McGraw-Hill.

Fields, G. M. (1988). You cannot delegate leadership. *ERIC, 45*(6), 33–35.

Foerch, D. B. (1989). *Predicting the outcome of a school bond election: An application of the dissatisfaction theory*. Unpublished doctoral dissertation, East Texas State University, Commerce.

Follett, M. P. (1924). *Creative experience*. New York: Longman.

Freeborn, R. M. (1966). *School board change and succession pattern of superintendents*. Unpublished doctoral dissertation, Claremont Graduate School, Claremont, CA.

Freund, S. A. (1988). Superintendent: Here's how I stay friends with the board president. *American School Board Journal, 175*(6), 39.

Garberina, W. (1975). *Public demand, school board response and incumbent defeat: An examination of local school districts in Massachusetts*. Unpublished doctoral dissertation, Pennsylvania State University.

Geertz, C. (1973). *The interpretation of cultures*. New York: Basic Books.

Gittell, M. (1967). *Participants and participation: A study of school policy in New York City*. New York: Center for Urban Education.

Gleick, J. (1987). *Chaos: Making a new science*. New York: Viking.

Good, H. G. (1960). *A history of Western education*. New York: Macmillan.

Goodenough, W. H. (1963). *Cooperation in change: An anthropological approach to community development*. New York: Sage.

Gouldner, A. (1957/1958). Cosmopolitans and locals: Towards an analysis of latent social roles I and II. *Administrative Science Quarterly, 2*, 281–306, 444–479.

Hamilton, H. D., & Cohen, S. H. (1974). *Policy making by plebiscite: School referenda*. Lexington, MA: D. C. Heath.

Harrington-Lueker, D. (1990). Coming to America. *The American School Board Journal, 177*(5), 17–20.

Hartley, H. J. (1989). Budgeting for the 1990s. *ERIC, 46*(4), 31, 34, 36.

Hentges, J. T. (1986). The politics of superintendent-school board linkages: A study of power, participation, and control. *Spectrum, 4*(3), 23–32.

Herzberg, F. (1959). *The motivation to work*. New York: Wiley.

Homans, G. C. (1960). *Social behavior: Its elementary form*. New York: Harcourt Brace and World.

Hunt, B. (1980). *An inductive approach to the dissatisfaction theory in the governance of local school districts: Predicting incumbent defeat*. Unpublished doctoral dissertation, Pennsylvania State University.

Hunter, F. (1959). *Top leadership, U.S.A.* Chapel Hill: University of North Carolina Press.

Iannaccone, L. (1970). Norms governing urban state politics of education. In F. W. Lutz (Ed.), *Toward improved urban education*. Worthington, OH: Charles A. Jones Publishing Company.

Iannaccone, L. (1983). Community education and turning point elections. In D. Schoeny & L. Decker (Eds.), *Community educational and social impact perspectives*. Lanham, MD: University Press of America.

Iannaccone, L. (1990). Callahan's contribution in the context of American realignment politics. In W. E. Eaton (Ed.), *Shaping the superintendency*. New York: Teachers College Press.

Iannaccone, L., & Lutz, F. W. (1970). *Politics, policy and power: The governance of public schools*. Columbus, OH: Charles E. Merrill Publishing Co.

Ianni, F. A. (1967). *Culture, system, and behavior: The behavioral sciences and education*. Chicago: Science Research Associates.

Institute for Educational Leadership. (1986). *School boards: Strengthening grass roots leadership*. Washington, DC: Author.

Joyce, A. B. (1991). *Written communications and the school administrator*. Boston: Allyn and Bacon.

Katz, M. (1985). Match working styles and find your way to board/superintendent harmony. *American School Board Journal, 172*(2), 33–34.

Kerchner, C. T., Mitchell, D., Pryor, G., & Erck, W. (1981). *The logic of citizen participation in public school labor law*. Paper presented before the International Project for Education Network, San Francisco.

Kimball, S. T. (1974). *Culture and the educative process*. New York: Teachers College Press.

Kimbrough, R. B. (1964). *Political power and educational decision making*. Chicago: Rand McNally and Company.

Kimbrough, R. B., & Nunnery, M. Y. (1988). *Educational administration: An introduction*. New York: Macmillan.

Kirkendall, R. (1966). *Discriminating social, economic and political characteristics of changing versus stable policy-making systems in school districts*. Unpublished doctoral dissertation, Claremont Graduate School, Claremont, CA.

Kirst, M. (1989, September 8). "Chicago's radical school plan," as quoted by Isabel Wilkerson. In *Dallas Morning News*, p. A12.

Koch, A., & Peden, W. (Eds.). (1944). *The life and selected writings of Thomas Jefferson*. New York: Random House.

Krajewski, R. (1983). Nine ways a superintendent can corral a maverick board member. *American School Board Journal, 170*(11), 29–30.

Kunesh, L. G., & Bakker, J. B. (1990). Parent involvement in school restructuring. *Policy Briefs, 9*, 1–4.

LeDoux, E. P. (1971). *Outmigration: Its relation to social, political and economic conditions and to the governing of local school districts in New Mexico.* Unpublished doctoral dissertation, University of New Mexico, Albuquerque, NM.

Lewis, O. (1951). *Life in a Mexican village: Tepoztlan restudied.* Urbana: University of Illinois Press.

Lisser, S. P. (1970). Community control: A case in point. In F. W. Lutz (Ed.), *Toward improved urban education* (pp. 63–79). Worthington, OH: Charles A. Jones Publishing Company.

Lutz, F. (1962). *Social systems and school districts.* Unpublished doctoral dissertation, Washington University, St. Louis.

Lutz, F. W. (1980). Local school boards decision making: A political anthropological model. *Education and Urban Society, 12*(4), 452–464.

Lutz, F., & Iannaccone, L. (1978). *Public participation in local school districts.* Lexington, MA: D. C. Heath.

Lutz, F. W., Lutz, S. B., & Tweeddale, P. G. (in press). Rural education: Kinder and gentler world. *Journal for Rural and Small Schools.*

Lutz, F. W., & Mize, G. (1990). Texas voters claim to vote more often for school bond issues than against. *The Journal of Educational Public Relations, 13*(2), 33.

Lutz, F., & Wang, L. (1987). Predicting public dissatisfaction: A study of school board member defeat. *Administration Science Quarterly, 23*(1), 65–77.

Magill, F. N. (1981). *World philosophies.* Englewood Cliffs, NJ: Salem Press.

Mann, D. (1975). *The politics of administrative representation: School administrators and local democracy.* Lexington, MA: Lexington Books.

March, J., & Olsen, J. (1979). *Ambiguity and choice in organizations.* Bergen, Norway: Universitetsforlaget.

Marcus, G. E., & Fischer, M. M. J. (1986). *Anthropology as cultural critique.* Chicago: University of Chicago Press.

McGehee, K. (1990). *The dissatisfaction theory: An application of Herzberg's motivation theory.* Unpublished doctoral dissertation. East Texas State University, Commerce.

Merton, R. K. (1949). *Social theory and social structure.* Glencoe, IL: Free Press.

Merton, R. K. (1968). *Social theory and social structure.* New York: Free Press.

Merz-Hosman, C. S. (1989). Electoral challenges as indicators of community dissatisfaction. *Urban Education, 24*(1), 77–92.

Michels, R. (1966). *Political parties.* New York: The Free Press.

Mills, C. W. (1964). *Sociology & schooling.* New York: Whitman Publishing Co.

Minar, D. (1966). The community basis of conflict in school system politics. *American Sociological Review, 31,* 822–835.

Mitchell, D. E., & Thorsted, R. R. (1976). Incumbent school board member defeat reconsidered: New evidence for its political meaning. *Education Administration Quarterly, 12,* 31–48.

Mitzman, A. (1970). *The iron cage.* New York: Knopf.

Moen, A. W. (1971). *Superintendent turnover as predicted by school board incumbent defeat in Pennsylvania's partisan elections.* Unpublished doctoral dissertation, Pennsylvania State University, University Park.

Moore, D. E. (1988). Change strategies in a rural school district: A case study. Unpublished doctoral dissertation, East Texas State University, Commerce.

Nash, P. (1970). *History & education: The education uses of the past.* New York: Random House.

National Association of Elementary School Principals. (1984, September). *Here's How, 3*(1). Reston, VA: Author.

National School Public Relations Association. (1979). School communications workshop kit. Arlington, VA: Author.

National School Public Relations Association. (1980). *Basic school PR kit.* Arlington, VA: Author.

National School Public Relations Association. (1986). *Building confidence for your schools.* Arlington, VA: Author.

New York Civil Liberties Union. (1969). The burden of blame: A report on the Ocean Hill–Brownsville school controversy. *4*(1),

Nowakowski, J., & First, P. F. (1989). A study of school board minutes: Records of reform. *Educational Evaluation and Policy Analysis, 2*(4), 389–404.

Nunnery, M. Y., & Kimbrough, R. B. (1971). *Politics, power polls and school elections.* Berkeley, CA: McCutchan.

Ortiz, F. I. (1982). *Career patterns in education.* New York: Praeger.

O'Sullivan, J. L. (1839). The great nation of futurity. In College of University of Chicago (Ed.) (1949), *The people shall judge,* Vol. 1. (pp. 715–717). Chicago: University of Chicago Press.

Parsons, T., Bales, R., & Shils, E. (1953). *Working papers in theory of action.* New York: The Free Press.

Peterson, P. E. (1985). *The politics of school reform, 1870–1940.* Chicago: University of Chicago Press.

Plank, D. N. (1986). The eyes of Texas: Rhetoric, reality, and school reform. *Politics of Education Bulletin, 13*(2), 13–16.

Plunker, O. L., & Krueger, J. P. (1987). Heed these commonsense tips, and get along with your board. *Executive Educator, 9*(6), 26, 29.

Rada, R. (1984). Community dissatisfaction and school governance. *Planning and Changing, 15*(4), 234–247.

Redfield, R. (1941). *The folk culture of the Yucatan.* Chicago: University of Chicago Press.

Reihl, T. (1991). *A study of voter behavior of Catholics in school bond elections.* Unpublished doctoral dissertation, East Texas State University, Commerce.

Richards, A., & Kuper, A. (1987). *Councils in action.* Cambridge, England: Cambridge University Press.

Rogers, D. (1968). *110 Livingston Street: Politics and bureaucracy in the New York City school system.* New York: Random House.

Saxe, R. W. (1975). *School community interaction.* Berkeley: McCutchan.

Schattschneider, E. E. (1960). *The semi-sovereign people.* New York: Holt, Rinehart and Winston.

School boards in an era of conflict. (1966, July). Education USA (Special Report) Highlights of the Cubberley Conference, Stanford University.

Shannon, T. A. (1989). What a superintendent can do about conflict with the school board. *American School Board Journal, 176*(6), 25–27.

Smith, M. D. (1989). *Voter behavior of older adults in school bond referendum.* Unpublished doctoral dissertation, East Texas State University, Commerce.

Spindler, G. D., & Spindler, L. (1987). *Interpretive ethnography of education at home and abroad.* Hillsdale, NJ: Erlbaum.

Spinner, A. (1967). *The effects of the extent of voter participation upon election outcomes in school budget elections.* Unpublished doctoral dissertation, New York University, New York.

Spring, J. (1986). *The American school 1642–1985.* New York: Longman.

Spring, J. (1988). *Conflict of interests: The politics of American education.* New York: Longman.

Spring, J. (1989). *American education: An introduction to social and political aspects.* New York: Longman.

Summerfield, H. (1974). *Power and process.* Berkeley: McCutchan.

Tallerico, M. (1989). The dynamics of superintendent–school board relationships: A continuing challenge. *Urban Education, 24*(2), 215–232.

Taylor, F. W. (1947). *Scientific management.* New York: Harper & Row.

Thorsted, R. R. (1974). *Predicting school board member defeat: Demographic and political variables that influence board elections.* Unpublished doctoral dissertation, University of California, Riverside.

Tocqueville, A. de. (1945). *Democracy in America.* New York: Knopf.

Tonnies, F. (1957). *Community and society* (C. P. Loomis, Trans.). Lansing: Michigan State University Press. (Original work published 1887).

Trotter, A., & Downey, G. W. (1989). Many superintendents privately contend school board "meddling" is more like it. *American School Board Journal, 176*(6), 21–25.

Valesky, T. C., Smith, D., & Fitzgerald, R. (1990, October). School-based decision making in Tennessee public schools. *Policy/Practice Brief,* Paper no. 9101.

Vidich, A. J., & Bensman, J. (1968). *Small town in mass society.* (Rev. Ed.). Princeton, NJ: Princeton University Press.

Walberg, H. J., et al. (1989). Reconstructing the nation's worst schools. *Phi Delta Kappan, 70*(10), 802–805.

Waldon, J. C. (1966). *School board changes and involuntary superintendent turn-*

over. Unpublished doctoral dissertation, Claremont Graduate School, Claremont, CA.

Wang, L. Y. (1989). *School board election prediction in Texas*. Unpublished doctoral dissertation, East Texas State University, Commerce.

Wang, L., & Lutz, F. (1989). The dissat-factor: Recent discoveries in the dissatisfaction theory. *Educational Administration Quarterly, 25*(4), 358–376.

Wayson, W. W., Achilles, C., Pinnell, G. S., Lintz, M. N., Carol, L. N., Cunningham, L., & the Phi Delta Kappa Commission for Developing Public Confidence in Schools. (1988). *Developing public confidence in the schools*. Bloomington, IN: Phi Delta Kappa.

Weber, M. (1964). *The theory of social and economic organizations* (T. Parsons & A. M. Henderson, Eds. and Trans.). New York: Free Press.

Weick, K. (1983). Administering education in loosely coupled schools. *Phi Delta Kappan, 63*(10), 673–676.

Weninger, T. A. (1987). *Dissatisfaction theory of democracy: Policy change as a function of school board member turnover*. Unpublished doctoral dissertation, Arizona State University, Tempe.

Weninger, T., & Stout, R. (1989). Dissatisfaction theory: Policy change as a function of school board member-superintendent turnover. *Educational Administration Quarterly, 25*(2), 162–180.

White, L. A. (1959). The concept of culture. *American Anthropologists, 61*(1), 227–251.

Wilkerson, I. (1989, September 8). Chicago's radical school plan. *The Dallas Morning News*, p. A12.

Wilson, W. (1941). The study of public administration. *Political Science Quarterly, 51*(4), 481–506 (reprinted from a 1887 issue).

Wirt, F., & Kirst, M. (1982). *Schools in conflict: The politics of education*. Berkeley: McCutchan.

Wirth, A. G. (1966). *John Dewey as educator*. New York: John Wiley & Sons.

Wirth, L. (1938). Urbanism as a way of life. *American Journal of Sociology, 44*, 1–24.

Wolcott, H. F. (1973). *The man in the principal's office: An ethnography*. New York: Holt, Rinehart and Winston.

Zeigler, H., & Jennings, M. K. (1974). *Governing American schools: Political interaction in local school districts*. North Scituate, MA: Duxbury Press.

Zeigler, L. H., Kehoe, E., & Reisman, J. (1985). *City managers and school superintendents: Response to community conflict*. New York: Praeger.

Index

About the Authors

Frank W. Lutz is a professor of educational administration and director of the Center for Policy Studies in Elementary and Secondary Education at East Texas State University. He received his doctorate from Washington University (St. Louis) in 1962 and has taught and held administrative positions at New York University, Pennsylvania State University, and Eastern Illinois University. Prior to entering higher education, he taught in both elementary and secondary schools and was president of a local school board. His major area of research is the politics of education and he has edited, authored, or co-authored six books and numerous articles in professional journals.

Carol Merz is dean of the School of Education at the University of Puget Sound in Tacoma, Washington, where she teaches students preparing to become teachers and administrators. She received her bachelor's and master's degrees from Stanford University and her doctorate from Washington State University. She has been a classroom teacher, principal, and district administrator. She is president of the Washington Association of Colleges for Teacher Education and a past president of Northwest Women in Educational Administration. She serves on the Governor's Task Force for Washington State Schools for the 21st Century and is a regular contributor to the American Educational Research Association. She has published numerous articles on the politics of education.